Best Practices in Access Services

Access Services departments in libraries have become highly complex organizations responsible for a broad range of functions, often including circulation, reserves, interlibrary lending and borrowing, document delivery, stacks maintenance, building security, photocopying, and providing general patron assistance. This book offers effective solutions to familiar problems, fresh ideas for responding to patron needs, and informed speculation on new trends and issues facing access services departments.

This book was originally published as a special issue of the *Journal of Access Services*.

Lori L. Driscoll has been Associate University Librarian and Chair of Access Services at the University of Florida Smathers Libraries since November of 2001. She has been a presenter and panellist on topics related to library technology and copyright at a variety of national conferences in addition to publishing articles of interest to the field of Access Services.

W. Bede Mitchell has served as Dean of the Library and University Librarian at Georgia Southern University since August of 1999. He served as the 2007-2008 president of the Library Administration and Management Association.

T0346687

Best Practices in Access Services

Edited by Lori L. Driscoll and W. Bede Mitchell

Routledge
Taylor & Francis Group

LONDON AND NEW YORK

First published 2009 by Routledge
2 Park Square, Milton Park, Abingdon, Oxfordshire OX14 4RN

Simultaneously published in the USA and Canada
by Routledge
711 Third Avenue, New York, NY 10017, USA

First issued in paperback 2016

Routledge is an imprint of the Taylor and Francis Group, an informa business

© 2009 Edited by Lori L. Driscoll and W. Bede Mitchell

Typeset in Times by Value Chain, India

British Library Cataloguing in Publication Data
A catalogue record for this book is available from the British Library

ISBN 13: 978-1-138-96454-9 (pbk)
ISBN 13: 978-0-7890-3852-4 (hbk)

CONTENTS

INTERLIBRARY LOAN & DOCUMENT DELIVERY

EVOLVING LIBRARIES

Reflections on Academic Libraries in the 21st Century

W. Bede Mitchell

As The ALA Glossary of Library and Information Science states, a library is "a collection of materials organized to provide physical, bibliographic, and intellectual access to a target group, with a staff that is trained to provide services and programs related to the information needs of the target group" (p. 130). A library is not worthy of the name if it is not organized and administered according to sound principles of library and information science. Without such organizing principles, collections of information resources of any substantial size cannot be used effectively or efficiently. Without such organizing principles, you don't have an effective library–you have the Internet. Information retrieval becomes an arduous process of hit and miss, of trial and error, with no assurance that the search-engine-of-the-day has really turned up all relevant sites. But organizing and administering information resources is becoming increasingly challenging due to the explosion in recent years of new publications, both in paper and electronic formats. In reality, no academic library is capable of meeting all the needs of its users, if that was ever possible. Even the great research libraries log thousands of interlibrary loan and document delivery requests every year. In short, truly effective academic libraries are more reliant than ever on highly skilled and well trained professionals who are sensitive to the needs of library constituents. The primary mission of the library faculty and staff as we enter the 21st Century should be to support educational goals and priorities through whatever media, means, and services are most appropriate, and to accomplish this mission the library faculty and staff must be an integral part of institutional planning and decision making.

I believe that while the surface veneer of our work will continue to change in dramatic and often stressful ways, we will also continue to be guided most wisely by the values and principles that have been the library's bedrock for decades. Consider S. R. Ranganathan's five laws of library science, which he published in 1931:

1. *Books Are For Use.*
2. *Every Reader His/Her Book.*
3. *Every Book Its Reader.*
4. *Save The Time Of The Reader.*
5. *The Library Is A Growing Organism.*

Maurice Line underscored the validity of these laws by turning them on their heads to describe what he believed to be the reality of too many libraries:

1. *Books Are For Collecting.*
2. *Some Readers Their Books.*
3. *Some Books Their Readers.*
4. *Waste The Time of the Reader.*
5. *The Library Is A Growing Mausoleum.*

The laws of Ranganathan and Line assert in their own ways that academic libraries should be measured by the extent to which they select resources on the basis of user needs, organize the resources so they may be identified and accessed efficiently, promote and expose resources to potential users, engage users in an ongoing dialogue regarding evolving user needs, and respond to social and technological trends affecting higher education. Not only does that describe the ideal academic library of today, but I believe Ranganathan's laws will continue to provide the best guide to achieving the ideal library in the 21st Century. The balance of this paper will expand on that assertion.

Consider the first law, *Books Are For Use*. This means there should be no unnecessary barriers or constraints on the use of information resources. The ideal academic library seeks the best balance between preservation and the need for patrons to use materials efficiently and effectively. Rare or irreplaceable materials require greater emphasis on preservation than on user convenience, but so far as our general collections are concerned the ideal academic library tailors its loan and related service policies to maximize the opportunities for students and faculty to use materials. A new but very important aspect of eliminating barriers and constraints on access is the negotiation of favorable license terms for electronic databases. Many of the standard contracts which vendors present us contain restrictions that go beyond a copyright owner's statutory rights and infringe upon fair use. In response, we should insist upon license terms that protect fair use without affecting the vendor's right to a fair profit or its competitiveness in the marketplace. I am encouraged that a number of experts have published sample license terms that are intended to accomplish just that task. I hope that as academic libraries in the 21st Century assert their rights and reject such dangerous requirements as indemnification of vendors against lawsuits, we will find standardized language in license agreements that is more realistic and less one-sided.

Another constraint on access involves the authentication of eligible users of electronic resources. As we rely more and more on electronic databases, both for users on campus and for remote students enrolled in distance learning programs, we must perfect authentication techniques such as web access management programs.

The academic library will continue to be a vanguard in the protection of free access to knowledge. First, consider that the people in the future will only know about us that which we preserve. Allowing the records of the past to disappear is a form of censorship. We must beware of being too selective about what we collect and preserve. The universe of academic libraries must preserve all records of all societies and communities and make those records available to all. This will be a major challenge in the future since we can expect the trend toward managing and controlling information as a commodity will continue. Libraries must be responsible for ensuring information is archived and doesn't simply disappear because a commercial vendor goes out of business. And libraries must strive to make information as accessible as possible, so that in the Information Economy about which we hear so much, there is not an unnecessary chasm between haves and have-nots.

A related issue of information preservation is that of data permanence. Stephen Sottong's article in the May 1999 issue of *American Libraries* records some facts that should give pause to anyone who thinks the paperless society will be within reach in the first decade of the 21st Century:

- Magnetic media such as floppy disks have a data life span of five years or less. According to data-preservation scientist J. W. C. Van Bogart, even in extreme circumstances high quality paper lasts 10 times longer than the best magnetic media used for commercial and scientific data storage.
- Optical media, such as CD-ROM and DVD-ROM, are proving to be far less durable than originally expected. The longest warranty in the industry for CD-ROM products only guarantees for 25 years, in spite of the claims that CD disks are good for more than a century. DVDs can be expected to have a shorter life span since increased data density has been proven to be associated with shorter life spans. In contrast, the life span of acid paper, which libraries have tried to avoid collecting for decades, is 50 to 100 years.
- As of the end of 1999, Kodak still advised libraries seeking to use digital media for long-term data and information storage could be faced every 10-20 years with either:

a. copying such data to the latest formats, or
b. purchasing the latest program for uploading data on obsolete formats to the latest medium.

Even given the obvious advantages of electronic media for remote access and searching for specific information, will we be able to justify this new kind of "planned obsolescence" to our funding authorities? The academic library in the first five years of the 21st Century will need to make tough decisions about what resources will need to be archived for the long term, and in what format. I suggest to you that paper will continue to be one of our most important long term data storage formats.

Let us now reflect on the second law, *Every Reader His/Her Book.* Here Ranganathan is telling us we are obliged to help find the resources that meet a user's need, and that may include going beyond the resources that are easily at hand. As I asserted above, no academic library is able to collect comprehensively. We must engage our constituents in the development of our collection development policy and ensure that when class assignments are made there will be adequate information resources to support them. We should try to stay abreast of the research needs of the faculty and support those needs as much as possible through materials purchases and subscriptions, and also through fast, accurate, and (to the user at least) free document delivery systems. The ideal academic library, particularly one that is a member of a state-supported university system, will help build an infrastructure of policies and procedures that facilitate resource sharing among the system's libraries.

The library should take full advantage of the dialogues that are possible with library advisory committees, through focus groups and surveys, suggestion boxes and e-mail addresses, informal communication of all kinds, and by the library faculty and staff being fully engaged in the academic community. The dominant ethic of librarianship is service to the individual, community, and society as a whole. This is especially true for publicly supported academic institutions. This requires attention to quality and living up to–and even surpassing–the expectations of library users. I would add that it also requires a commitment to human diversity and multiculturalism, which should be reflected in collection development policies and respected in our patron services.

The third law is *Every Book Its Reader.* In the ideal academic library, the librarians seek to match information materials with their potential users. New acquisitions which could be helpful to someone's ongoing research should be brought to that individual's attention. We should be as concerned with the exposure and promotion of our resources as we are with their accessibility. This goal is not only difficult but urgent due to the remarkable proliferation of paper and electronic publications. How many of us feel awash in information, and overwhelmed at the prospect of sifting through dozens if not thousands of search results to find the information that best serves our needs?

Through such means as electronic and printed bibliographies, current awareness services, and liaison programs with academic departments, librarians should be the matchmakers that bring materials to the people who could use them.

Law number four is *Save The Time Of The Reader*. Information services must satisfy needs as efficiently as possible. Clearly this relates back to my earlier comment about the difference between a library and an unorganized collection of materials.

An important way in which an academic library will save the time of the reader is by bringing greater bibliographic order to the Internet and World Wide Web. As marvelous as these are, they leave much to be desired as efficient and orderly means of archiving and retrieving information. I enjoyed Will Manley's humorous take on the Internet, to wit: "If we were to go about acquiring the Internet like any other resource we would probably try to read a review of it. What would the objective reviewer say? 'The Internet is a vast informational network with millions of entries on a myriad of diverse subjects. It is loosely and unreliably indexed and is awkward to use because of the increasingly slow response time. While some of the entries are well researched by reliable authors, many others are poorly written by people with no literary or academic credentials who have a pronounced proclivity to punctuate their points with the repeated use of the words cool and suck.'" In summary, says Manley, "the Internet is the global village's vanity press. It has no editorial board and no editorial principles."

Given the vastness of the Internet and its resources, we cannot rely on existing Internet search engines to help us find all of the best information available to meet our needs. The most effective search engines index only a portion of the World Wide Web. I think over the course of the next several years we will need to re-double our efforts to save the time of our users by identifying those reliable Internet sites that are likely to be of the greatest utility and facilitating access to those sites. This can be done through subject bibliographies that are printed as well as mounted on the library's web page with links to the sites. It can be done through creative proposals like Dan Hazen's selective scanning. In this scheme, digitizing front matter like tables of contents could result in quicker and cheaper cataloging, and in the enhancement of the information that cata-logers can provide users trying to make informed choices of which ma-terials to examine in depth. It can also be done by helping users learn advanced searching skills and evaluate critically the results of their searches. And it certainly should be done through working as partners with commercial vendors and campus computer centers to design, test, and implement improved search capabilities, user interfaces, and ergonomic hardware.

Naturally we must continue using technology intelligently to en-hance our services, but must reject the false dichotomy of either/or choices. In reality, we do not have to be either a Luddite or a technocrat. Each medium has its place. Electronic media are excellent for accessing data and short, discrete textual, numeric, and visual information, while traditional paper-based documents are still the best vehicles for sustained reading.

Finally, law number five states that *The Library Is A Growing Organism*. While all of Ranganathan's laws, as I interpret them, imply the need to be prepared for change, this fifth law reinforces that need ex-plicitly. We need to continue adapting to new social conditions, techno-logical developments, and changing needs of the clientele. The number of challenges we face can seem daunting at times, but change is the norm in the library world and we must not delude ourselves into hoping that we are ever going to reach a steady-state plateau. A clear implica-tion of this law is that the ideal academic library will make a major on-going investment in the continuing development of faculty and staff knowledge and skills. We must take advantage of workshops and semi-nars offered on and off campus–some of which are now offered elec-tronically. We must attend professional conferences, engage in informal networking with peers, and learn from the literatures of our own and other appropriate disciplines.

As noted above, we will need to judiciously select from among many new and evolving media which are best for a given storage need. The academic library of the future will use all kinds of carriers of knowledge and information, with each new means of communication enhancing and supplementing the strengths of all previous means.

The academic library in a publicly supported university will find itself in-creasingly called upon to serve the citizens of the region and to engage in co-operative ventures with other post-secondary institutions in the state. For example, statewide consortia are the paradigmatic example of the benefits of libraries working cooperatively and with the state to establish an electronic network that brings enormous information resources to all citizens of the state, at a fraction of the full cost that the individual libraries would have paid for those resources. In the future, such collaborative efforts will become ever more important means of maximizing access to information and controlling costs. Within such initiatives, an individual academic library must be prepared to demonstrate leadership, contribute whatever strengths of personnel and collections it may have, and continue to keep its primary users' unique set of priorities in mind as it works with other libraries for the good of the entire state.

Another intriguing challenge to academic libraries is the growing tendency of superstores like Barnes & Noble (B & N) or Borders to usurp the academic library as the favored location for students to study. Renee Feinberg, a reference librarian at Brooklyn College, has reported on her interviews with college students she encounters at B & N superstores, and not surprisingly to those of us who have enjoyed patronizing these stores, the students indicate a preference for B & N over their campus libraries because of the more comfortable and congenial settings, good coffee, the buzz of conversation, and in some cases even the more convenient hours of operation. Perhaps most disturbing, however, is the recurring statement that B & N has better and more accessible monograph holdings, especially of recently published materials. This is worth bearing in mind when we hear the stories of how students are plugged into technology to the point of ignoring printed resources. The truth may fall somewhere in between these two extremes. As Feinberg states: "Students want their books. If libraries choose to weaken their book collections in favor of increased electronic information, they will lose patrons who would support them as they argue for protection of collections." Fortunately, we are seeing new libraries being built with the niceties found in contemporary bookstores: tasteful signs, cozy spots, comfort, elegance, and the human touch. We in academic libraries should concede nothing to Barnes & Noble in terms of comfort, convenience, and service, and we certainly should not bow to B & N's holdings of scholarly books.

CONCLUSION

As academic libraries evolve to meet new challenges, they must retain the best of the past and a sense of the history of libraries and of scholarly communication. With a sense of history, and knowledge of enduring values and the continuity of our mission, there must also be the acceptance of the challenge of innovation. If the library ever ceases to be a growing organism, then it really will become Maurice Line's growing mausoleum.

REFERENCES

Feinberg, R. (1998). "B & N: The New College Library?" *Library Journal*, 123 (2), 49-51.

Hazen, D.C. (1998). "Making Collections Work: Remote Access and Browsing." *College & Research Libraries News*, 59 (2), 97-99.

Line, M.B. (1979). "Review of Use of Library Materials: The University of Pittsburgh Study." *College & Research Libraries*, 40 (6), 557-558.

Manley, W. (1998). "The Worldwide Vanity Press." *American Libraries*, 29 (1), 136.

Ranganathan, S.R. (1931). Five Laws of Library Science. Bombay: Asia Publishing House.

Sottong, S. (1999). "Don't Power Up that E-book Just Yet." *American Libraries*, 30 (5), 50-53.

People First:
A New Zealand Approach
to Staff, Structure and Service

Jane Hill

INTRODUCTION

To set the scene, Wellington is in the Pacific, the capital of New Zealand and the seat of power for central government. Wellington City has a population of 182,000 and is within a region of 350,000. Wellington City Libraries is a network with a Central Library and eleven Branch Libraries. Wellingtonians "love their libraries" and see them as "the jewel in the City's crown."[1] Sample annual measures of our business show that 2.8 million people visit the libraries and currently 1.3 million visit our website. To complete the snapshot, we have an annual budget of $20 million New Zealand dollars, a collection of 800,000 items, seventy-seven percent of Wellington residents are active members and an annual circulation of 3.5 million items.

CHANGE

With Martin Luther King's words–"I have a dream"[2]–in 2000 I launched our extensive change process within Wellington City Libraries. Why? In 1993 the Library had celebrated 100 years as a Wellington City Council (local government) owned and operated service. We had added staff, Branch Libraries, new services and a new Central Library. We had been through 5 reviews in 7 years between 1993 and 2000. The budget cycle did not take account of major investment funding for entirely new projects.

Within the national and international libraries market and the information environment generally, Wellington City Libraries had lost its standing. There was an urgent need for the Libraries to become more "businesslike," that is demonstrating value using standard business or customer tools, principles and practices, and businesslike in attitude to treat every customer and every customer transaction as the key to our "business."

THE APPROACH WE TOOK

Eleanor Roosevelt said that "you must do the thing you think you cannot do."[3] All City Council units were facing a new change process. I volunteered the Libraries to go second. It began initially as a Business Process Re-engineering Review and developed as a library process led by me and a change team. The governing body, the Wellington City Council, approved the implementation of the Libraries change with the project to be undertaken over two years.

ANALYSIS

Our work gave us a chance to look at the business as a whole, which was important for redesigning processes and ensuring all the elements worked together. We entered a period of extensive analysis–consultation, interviews, dissecting the business and future planning. The analysis took eight months. We started with a blank sheet of paper. It was imperative that we found out what residents, customers, city councilors (that is elected representatives) and staff wanted.

The consultation and stakeholder interviews resulted in process, communications and culture changes, establishing new processes and devising a new organizational structure. While wanting a "business-like approach" we wanted to establish a team culture that encouraged innovation and ideas. We wanted people to be empowered. We wanted to see if we could achieve a flat organizational structure.

Three key performance areas were agreed–service levels as measured by resident and customer satisfaction, staff satisfaction as measured by staff surveys and staff feedback and reduction in the cost to council as measured by financial results detailing cost savings and additional revenue.

VISION

This was an essential first element. Our work in this area gave us focus, an opportunity to look at the business strategically as a whole and to examine present and future perspectives. Our choice of vision was to be "the first choice of Wellingtonians seeking to enjoy and benefit from fact and fiction."

To achieve the vision we needed to ensure all the elements worked together–the delivery of quality services, the use of quality information systems, the employment of highly skilled, versatile staff to work in high performance teams, the use of streamlined customer focused processes and support, cooperation, innovation and continual learning.

LEADERSHIP

I made a decision to lead the change. I believed and believe passionately in public libraries. I wanted to have the advantage of leading/steering the change. I was given the delegated authority from the Chief Executive and involved in all high level, weekly change planning meetings. This was vital. I undertook to make the difficult decisions (usually people centered.) I made a commitment to the staff that communication and honesty would be how the process was handled. I arranged for extensive support networks, counselors and change management courses for staff to attend. I spoke to every staff member who was made redundant at the end of the full appointments process (This process combined the use of recruitment protocols with interviewing all the staff for the new positions. Fifty-one staff were made redundant.)

A Libraries Change Team, with a Change Manager from another City Council area, worked actively on promoting and coordinating the change implementation and processes with me. A year before the main staff appointments were made we advertised for three Coordinators to manage aspects of the Libraries operation and change processes for two years.

We underwent change in a fishbowl–media, customers, councilors, lobby groups, other national and international library managers watched very closely. My first experience of handling the television media was when the public announcement was made by the Mayor and the Chief Executive that the change process was to begin. The media turned to me at the back of the room and only wanted to know about the Libraries' changes. The other Council areas were of no apparent interest. I was on camera! It was a steep learning curve. There were public meetings where the integrity of me and my staff was questioned often by former library staff concerned that things were changing. Time and time again our change messages were repeated. We held on to the vision we believed in.

RESPONSIBILITY AND ACCOUNTABILITY

I believe that responsibility and accountability are key in any change that involves staff. I was accountable to the Chief Executive, my peers and to the staff and responsible for steering the change. Risk taking was part of the process and brought benefits.

UNION INVOLVEMENT

Ninety percent of the Library staff were members of the New Zealand Public Service Association Union. The Libraries had already been through several reorganizations and management was only too aware of the burden and cost to staff. The prospect of job losses, retraining for different jobs, redundancy and other "fall-outs" painted a scenario for potential disaster.

I had inherited a climate of "union versus management" where each took a stance and approached problem solving with a confrontational attitude. Staff had been on strike after a round of unsuccessful employment contract negotiations. Given this scenario, we opted for a new approach–one that would achieve the stated objectives. We made a commitment to look at the benefits for the individual staff member so they complemented those of the business. The Libraries Leadership Team viewed this exercise as an opportunity to develop a new relationship and partnership with the Union and the delegates.

To initiate the process we did our homework first. Using De Bono's colored hat methodology, my team and I set out the issues. Such a method identified the possible situations, emotions, consequences, trigger points and uncertainties of the prospective appointment process. Secondly, we involved the Union delegates and representatives in the change process. The Union became a sounding board for possible options.

Communication used with integrity was key. The ground rules were that confidentiality was respected, open communication of problems, active listening for problem solving and no hidden agendas. We developed and maintained a transparent process. The Union adopted the change process and "work together" attitude and developed with us a platform for future business development and growth. They assisted the process by continual discussion and active problem solving with staff. Any unexpected problems that arose were efficiently resolved.

The real two-way meeting point was that the Union was party to the Library management's organizational structure proposal. We met weekly and discussions resulted in frequent joint newsletters. A jointly agreed *Libraries and Union Protocol* was developed that led to the Library winning the *Local Government Award for Management Excellence*. It provided the Union with a model for other union/management working patterns around New Zealand. The result of working together was a smooth change from one structure to another and an enhanced customer-focused culture. Today we have a living, working, ongoing relationship with a genuine willingness to work together.

COMMUNICATION

The key words were and remain honesty, integrity and communication. Open and continuous communication led to transparent discussions between the staff and management.

During the change, we had a weekly *Change* newsletter, a *Change* telephone hotline whereby calls came into my office and I replied within twenty-four hours, and regularly scheduled team meetings. There were meetings with individual staff who had questions or concerns. The Change Team members became a vital contact point for questions and discussion with colleagues and our customers and a link with the rest of the Council staff. Today we have an internal newsletter, intranet, email lists and I visit each team regularly for team briefs and exchanges of views to keep communication going.

KEYS TO OUR SUCCESS

A clear vision was crucial. The business direction "eye on the present, view to the future" underpinned the Libraries' five year strategy. We have placed people first–customers and staff. We have made a shift from a collection focus to a customer focus. Customer interaction has become a key driver for the business. Surveys, focus groups and on-going dialogue allow us to find out what is needed. Our customers maintain that staff, books, services, technology and community buildings are important.

Staff were actively encouraged to be involved in the change process and in process designs. Their continued initiative, attitude and skill resulted and results in new ways of acting and accomplishing goals. For example, a team designed a process whereby new items would be available on the shelf five days after delivery rather than the previous three month timeline. New services, technology, collection layouts and stock set a new base line for better customer service.

Staff involvement can be seen more easily in terms of the organizational structure changes. We made a conscious decision to leave behind the old hierarchical structure. It was building based, and each building had its own hierarchical structure with little overlap between buildings. There were eleven layers in the organization in 2000. There were power brokers, "gate keepers," and no personal responsibility was taken. Decisions were made by a few people and new ideas were "filtered out." Length of service mattered, not competencies. The service model had stagnated, morale was low and staff were not growing and developing. The restructuring of the Libraries' organizational structure has resulted in a future-focused flat structure. We have a smaller management structure and staff work in customer focused teams. We work as one network across the Central and Branch Libraries. Following the initial change, we made fifty-one staff positions redundant as we had developed smarter processes. Staff often devised the new processes themselves.

There are new staff positions and line responsibilities. The structure has a Libraries Leadership Team comprised of seven library managers, a marketing manager and a strategic business advisor who report to the Director. This team has negotiated and assigned service areas, financial responsibilities and strategic portfolios for the Leadership Team members. For example, one person has overall responsibility for children's and youth services and portfolios such as building management and occupational health and safety. The individuals have also staff team responsibilities (a human resources legislation requirement). As a team, the library managers can negotiate to change roles with each other. This keeps them fresh and new services can be created easily.

Below the Libraries Leadership Team is the rest of the organization. There are specific roles with different pay rates, but organizationally the structure is flat. For example, a specific Technology Coach works with teams across the network, not only on one site. The coach role was new and has resulted in a positive attitudinal change by the staff members. The coach position was a response to the challenge of developing and empowering staff. The coaches are critical for tactical, day-to-day operational leadership. Their roles encompass facilitation and training, matching business and staff development needs. They mentor, coach, motivate and identify opportunities for improving internal and external customer service.

There is a culture of participation. The managers lead by example. Staff report that they feel part of the whole network. Each person does ten percent of their time serving at public desks. Their ideas and initiatives are valued. The most junior staff member can make a suggestion, investigate it through an Ideas Process and present it through to the leadership team or to their service team, as appropriate. Staff are empowered to make decisions and take personal responsibility for those decisions. A staff member on a front line desk is able to implement policy without referral to a senior staff member. The culture did not change overnight. It has taken five years. There are project teams that work across the network and involve a variety of staff. They become part of the decision making process and learn and develop. Staff are encouraged to develop and grow through an extensive training program. A new Library training program was developed to meet business needs and staff development. In-house teams have presented their approaches to training at national, library conferences. Each staff member has training and development tasks set as part of their six monthly tactical objectives. An individual's training needs flows through to the larger plan.

Recruitment is based on competencies. A "can do" attitude is crucial. We recruit for this attitude and provide the library training if necessary. Sixty percent of the newly hired staff have library qualifications. The Library is seen as a great place to work and we are attracting graduates from other disciplines. Our staff mirrors the diversity of the community. There is constant challenge and planning to achieve results with people. Staff will continue to be developed to support the Libraries' strategic direction and services by being able to fully exploit and adapt to the challenging digital environment.

WHAT HAVE WE ACHIEVED?

1. A state-of-the-art library service for Wellingtonians with a platform for future development and growth.
2. We have shifted from involvement to people investment.
3. We have an entrepreneurial environment.
4. Wellington City Libraries has become a leader in the provision of public library service in New Zealand. We have won several awards for new initiatives and products.
5. We have a high level of customer satisfaction.
6. Staff are positive and the morale is good. Those that went through the change say they would never want to return to the old ways.

To quote from Nelson Mandela–"(we) have tried not to falter. (We) have made missteps along the way. But (we) have discovered the secret is that after climbing a great hill, one only finds that there are many more hills to climb."[4]

I believe that Wellington City Libraries network is customer focused, business-like and with empowered staff. I lead a vibrant libraries network and share a passion and commitment for public library services with my library colleagues–all two hundred and five of them.

NOTES

1. BRC Marketing and Social Research. *Wellington City Libraries Users Survey,* Appendix B: Verbatim reports. May 2003, p. 86.

2. King, Martin Luther Jr. *I Have a Dream* speech, Washington Civil Rights Rally, 15 June 1963.

3. Roosevelt, Anna Eleanor. *You Learn by Living.* New York, Harper, 1960.

4. Mandela, Nelson. *Long Walk to Freedom.* United Kingdom, Little Brown and Company, 1994, p.617

Mildly Delirious Libraries: Transforming your Library from Top to Bottom

Pam Sandlian Smith

Imagine this scenario: you walk past a public library and you see a drab, unkempt building. From the outside, it looks dirty, there is a faded handwritten sign taped to a window. You wander in out of curiosity and get an overwhelming sense of disrepair, old furnishings, and confused organization. The carpet is dirty, the beige paint is chipping. There are piles of clutter everywhere. A few people are reading newspapers, but the library is essentially empty. You wander into the children's department which is drab and devoid of joyful noise of children's chatter. There are signs taped throughout the library: no children allowed without parents or guardians, no running, no talking, you are limited to 10 items per card, $20 fee for nonresidents. The overwhelming sense you get is that this library is a place that has become irrelevant.

This is a description of the West Palm Beach Library in the mid-nineties. The library was stuck in a sixties time warp. Old rules, old furniture, old building. Unfortunately, this situation is an all too familiar scene in public libraries throughout the country. As library funding is cut, the physical environment is allowed to deteriorate. This sends a negative message that unfortunately can become self-perpetuating.

From the moment that I saw the West Palm Beach Public Library when I took over as Library Director in 1997, I knew we had our work cut out for us. The 1960's building had not been maintained, the collection was dismal and overcrowded. It had been twenty years since weeding had occurred and the marginal book budget simply didn't keep pace with the need for current books and media. There was no technology support and a computer system that had been down for six months. Everywhere one looked there were piles and files of irrelevant aging paper and machinery. The original furniture was vintage sixties. The walls were beige and dirty. The Children's department was attempting to hold things together, but there was one missing ingredient: children. You get the picture, a librarian's nightmare. This place was a mess.

THE LIBRARY THAT LOST ITS CUSTOMER BASE

While the West Palm Beach Public Library had a tradition since 1884 of being a lively, festive library at the edge of a park on the Intracoastal Waterway, it clearly had fallen upon years of bad times. It had become a forgotten institution which was almost closed due to a city funding crisis in the early nineties. The library building sitting in the center of Centennial Square was so non-descript, it was almost invisible, a stealth building. The children and families played joyfully in the new computerized fountain just outside the library's front door, but that joyful noise was not occurring inside the library. A security guard who resembled a WWF wrestler sat at the doorway inspecting visitors and making sure that children with bathing suits and flip-flops didn't sneak into the library. People had stopped coming to the library because it was no longer a safe, welcoming, friendly place.

I knew we could infuse new energy into the library and bring it back to life, but this job was going to be a challenge. Turning a library like this around was going to take more than a spark of creativity; it was going to take a structural, cultural, facilities and technological overhaul. We had to do something fast to save this patient from hemorrhaging. We started with a strategic plan developed with Aaron Cohen and Associates in 1998 which recommended shifting from basic services approach to an innovative, proactive library. City residents and businesses wanted a vibrant library. Systematically, we set out to bring the library back to life and the community back to the library.

HOUSECLEANING

First on the agenda: we rolled up our shirt sleeves and cleaned house, weeding over 50,000 books and documents. We reorganized our staffing, encouraging collaboration, speedy service delivery and customer service. The library had a tradition of excellent reference service and most of the staff were delighted to shift directions. It became apparent that some staff were not aligned with the new plan. Some elected to opt out of the team; some were encouraged to find more appropriate employment. A culture that seemed negative and somewhat stagnant needed to be redirected to focus on the looming task of reengineering and revitalizing this library. We jump started the process by focusing on staff who displayed sparks of creativity, and it soon became apparent that energy and positive problem solving attitudes were expected at the West Palm Beach Public Library.

Cataloging backlogs went from six months to a sprightly three week turn-around from the order date to receipt by a customer. The Library Advisory Board recommended a bold move: instituting a global library card. Anyone with a current picture ID qualifies for a library card at the West Palm Beach Public Library whether you live in Boston, Rome, Miami or Puerto Rico. This was the perfect solution to a snowbird community with an international seasonal population. It reminded us to welcome our guests into our library home.

We began partnering with local agencies to provide expanded services and programs. We connected with local museums, schools, businesses and media. Programs like Clematis for Kids brought children into the library while their parents were enjoying Clematis by Night, a weekly music event held in front of the library. We were willing to experiment with programs and services, from hosting authors, creating a business reference (which didn't fly), and visiting neighborhood groups to promote the library and receive feedback. Slowly but surely things began to change. More people began using the library; they even began complaining that it was too noisy, and in our case, noisy was a very good sign.

BADLY NEEDED: IMAGE REPAIR

All of our efforts to jumpstart the library were beginning to pay off, but we weren't getting any real traction in creating a significant change in attitude by the community. The mechanical side of the library was humming, but the building was still in a state of despair. Our sense of pride in our work was diminished by a grey gloom of institutional sameness, a lack luster environment. The image of the library still conveyed a sense of hopelessness. The physical appearance of the library was sending the wrong message.

We needed a makeover in the worst way, but we were on a very limited budget. Half a million dollars was allocated for the library from the city capital projects budget. The library strategically allocated $300,000 for a complete technology upgrade and $200,000 for a makeover.

The executive director of our local greenmarket was recommended. Peter Robinson, President of Mildly Delirious Design, has a background in the hospitality industry where he developed the GASP process (Graphics, Ambience, Style, and Presentation.) We contracted with Peter to assist us in creating a new environment that matched our enthusiasm. As badly as we needed to refresh our interiors, we also needed to refresh or more accurately, reinvent our image. We needed the entire package from furnishings to logo to website; we needed to establish a look, a brand. Our goal was to involve a team of staff and management to develop and then deploy a common vision and image for the library.

CREATING A VISION

We used the GASP process as a tool or vehicle to achieve this cohesive vision. The process on the surface is quite simple, Peter previews the GASP program and then gives the participants homework: list ten adjectives that represent your concept of how graphics, ambience, style and presentation should feel. The kicker is adjectives. It is so easy to insert verbs, nouns, adverbs, but he asked that we stick to adjectives and he gave us about a week to accomplish our assignment.

When the staff reconvened, (we had a team of about ten members including management and librarians) we reviewed our descriptive words, patiently listening to each other's concepts. To our amazement, our words were surprisingly similar in tone. The library that we were describing was vibrant, colorful, tropical, invigorating, refreshing, and innovative. I would never have guessed that an eclectic mix of fairly traditional librarians would simultaneously and independently imagine such an intriguing space. From that moment, a huge sigh of relief occurred. We discovered that we had a common vision, one that we could work toward together. By taking the time to create that vision, we have formed a common language, a common bond of decision making criteria that has served us now for over seven years. This vision has helped us create a cohesive personality for the library that helps us define not just how we look, but how we deliver services and our inspiring programs.

The next step was to get a design contract approved with our Board and City Commission, and then we worked on design concepts by developing a bubble diagram of traffic flow, anchors and collections. Within a limited amount of space, we needed to create more of retail, hospitality environment for the main floor which hosts the adult and teen services and collections. Once we had agreed upon a new workflow layout, Peter went to work developing concepts and color palettes. He researched carpet, furniture, mill work, and retail display fixtures. We went through two or three complete schemes of colors and carpets which needed approval by staff, Library Board, City Administration and finally City Commission.

DRESS THE LIBRARY FOR SUCCESS

As we went through the process of deciding on colors and carpets, human nature took its course and people reverted back to personal preferences when asked to decide on samples. At one point we had a huge carpet dilemma, so many choices and everyone had their favorite. Peter brought a group of twenty carpet swatches to a staff meeting, asking everyone to stand on their favorite. Choices were eclectic: pink, navy, beige, and turquoise. Then Peter began reading our adjectives and asked us to move toward the samples that met our criteria. One by one, we eliminated the carpets that didn't fit and we narrowed our choices to the ones that met our tropical identity. The guidance of our adjectives: tropical, crisp, and fluid kept us on task when it came time to make hundreds of critical decisions.

Because we were on a very tight budget ($200,000) for the main floor, (including ceiling tiles) and then $100,000 (from our annual Florida Library State Aid funding) for the children's department, we had to maximize every purchase. On the main floor, the decision to open the library up to our beautiful waterfront view guided our color scheme of ochre, sea blue and green, which ultimately guided the carpet decision. We found a carpet company that allows you to customize your carpet through a computerized process. The client selects the pattern, the yarn colors and the weave. This carpet was more expensive than typical state contract government carpet, the quality of the product eventually won over our procurement director.

Fortunately for this project, there were no structural changes, and minimal electric work. Other key items in establishing our look were paint, millwork for a new circulation and reference desk, display furnishings for media, signage and computer furniture. We reused existing tables and chairs out of budget necessity. The floor was finished off by purchasing outdoor furniture and tropical fans to create the casual, tropical, welcoming atmosphere. Peter Robinson very generously helped us stay on budget by shopping at thrift stores for used furniture and brought fabric swatches at bargain stores to upholster cushions and chairs.

The results: magnificent. The makeover was so cost effective and it produced inspiring results overnight. Our grey boring space was as luxurious as a hotel lobby, cozy, warm and welcoming. The space was so beautiful it received rave reviews, even from our toughest critics. Palm Beach residents sat in front of our gorgeous water view reading next to our homeless customers and everyone seemed contented. Teens started noting that the library was one of the coolest places in town.

GRAPHICS TO THE RESCUE

In tandem with the interior work, we created a graphics scheme involving logos, signs, and banners. We went through three graphic designers before we found a graphic representation that fit our concept. Since the initial logo design, we have evolved into yet another logo which provides even more fluidity for our image and all of our communications.

Staff used the GASP concept statement as we developed our website, our publications, business cards, library newsletter, program flyers and ads placed in our local newspaper. The repetition of our image is communicated in a professional, cohesive manner–aiding in our branding as

FIGURE 1. West Palm Beach Public Library Graphic

GASP

G = Graphics – image projected

A = Ambience – the feeling in the air

S = Style – service approach

P = Presentation – personality and programs

Used with permission.

a unique tropical, innovative library. The discipline of utilizing a style sheet, so to speak, sometimes provoked a concern that we were stifling creativity. However, after years of working through many hits and misses, staff understand the value of a cohesive look to all of our materials. The graphics changes have evolved over a number of years; as funding became available we have added additional elements. Each element that we add builds on the branding of the library and creates recurring value and image recognition. I see people all over town carrying our beautiful library bags. Families walking to the store, people on bicycles, business men walking downtown, all carrying our recognizable bag with the West Palm Beach at the cost of about twenty cents a bag.

DON'T FORGET THE CHILDREN'S LIBRARY

Once the main floor was complete, we gathered the children's staff and completed a complimentary round of GASP. We wanted the children's department to provide a continuum of the adult space, but have its own identity and sense of frivolity. Adjectives from the children's team included: submerged, snorkeling, calming, nourishing, intriguing and approachable, magical, dancing, curiosity generating and adaptable.

The challenge of the children's department may have been even greater than on the main floor. Unlike the adult services area, the children's department had no great view, just a concrete jungle and about 2,500 square feet of fixed book stacks with poles supporting the main floor. This severely limited our options for creating the multiple zones required for a dynamic children's department serving babies, parents, grandparents, toddlers, preschoolers and older kids. Attempting to create both quiet and active spaces challenged our best sense of space planning. Once again, using an out of box thinking style, our designer pushed some of our barriers by removing shelves from the shelving units and converted the remaining "poles" into desks for a homework or quiet game space.

As in the adult area, key features in the children's department are the carpet, warm tropical paint colors, millwork that turns the reference desk into the bow of a pirate ship. Accents to complete the package include tropical Adirondack chairs, mesmerizing water bubble fountains, and aquatic murals to give the sense of being underwater, or the calm of snorkeling. Built into the reference desk is a series of snorkeling masks set at toddler height for gazing into an underwater diorama.

PHOTO 1. West Palm Beach Public Library: Before

Used with permission.

PHOTO 2. West Palm Beach Public Library: After

Used with permission.

If it is possible, the response from the redo of the children's department might be even more positive than the adult makeover. The colors are warm and engaging, almost like a bright porcelain bowl. They draw you in as you walk into the space. We wanted to highlight the books in age appropriate zones and bring out the non-fiction that had been buried in the prison-like stacks. The computers are always a draw, but we wanted the entire library to have a sense of discovery. We splurged on some beautiful Italian fish lighting that set the stage for an underwater cove. The space features a craft area with rubberized flooring for easy clean up, a small story hour area, a movie space, a pre-school-toddler-baby space with grownup chairs for parents to spend time reading or chatting with each other.

IT GOES BEYOND PAINT AND CARPETING

Changing our interiors has gone beyond new carpets and furniture; it has changed the way we do business. Staff defined the library that we wanted to become and this language has guided our design process and continues to guide our thinking as we develop and grow into a refreshing library that strives to make its customers happy. A library has to deliver more than a pleasing look; it has to work to continuously to deliver great products, services and programs. Just like a company, a library cannot rest on past laurels; it must stay ahead of the curve.

PROGRAMS INVIGORATE THE LIBRARY;
CREATE AN EXPERIENCE

Adjacent to the children's department is a meeting room which has been commandeered by the children's staff as their black box theater like space. They stage impressive theater-like interactive book experiences for special occasions like summer reading or holiday programs. The Polar Express program has become a huge hit with families over the past two years. This summer reading program features the book, *Eragon* by Christopher Paolini and encourages children to become dragon riders. The entire library is participating in the summer reading theme: Ignite your Imagination.

Establishing the library as place is sometimes more difficult with adult programs. One huge success that the library has encountered is a Friday Night Jazz series sponsored by the Palm Beach Post. The event turns the library into a jazz club for two hours a month, the second Friday night of the month, where we host a local jazz combo arranged by JAMS (Jazz Arts Music Society) and serve wine by the glass through a local wine merchant, Wine Living. This program consistently draws crowds of over 200 people who simply enjoy listening to some fabulous music while sipping a drink. The occasion brings people who never have visited the library and turns them into regular users and adamant supporters of a library that is filled to the brim with a sense of *joire de vivre*.

AT YOUR SERVICE

Focusing our attention on an image makeover provided new interiors, but more significantly, a revision in the way staff interacted with customers. Over the past years, our customer service approach has been developing in an organic fashion. The management team has developed a series of customer service training packages which draws on staff experiences in the hospitality field. We treat our customers as guests, welcoming them into our library as if it were our home. The management team visited the Ritz Carlton for a day of concierge training. We analyzed the Ritz Carlton customer service style and decided it was too formal: ladies and gentlemen serving ladies and gentlemen. That did not fit our casual style that was a bit more informal and whimsical. We developed a customer service card that outlines our service expectations and guidelines that is used in training and mentoring staff.

THE BOTTOM LINE

So what? The result of paying attention to our presentation and service style pays off daily. The most common comment from library customers is "I love this library." We regularly receive customer comment cards such as the following:

"Awesome."

"The best library ever!"

"Amazing. I am so pleased to have an amazing library for this region. The staff are problem solvers and courteous. The movies are first class and the book selection is ever improving."

The library statistics reinforce these comments. An underutilized library that was barely holding its own now displays a robust community support and use. Circulation has tripled, customer visits have doubled, and our budget has more than doubled since 1997. Library card registrations have climbed from 15,000 to our current 80,000.

The take-away from this experiment? Appearances count. When a library looks worn out, it can be more easily dismissed as non-essential. If we want our public to take the library seriously, we have to respect ourselves enough to invest in regular physical maintenance and upgrades, fresh paint, and colors, clean furnishings and tidy surroundings. Looking good is not an option, it is a requirement.

Ambiance is key. When you walk into a space, you immediately generate an impression from the space. Some libraries generate a sense of formality or aloofness, a sense of superiority that intimidates people. In West Palm Beach, we work on creating a sense of welcome. We want to be respected, but approachable. When I walk into the library, which is many times each day, I always feel like I want to smile, I feel a sense of warmth, and an invigorating charge of curiosity, a sense that everything is right in the space.

Cohesive, integrated planning pays off. When everything and everyone work together in a cohesive manner, each element supports the brand, and the result is greater than the sum of the individual parts.

Language is a powerful tool. By using language to paint our vision, we began imagining our future. Instead of beige, bureaucratic institution, we became a surprising oasis of knowledge. The West Palm Beach Public Library will never have the best or largest collection and cannot begin to compete with the large, popular library systems, but by claiming we are the nicest library in the world, we have set our sights high, and it gives us a mission, to try to offer the friendliest service to each and every customer. Words are remarkable. They can create powerful energy and direction. They pointed us in the right direction and they reinforce our every move. We have become that generous, whimsical, innovative, approachable, energetic library. It all started by creating that word picture . . . and then connecting all the pieces into a cohesive, thoughtful package.

The New Academic Library
and Student Services

Jim Morris

There is a new model for the academic library and how it can support student services, especially through student activities. In developing this model, I came to the same conclusion as did James Joyce in the final pages of *Ulysses* . . . the need to say "yes" instead of "no." What follows are a few of the things that have worked for us at Lake City Community College.

Most libraries, their librarians, directors, and staff, have remained current with the latest library trends . . . the move toward a Barnes & Noble, Borders model with coffee shops and comfortable seating. I believe that all of this is really about letting go . . . of old ideas and beliefs concerning what the library should be and where the boundaries of its limitations should be drawn. The responses fall along a continuum, not surprisingly.

I have discovered upon growing older that life itself is a process of letting go; letting go of things we once thought we could not live without: ideas, pre-conceptions, even people and places. This truth extends to the library, and really to our institutions as a whole and how they relate to today's students. So I want to begin by describing the evolution of my library, and my personal evolution as a librarian.

Lake City Community College has had three presidents and three college librarians. Our first, founding librarian was there during the Lyndon Johnson years and the Great Society, when funding for library materials at Lake City was $175 thousand per year, in federal flow through money. That would be a half million in present day dollars, so it is no surprise that our first librarian was on the same standing order plan as the University of Florida. We got nearly everything that was printed, and a vast collection of educational films.

When I show people a melted bookend, mounted on a wood plaque, some think it is a rendering of the African continent or an example of contemporary abstract art. It was melted in the fire that burned the old main building on our campus in 1960. That building housed the library. According to what I thought was legend, Ella, our first director, was inside the burning building tossing books out the window to staff and student assistants on the lawn. Several months ago, I was giving a talk on the history of academic libraries to the Columbia County Historical Society, and I mentioned the story of Ella and the fire. One of the members said, "That isn't just a legend...I was one of those student assistants."

Ella was old school. Grab that noisy student and toss him out the door. No one made noise in Ella's library. Her successor, Noah, was more moderate, but still adhered to traditional notions about the academic library and how it should operate. Reference materials do not circulate . . . the building should remain quiet (which was difficult . . . our building is a Wright-influenced, Sarasota School of Architecture wonder of sixties design, but every word spoken anywhere in the building is heard throughout. It is a great setting for a music concert, and more about that later.)

When I became director in 1988, I followed in the same traditional approach. I would speak to students who were making a racket, and if that did not work I would ask them to leave. Occasionally, I would have to refer them to the Dean of Students.

The chairs in the library were hard wood, and it was altogether a rather austere, monastic environment. I am not sure how the changes started to come about. Like all other libraries, we had rules against food or drinks and of course, no tobacco products. We kept finding spills, stains on the carpet. Lake City is in North Florida, and chewing tobacco is popular here. Without being too graphic, I will only say that Gibbon's *Decline and Fall of the Roman Empire*, situated on a bottom shelf in the 900's section, became an unfortunate, if ironic target. Also, students found ways to steal our books at the rate of about two hundred and fifty per year. Or, they would use a razor blade to cut pages from expensive reference sets because they could not check them out or did not have money for copies. One day we realized that all of the controls and rules were not working. Then it occurred to me, why not let go and see what happens? The initial changes cost us little or no money. We requested donations of couches and comfortable chairs, as we had no budget for them. As a result, we now have a library full of comfy couches, and students are allowed to nap undisturbed between classes or while waiting for rides. We still seek donations of couches and have asked for recliners as well. We allow food and drinks, and yes, even at the computers. To nearly everyone's surprise, we have had only one damaging spill that ruined a thirty dollar keyboard. We consider it a small price to pay for the comfort and good will that we have generated. As for the rest of the library, spills have gone down and now are negligible.

Information finding for our students and other library users remains a central part of our mission. However, we have come to understand that the social element of the library, even the academic library, cannot be ignored. Other libraries, such as the W. E. B. Du Bois Library at the University of Massachusetts, have started emphasizing social activities.

At the same time, the UMass Library has experienced an increase in circulation. Students come and stay in a comfortable place, and they check out more books. We have initiated an aggressive weeding project and it is resulting in more space on the shelves to present new and attractive books, much in the same way that bookstores present "checkout" items. Special shelving areas for our new books and for our growing DVD collection of foreign and independent films, all of which circulate, should have a positive effect on circulation. And we have noted that while there has not been an increase in out-the-door circulation, in-house circulation has grown . . . more students are coming in and staying, while browsing our books and magazines in the library.

We have the reputation, of which we are proud, of being the most permissive building on campus. It is a place where students feel safe enough to go to sleep, or to visit with friends. And somehow, in this new welcoming environment, it is almost always fairly quiet. Usually, if there are complaints about noise, it is from students about us, the staff. We often forget we are working in a library. In fact, sometimes it has the feel of a sitcom . . . something between "Seinfeld" and "McHale's Navy."

We have original art on the walls. We encourage receptions for other college events, like Women's History Month, African American and Hispanic Heritage months. We now offer a gaming night each semester, on Friday night when the library typically is closed . . . and we have 50 to 70 students, including potential students from the local high schools, coming to play video games, X Box, Halo II. We serve energy drinks and pizza. Parents come and watch, amazed, while enjoying the pizza.

We include a Digital Dance Revolution machine and pad, and the music that accompanies it. Students take a break from Halo and unwind on the DDR. We have the lights turned down and instead use color gel stage lighting, to give the library more of a club atmosphere. We use this lighting for our other evening, musical events.

During the day, we allow students to play computer games, do e-mail, MySpace, and other electronic pastimes not directly related to their class work. However, a growing body of literature suggests that these activities are not a waste of time, but instead they contribute to critical thinking skills and effective access to the digital world. If there are no computers available for a student to do legitimate class work or research, we bump first a community member and then a student who is playing or e-mailing. We make this clear in our faculty and student orientations and on the form signed by community members prior to taking a station.

Each fall we host Jazz and Java in the library . . . an evening of poetry reading and live jazz sets, and we have had as many as 250 in attendance. The Student Activities Department supports these events with food and drinks, because we are supporting their purpose of providing meaningful and interesting student activities. Such events require broad institutional support, from the President who may have to field complaints about material read at the open microphone, to the art instructors who have their students' work on display, to the music instructor who brings his jazz band, to the liberal arts faculty members who come and support the event and who grant students extra credit for participation.

An event planned for the coming Spring will be our first "Rockin' the Stacks," a rock band in the library on a Friday night. This will be combined with another gaming event in an attempt to create synergy. When my colleagues heard about this they said, "of course you mean an "unplugged" group. No, I don't. I mean, hard, loud, southern rock and roll. I heard a quote recently . . . 'Don't trust anyone under 30 . . . (decibels)!'" I want to see the stacks rocking, and the windows vibrating. Once again . . . this will happen on a Friday night when we are closed for regular business.

One final comment about food in the library: so often I have heard librarians say, "Oh no, it will draw bugs! We can't have that! Whatever shall we do?" Let me tell you about bugs in the library . . . The covers of hardback books are a little bit of fabric, but mostly starch. This is delicious dining for insects. Or as we say in North Florida, "Good eating." If you do not spray, the bugs will come anyway, without the pizza and cookie crumbs. Clean up, spray, and forget about it!

We have built a major foreign and independent film collection, which is available for checkout and interlibrary loan. Now that many of the video outlets have become a mile wide and an inch deep in their collections, with hundreds of copies of the latest releases and little else, this is a real service for our students, staff, faculty, and community. And regarding checkout . . . now there is literally nothing that will not check out of our library, including audio visual items. Regarding reference books, my staff members have authority to let them go out. I have told them I will always back them for saying "yes," and for expanding rather than limiting access for our students. And our reference books do not get cut with razor blades anymore, either.

During finals week for each of our academic terms, we sponsor "Burning the Midnight Oil," with extended hours, snack food and pizza, soft drinks and coffee and free copies. During the most recent late night study event, over a three night period, we logged a gate count of 475 library users. And regarding gate count, it is now the highest in the history of our library . . . up by a thousand a month over the previous year.

Lastly, each month we sponsor Café Politico, an open discussion group that brings together students, staff, faculty, and the community to discuss current topics of political and social relevance . . . our topics have included same sex marriage, the world response to the east Asian Tsunami and to Hurricane Katrina, Civil Liberties and the Patriot Act, and the war in Iraq and world terrorism. We call Café Politico a place where you *can* discuss politics and religion. These discussions can get fairly heated, and we have moved them to the student lounge in our student center, but the library is still the sponsor. Civil discussion and debate is at the heart of democracy. These events provide students and the community with a chance to participate in one of democracy's most basic elements . . . public discourse.

In closing I want to relate an incident that our president, Dr. Charles Hall, related to us at our Fall Welcome Back convocation for all faculty, staff, and administration. He went on a cruise this summer with his family. One afternoon they came to the dining room to be seated and the waiter directed them to a table where a wall occluded their view of the ocean. They asked to be seated in another section, which was empty and which had an excellent view, but the waiter told them that section was closed. They were disappointed, but the Maitre de overheard what happened, came over and said, "Please come with me . . ." and he removed the rope barricade and allowed them to take their seats at the table they wanted. Dr. Hall thanked him, and the head waiter sighed and said, "Ah, yes . . . my staff . . . if they could only learn to say 'yes' more often, they would all be Maitre de's . . ."

So I suppose that the message for our libraries in the coming decades as we reach out more to our students and others, is not just letting go of the old ways, but saying "yes" to the new.

An Evaluation
of Selected ASERL Web Pages:
"Best Practices"
for Serving Distance Learners

Melanie Thomas

INTRODUCTION

"If you have built castles in the air, your work need not be lost; that is where they should be. Now put the foundations under them." By following the advice of Henry David Thoreau, the distance education learner can be supported with those essential resources needed for success. The number of opportunities for virtual learning in higher education has exploded during recent years. NCES statistics report that over 3,077,000 students were enrolled in distance education programs in 2000-2001 (NCES, 2004). There are many types of distance situations imaginable–intrastate, interstate, and international and just as many local arrangements established to accommodate the library and information needs of the distance learners, regardless of their location. Library customers demand the proper infrastructure in order to achieve their academic aspirations; thus, the provision of the proper foundations must be ensured. With all library resources that are already accessible for the end user's convenience and choice, it almost seems a trivial matter to quibble over the few cents per page for the small luxury of the provision of photocopied materials. In a recent OCLC Report, the "production of print journals is expected to remain steady and online journals are expected to increase substantially" (OCLC, 2003, p. 3); however, the report goes on to say that the traditional information formats are not going away. So that all formats of information can be effectively accessed and utilized, this writer feels that university libraries responsible for serving distance/off-campus students warrant some special consideration, due to their unique circumstances. The aim of this article is to examine and compare the web pages designed to serve distance learners or off-campus students enrolled at ASERL (Association of Southeastern Research Libraries) libraries and to evaluate their policies on the provision of print resources to their constituents. There were almost as many scenarios and local strategies at each institution. ASERL has several examples categorized as "best practices" that provide excellent examples.

METHOD

The Association of Southeastern Research Libraries' web site lists a link to each of the 38 member libraries, most of whom have some responsibility of serving distance education students, or extended campus or off-campus students. Consider ALA's definition of distance education:

Distance learning library services refers to those library services in support of college, university, or other post-secondary courses and programs offered away from a main campus, or in the absence of a traditional campus, and regardless of where credit is given. These courses may be taught in traditional or nontraditional formats or media, may or may not require physical facilities, and may or may not involve live interaction of teachers and students. The phrase is inclusive of courses in all post-secondary programs designated as: extension, extended, off-campus, extended campus, distance, distributed, open, flexible, franchising, virtual, synchronous, or asynchronous. (American Library Association, 2007, Para 6)

Libraries have the obligation to serve this population of students as appropriate to their own institution. ASERL member libraries were examined based upon the following criteria: utilization of a request management system to automate repetitive tasks, provision of clear definitions of whom is eligible for distance services, thorough explanations of the level of services offered, the availability of web-accessible online forms to help expedite the process, and description of policies on charges, if any, for the provision of non-returnables (i.e., photocopies of materials available within the library's print collection).

I was particularly interested in exploring ASERL library policies on furnishing to distant constituents print materials that are owned and readily available within the library. A cursory polling of members of the Off-Camp list-serv (for practitioners who serve the library and information needs of patrons at a distance from the main library operations) revealed that the majority of its members serving distance clientele do not charge for photocopies, or at least offer them various types of subsidies. The precepts of the *ACRL Guidelines for Distance Education* state that, "the sponsoring library must provide for equivalent services for the distance student." Provision of equivalent services within the context of the *Guidelines* does not necessarily mean that the library should provide exactly the same services as it would offer the on-campus students, as their needs are slightly different; thus, a wide variety of methods of document delivery of library-owned printed materials was represented per institution.

EVALUATION OF ASERL
DISTANCE EDUCATION WEB PAGES

Of the 38 ASERL member libraries that serve patrons identified as distance learners, practically all utilize ILLiad to streamline the process of electronic delivery and facilitate the sharing of resources. Most of the ASERL institutions utilize the customary electronic forms within ILLiad for all-in-one record keeping of the patron's account. Request management systems like ILLiad help to automate many repetitive, time-consuming chores (Hilyer, 2006, p. 78). It is a powerful one-stop shopping interface that can be used to automate and streamline the workflow for both types of materials (library-owned and non-owned material). In addition to being of great convenience to the user, this enables the access services professionals to ensure that the requests are routed through the proper channels. At least 16 of the 38 libraries represented in the ASERL list, indicated on their web sites that they provide their distance education users with photocopies of articles available within their print collections at no charge. At the very minimum, the library should have clearly posted on its web page some indication of the fees, if any, that will be assessed for photocopy service.

There should be some language that delineates between the types of material to be photocopied for the patron. Often both types are handled through the same ILLiad interface, which may cause some confusion, as to charges assessed and for which user group–on or off-campus users. Many libraries offer the free delivery photocopied of journal articles or book chapters service for both types of materials (library-owned and non-owned materials). Since it is commonplace for interlibrary loan materials to be photocopied and made available at no charge to the user, it is important that the web site show delineation between the types of material requested. On-campus students may attempt to circumvent the system to evade any per-page charges, if such expenses are required. A clear definition of whom qualifies for which level of service and at what cost should be posted.

SOME "BEST PRACTICES"

Among the libraries that facilitate photocopies for free or at least subsidize the costs, the Florida State University Libraries have a web page that does a good job of defining who is eligible for distance learning students services. It states that any student who is enrolled in the university's distance learning program and resides at least 50 miles away from the main facility at Tallahassee is eligible. The interlibrary loan department photocopies articles that are not available electronically through the databases and delivers them to the patron. Library web sites, such as that of Florida State University, establish their parameters and potentially reduce the numbers of students closer to home–perhaps within the library building or nearby dorm building who might attempt to defeat the system. The ILL Department does not charge eligible remote customers for the delivery of photocopy articles, electronic or in print format. Their web site states, "Distant customers have a single point of contact for obtaining library materials regardless of the location of those materials."

The University of North Carolina–Raleigh's aptly named "Tripsaver" service provides photocopy services to its distance learners at no charge. Articles and book chapters may be delivered to the web. To take advantage of this convenience, all distance education users need do is log in and specify their status in their profile. There is a separate link about the five types of services available for requesting items through "Tripsaver." Tiered charges for various user groups served signify that not all services are open to everyone. Some services are open to users unaffiliated with the University. They may register for an account and are billed for the materials requested. University of North Carolina-Charlotte's web site reminds students who are enrolled in distance education programs to type their status as "distance user," as they "don't provide this service to on-campus students." Similarly, University of Louisville currently assesses no charge to supply its users with library resources that are not readily available online. This web site enables the user to identify the program and department served through the University's online distance education program and log in with the proper authentication. Only when the cost exceeds $25 are distance library users charged for obtaining library materials.

The Thomas Cooper Library of University of South Carolina, Columbia promotes its "Scan and Deliver" service. The web page appears clear and concise with links to details about policies, fees, turn-around times, what is available for photocopying and method of delivery and there is no charge to the user for this service. If an article is only available in print format, students living outside of the designated counties and enrolled through the Distance Education program may register to use "Scan and Deliver" (through *ILL Express*) and enjoy journal articles and book chapters delivered to their desktop. There are even provisions available for students who are unable to come to the library in person because of a disability or other medical condition. According to the ILL librarian at University of South Carolina, the faculty and distance students already appreciate the new service and its use is expected to flourish.

Virginia Commonwealth University provides a simple and clear web page for its distance education students. Three main paragraphs comprise Interlibrary Loan, Copy Service, and Book and Media Delivery Services and Fees page. The links at each service point connect the user to the common ILLiad interface. According to the web page, there is no cost to those employed by or enrolled in a distance program at Virginia Commonwealth.

Due to local circulation and document delivery policies, some ASERL institutions adhere to a charge-for-photocopy service. Auburn University requires a fee to obtain materials owned within the Library. The *AubieExpress* document delivery form initiates a request for materials photocopied and delivered by fax or by e-mail. University library sites, such as Mississippi State University's encourage the user to first check the online catalog to determine whether the library owns the material. Once it is determined that the material is owned, the user is queried if he wishes to proceed with the request, since there is a per-page charge for the material. Photocopy service at Mitchell Memorial Libraries of Mississippi State University is available to distance learners at a reduced price, as compared to on-campus charges. The user is billed through the university business office. Many other colleges and universities use various automation tools to archive the financial tasks of collecting money, maintaining the records, and issuing receipts. Automated and integrated accounting and student record systems offer two-fold benefits: its use saves the library personnel from the tedious and repetitive tasks of collecting money for copies, and the library user is spared form the 100 or more mile drive to access the material in person.

It is always a "best practice" to ensure that the user is informed about the library's policies, and particularly to be forewarned of any potential charges. It is the responsibility of the library user to find out about the policies and the level of services to which he is entitled. Too often, circulation or document delivery procedures are misinterpreted or misunderstood; thus, it is essential to explain the local policies. Distance and extended programs and the arrangements for library support added to the mix can further complicate matters. Leung concedes that circulation and access services policies are sophisticated and complicated because of the "the diverse and growing clientele that libraries serve and the variety of circulation services to serve users better." (p. 29) Distance education, extended campus, off-campus, open, and distributed learning arrangements have certainly grown and we must accommodate their library and information needs within the parameters of the university's policy to enable equivalent access to those enrolled.

CONCLUSION

Anecdotal evidence suggests that since so many publications have been made readily available online, requests from distance users for photocopies of printed materials are declining. Sometimes, the distance student can feel disenfranchised when not having ready access to the material that happens to be not included in some of the electronic resources and without ready access to the main library. Too often, patrons will likely disdain significant research materials simply because they exist solely as part of the library's print collection miles and miles away.

In an age of the perception that all information can be obtained at any time, from any place, and all at no cost on the Internet, the human factor is what makes all the difference. The true access services experts are at the foundation, providing appropriate support for off campus users at any geographical location that they serve and are ready to provide services in a variety of means. Intangibles, "such as the attitude of the person answering the phone, neatness of the photocopy, consistent accuracy of order fulfillment, the cheerful and helpful resolution of errors and the flexibility of the staff to accommodate special requests . . . can be attributed to the commitment and dedication of the people providing this service" (Fong, Ward, & Dearie, 2002, p. 209). It is essential that the sponsoring library provide sound and reliable foundations for the support of its distance users.

REFERENCES

American Library Association. (2007, January 7). *Guidelines for distance learning library services.* Retrieved February 7, 2007, from Association of College and Research Libraries Web Site: http://www.ala.org/ala/acrl/acrlstandards/guidelinesdistancelearning. htm.

Association of Southeastern Research Libraries. http://www.aserl.org/ . Accessed February 6, 2007.

Fong, Y., Ward, S., & Dearie, T. (2002). Emerging trends in fee-based information delivery. *Journal of Access Services, 1*(1), 193-210.

Hilyer, L. A. (2006). Additional considerations. *Journal of Interlibrary Loan, Document Delivery & Electronic Reserve, 16*(1/2), 75-80.

Leung, Yau (2005). User education on circulation policies. *Journal of Access Services, 3*(1), 37-46.

NCES. (2004). *Distance education at degree granting post-secondary institutions 2000-2001*. Retrieved January 12, 2007, from National Center for Education Statistics Web Site: http://nces.ed.gov/pubsearch/pubsinfo.asp?pubid=2003017.

OCLC. (2003, March). *Five-Year information format trends*. Retrieved January 19, 2007, from OCLC Web Site: http://www5.oclc.org/downloads/community/informationtrends.pdf.

Thoreau, H. D. "Walden." (1976). In *The Portable Thoreau*. C. Bode (Ed.) (Revised ed.), New York: Viking Press.

APPENDIX
WEB PAGES CITED

ASERL Library	*ASERL Library Web Page Support for Distance Learners*	*Policy or instructions for obtaining photocopies of print material owned by the library*
Auburn University	Distance Education/Outreach Services http://www.lib.auburn.edu/hum/humweb/	AubieExpress http://www.lib.auburn.edu/access/ill/aubiexpressprocedures.html
Florida State University, University Libraries	Distance Learners: Resources http://www.lib.fsu.edu/distance_learner	Library Services for Distant learners http://www.illiad.lib.fsu.edu/
Mississippi State University, Mitchell Memorial Libraries	Distance Education Services http://library.msstate.edu/content/templates/?a=133&z=126	Request Books and Articles: Login to ILLiad https://saturn.users.library.msstate.edu/illiad/
University of North Carolina at Charlotte J. Murray Atkins Library	Distance Education Library Services http://library.uncc.edu/distance/	Distance Education Book and Article Delivery http://library.uncc.edu/display/?dept=access&format=open&page=1822
University of North Carolina, Raleigh	Distance Learning Services for Students http://www.lib.ncsu.edu/distance/	Tripsaver http://www.lib.ncsu.edu/tripsaver/index.html
University of South Carolina, Columbia Libraries	Resources and Services for Distance Education http://www.sc.edu/library/pubserv/disted.html	Scan and Deliver http://ill2.tcl.sc.edu/docdel/default.html
Virginia Commonwealth University James Branch Cabell Library	Distance Learners Toolkit http://www.library.vcu.edu/research/disted_toolkit.html	Services and Fees for VCU Distance Education Faculty, Students, and Staff http://www.library.vcu.edu/ill/distedfees.html
University of Louisville	Distance Learning Library Services http://library.louisville.edu/dlls/	U of L Distance Learning Library Services (U of L Login Required for each off-campus program/department)

Video Reference and the Library Kiosk: Experimentation and Evaluation

Char Booth

Recent innovations in academic library patron services have been influenced by a wide variety of factors–the common movement towards service point consolidation as well as radical advances in mobility-enhancing communication technology are among the most prominent. Combined with near-ubiquitous Internet connectivity these developments have motivated a general reexamination of information and access service models with an eye to efficiency and enhancement. The newer generation of patrons reflects a massive paradigm shift in information use patterns and a consequent repositioning of library-related expectations and needs. The popular concept of "point of need service" represents librarians' collective response to these changes. Widespread creative attempts to provide service where, when, and how users desire it has resulted in a shift away from solely providing static, location-based user access in the form of reference and circulation desks and towards supplementing this traditional model with a range of distinct and technologically innovative services. Recent advances in the development of point of need programs include IM reference, various applications of RSS feeds, "mobile" librarians enabled by smart phones and portable computing technology, as well as experiments in user-generated content, library gaming, social software, and virtual worlds such as Second Life.

The Ohio University Libraries Reference Department recently began experimenting with another type of service innovation–the video kiosk model–as a means of providing information and research help inside and outside of our physical library. Currently still in its testing and evaluation stages, our pilot kiosk program uses Internet video technology to establish a face-to-face connection between users and librarians using what can be best described as a virtual reference desk model. The pilot is taking place in Alden Library, the core library facility of Ohio University, which supports a student population of roughly 20,000 on its main campus in Athens, Ohio. The library is a large, centrally-located facility that enjoys heavy patronage and features a highly popular 24-hour Learning Commons.

Due to Alden's large physical size, an ongoing reduction in the overall number of service desks, and the typically daunting array of available information resources, the idea of an in-library information kiosk as a supplementary service point proved appealing to Reference staff. Additionally, we were motivated to gauge the utility of video kiosks as outreach tools because of their potential to create a library presence at remote campus locations. The inspiration for this program originally came from an individual in our Systems department who encountered video help terminals at a museum and was intrigued by the potential library applications of such a service. After investigating available specs and pricing of free-standing kiosks[1] he brought the idea to the attention of the Reference Department, who in a team effort began discussing scalable in-house testing measures to work out the technical kinks that would inevitably arise while implementing a service such as this. Because of the proliferation of inexpensive web cams and free or affordable video IM and video call clients such as Trillian Pro and Skype, creating an inexpensive test video kiosk system prior to purchasing a costly manufactured unit presented an attractive usability testing scenario.

Because few other libraries have experimented with kiosk and video call technology in this manner we developed our pilot to assess whether any of the several imaginable library applications of Internet video could offer a scalable and effective means of providing information and research help to our patron base. Best-case-scenario applications of video reference were defined as the following: (1) to offer video kiosk help services inside Alden Library, (2) to expand our use of Skype to enable library users to communicate with us via Internet video from their personal computers, and (3) to establish a library video help kiosk in the newly constructed, high-traffic campus student center. The video reference program both in its kiosk and "Skype a Librarian" incarnations were conceived as an innovative method of using a developing communication technology to provide meaningful outreach and reference help within and beyond our physical library. We approached this program much in the same way we adopted IM reference in the recent past, as a somewhat unfamiliar, interesting service that seemed to be gaining prominence and carried considerable potential as a service tool. As patrons increasingly adopt internet video IM and call technology as a communication method, it is our hope to accommodate users by offering services via the same medium to fill an anticipated reference need.

The idea of the video reference itself raises an intriguing point in terms of the nature of digital user services. Despite their demonstrated effectiveness other types of electronic reference services such as IM and chat create something of a virtual divide between librarians and users insofar as they don't enable a level of personal contact and communication that can vastly enhance the reference interaction.[2] Because of its visual nature, reference help via video has the potential to personalize virtual reference services in a way that has been difficult to replicate using chat or IM. Additionally, because most video call and video IM services also allow simultaneous text messaging it is possible think of video capability as a major enhancement to an already proven service. Finally, because Skype allows one-way video calling,[3] "Skype a Librarian" or a similarly configured service could easily augment the personal visibility of librarians in a time when many are seeking to effectively market their services to increasingly distant, electronically-based users.

During Winter quarter of 2007 and in collaboration with Systems and Circulation, the Reference department Technology Team set up a simple, temporary video kiosk on one of our stacks floors in a location where experience has shown that customers typically have immediate reference or catalog help questions. In its first incarnation, the "kiosk" was nothing more than a flat-screen monitor with a webcam mounted on top, a keyboard, and speakers arranged at eye-level on a small service desk and highlighted by a sign inviting patrons to chat with us should they have any questions. In determining the setup of our service, we opted for a "constant call" model, which effectively creates an open video connection that allows patrons to constantly "see" into our office as they pass the kiosk and approach us with inquiries as they would a reference desk. We kept the video window minimized to allow users to simultaneously access the Internet, which allowed us to recommend sites, send links, and suggest navigation paths while communicating. To staff the service we dedicated a cubicle in our office suite as a virtual reference station, where on an hourly rotation staff monitor both IM and video reference via a webcam-enabled laptop while also able to work on a remote-login desktop computer.

We launched the service using Windows Live Messenger as our primary video client, establishing a screen name for both the stacks kiosk and staff station so that once signed in the computers could in effect "communicate" with one another. We immediately found that Windows Live Messenger proved erratic and complicated with the open call model–calls were dropped frequently, which due to the limited customizability of WLM caused us to have to run upstairs several times a day to reestablish the connection. We also tested Trillian Pro, which offered a clear, more stable video connection but would have created overlap issues when we needed to answer traditional IM questions simultaneously from our MSN screen name. Of all the video services we have tested, the free internet calling program Skype has proven the most consistent by far, and is the one with the greatest number of other potentially useful applications (such as the extremely affordable fee-based option of long-distance and international calling from library computers). Among other benefits, Skype's preferences are customizable to the point that it is possible to configure accounts to automatically open video calls, thus neatly solving the prohibitively inconvenient issue of having to dispatch a librarian to physically "answer" kiosk calls to reestablish a failed connection.

The Alden Reference Department is currently entering the second phase of testing with a reconfigured, relocated video kiosk. The first kiosk was located in a somewhat obscure area within the library and was, due to its resemblance to a typical computer terminal, difficult to identify by sight as a service point. Likely due to these two factors it was our experience that the traffic generated by the kiosk was considerably less than desired. We also had several serious incidents of webcam tampering, another obvious risk of locating the initial kiosk in an isolated area. Those issues notwithstanding, our most positive interactions came from questions referred by stacks staff who directed users with information needs to the kiosk and explained the service; however, it seemed that users did not often independently approach the video terminal. Users seemed to experience some initial confusion and/or self consciousness while interacting with us via video, but this reaction typically quickly gave way to more comfortable communication and an overall appreciation of the service.

In an effort to mitigate these initial concerns and to assess the technology in a more frequently trafficked area we decided to relocate the kiosk directly opposite the 4th floor library entrance, a common access point near to our Circulation desk but two floors removed from our Learning Commons Reference and Technology Services desk. (Alden Library is somewhat unusual in that it features two main entrances on separate floors, each with a major service desk in plain sight. Thus, patrons are often frustrated by being referred from one desk to another–establishing this communication point between the desks may significantly reduce user dissatisfaction over this arrangement.) It is our hope that a more prominently located video kiosk with improved signage and design will better attract library navigation and quick information questions as well as more detailed interactions resulting from nearby Circulation referrals. In addition, the relocated kiosk will test a design configuration that differs significantly from the previous one–it enables only video communication with no keyboard or mouse navigation possible by the user, which we hope will offer additional insights into preferred methods of interaction with video service terminals.

Bringing this service to an operational point has been an ongoing lesson in cross-departmental collaboration. The kiosk necessarily takes up significant "real estate" in important zones of the library, thus requiring a continuing discussion between different constituents as to appropriate kiosk placement, setup, triage, and other important matters. Orienting staff and users alike to this still novel means of communication also requires a good deal of effort, and the question of whether video technology is a long-term and scalable means of providing reference via kiosk and as an aspect of our Ask a Librarian services has not yet been satisfactorily answered by our current experiment. A central question raised by the first phase of the experiment is whether users will feel comfortable approaching and conversing with a librarian via video kiosk to an extent that will justify the existence of the service itself. Conversely, the combination of a prevalent unfamiliarity with internet video among the general population (caused in part by the still recent development of this technology as a reliable and accessible means of communication) combined with the simple "freak factor" of librarians on camera may effectively deter users and motivate them to users seek out a "live" staff member for information. In light of these questions, placement of a kiosk within the campus student center will only occur once the alternate configurations have been tested and the viability of video help has been proven successful. Whether patrons will contact us using their personal computers via Skype a Librarian when it is enabled in the coming weeks is also a source of much curiosity, because this method of communication requires users either to download Skype or to be previously established with the program.

Although a final report on the success of video reference technology is not yet possible, when one considers the growing popularity of Internet video communication as well as our mixed yet positive experience with the project to date there are positive indications that this technology can provide a beneficial information service model for use by libraries in general. It is my sense that the success of video reference kiosks will depend heavily on location-based experimentation to achieve the best possible configuration, promotion, and staffing model for each individual context. However, the most important test of this type of service will inevitably play itself out over time as the technology gains precedence–as users in general become more acclimated to video communication their demand for, comfort level with, and reactions to video in library services will ultimately determine on a case-by-case basis the success and scalability of these projects.

NOTES

1. The quote we received for a graphically customizable, dual-monitor freestanding kiosk that would enable simultaneous video and Internet browsing came to roughly $3,500. Less expensive options are also available.

2. An interesting caveat to consider if and when implementing video kiosks–because of camera and screen configurations it is literally impossible using current technology to make eye contact with your users, which is a source of some discomfort when acclimating to these services.

3. In a one-way video call, a user without a webcam can still see the image created by another user's webcam.

Char Booth presented on the video reference pilot program at the Cyber Zed Shed, a component of the 2007 ACRL Conference; slides of the presentation can be viewed at http://charbooth.googlepages.com/home, and a short podcast interview about the service is available at http://www.palinet.org/lts_techupdates_podcasts.aspx#Tech.

Totem Kiosk,
Not Just for the Hotel Lobby

Kelly Broughton

Would you like to get away from unappealing easels in the lobby and signs advertising services and events taped to the walls and service desks? Want to expand and enrich your traditional physical exhibits with multimedia content? As part of an effort to improve the appeal of the entrance area of our main library, Bowling Green State University Libraries installed a multimedia kiosk, similar to what you might find in a hotel lobby or convention center. This article discusses the capabilities for such a kiosk, how we have used it to date and our future plans for better utilizing its capabilities to further engage our users.

Bowling Green State University is a residential university located in Northwest Ohio that serves over 21,000 students with an array of bachelors, masters, and doctoral programs. The University Libraries' William T. Jerome Library houses the main collection and a variety of special and archival collections, including the nationally recognized Browne Popular Culture Library and the Sound Recordings Archives. The library has only one entrance and exit and this is located in between the main circulation and reference desks.

During the summer of 2006, the main entrance area of the Jerome Library, which incorporates the reference desk, main circulation, the reserve room, exhibit space and computer access for users was given a facelift. An improved floor design incorporated new computer, lounge and study space furniture, new reference and reserve desks, and an updated accent wall color. This changed the entrance area of the library from institutional to inviting and has resulted in different traffic flows and even increased statistics at the reference desk. In addition to providing a much more attractive and contemporary look and feel to the first glimpse users have as they enter the library, it also provided more appropriate seating and study space for today's learners. With the updated learning space, we also needed a better way to inform users about our services and collections, as well as advertise our events. Offering a convenient, eye catching, and aesthetically pleasing way to advertise library events and services, as well as welcome patrons and offer directions were the goals of our installation of a totem-style kiosk in the updated learning space.

Computers or kiosks used in high traffic areas, primarily in the health care industry, have been described in the literature, although little has been written specifically about kiosk use in libraries. Ya Ni and Tat-Kei Ho (2005) describe three different purposes for kiosks: information dissemination and advertising (one-way information offered to users), interactive information (users input data to retrieve information), and transactions (interactive, but also involve user identity verification or money exchange). Slack and Rowley (2002) describe how new generation kiosks have evolved to offer both improved user experiences and more effective and efficient information provision. In an article about outreach, Fabian et al. (2003) explain how multimedia kiosks were used at the University of Buffalo libraries in conjunction with a variety of exhibits.

We selected a product called the "3Vue Totem" by Sheletron (http://www.sheletron.com/index_flash.html) that is distributed in the United States by Neil Nathanson & Associates (http://www.nathansonassociates.com/). It is currently in use at hospitals, hotels, retail locations, conference centers and other high-traffic areas. The product includes three seventeen-inch flat computer screens stacked vertically. The base of the totem contains a computer processor. It is tall and slim, about two feet deep at the base where the processor is located and about six inches deep on the tower where the screens are located. The screens are each seventeen inches and the width of the entire unit is twenty-one and a half inches.

Our purchase of the totem included a customized casing color and a customized graphic imprinted on the bottom panel that we designed and was manufactured with the aluminum casing.

The versatility of the 3Vue Totem is in the control software. It includes three components that allow for editing, controlling and managing the files that are displayed on the three screens. A wide variety of image, audio, video, and animation formats, as well as HTML can be used, including PowerPoint™ and Flash™. It operates on the Windows platform and includes a database structure for organizing and gathering your files. The totem can be operated directly from the internal processor in the base or can be networked to allow management from staff desktops where the software is installed. Timing of the files can be controlled in the editing program that includes calendaring features so that starting and expirations dates and times can be pre-set. Each of the three screens can be separately programmed, with unique times set for each individual file. Training on the use of the control software was included in the purchase price, although it is relatively simple to use. Any one or all three of the screens can be purchased as touch-screens at an extra cost.

FIGURE 1. Kiosk Totem

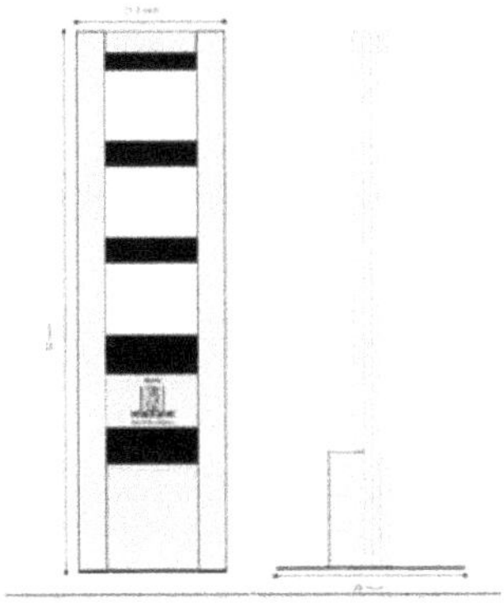

FIGURE 2. Customized Graphic

Used with permission.

Positioning of the kiosk is only limited by access to power and networking, should one choose to manage the kiosk from an office desktop. We originally installed the kiosk in our lobby area along the main traffic route to the elevators. After a short period at this location, it was determined that few people were noticing the kiosk, let alone stopping to read or interact with it. We then decided to move it directly across from the main entrance to the building, about equidistant from the circulation and reference desks. The kiosk is much more noticeable now as users enter the building, and more visitors do now stop to examine its messages and content. Even those who don't stop are still viewing at least three different messages or images just because of the kiosk's new location.

Staff in the libraries' administrative office manage the kiosk files and a staff member in the technology unit has also had training on the system and can serve as a back up. We currently rotate a wide variety of files on the three screens, including locally produced "READ" posters, events announcements, welcome messages for special visitors on campus or in the libraries, local weather information from the Internet, advertising of special services in the libraries such as research project clinics and "Did you know . . ." slides about general library services. Staff from many areas of the libraries developed this content. We discovered that when displayed they have somewhat of a disjointed look. Because of the variety of fonts and colors used, the kiosk looked a bit like an electronic bulletin board or a collection of different "ads" produced by different groups or individuals. In order to improve this, we are currently developing a set of templates for information to be displayed that will offer a set of complimentary fonts and colors. This will not only add some continuity to the look of the information, but allow staff to simply input text into preformatted slides.

In the near future, we hope to redevelop an interactive tour of the libraries that can be used both on our web site and on the kiosk using the touch-screen technology. Additionally, we would like to develop some visually stimulating content to highlight what can be found in the special and archival collections on the upper floors of the library. Another possibility is to develop special content for the kiosk that corresponds or enhances the nearby exhibits housed in traditional display cases. Nearly anything we develop for the libraries' web site can be used on the kiosk, reducing the amount of staff time needed to devote specifically to kiosk content development. While developing content for the kiosk that compliments the content of the exhibits would require additional labor, we should be able to develop it in such a way that it can also be used on our web site, creating another outlet and perhaps even attracting visitors to the library to see the related exhibit.

While we think we have not yet taken full advantage of the capabilities of the kiosk to engage our users, it is easy enough to provide and update content to make it a worthwhile addition to our library. Future content development for the kiosk should take full advantage of multiple outlets for that content and be useful for both the kiosk and the libraries' web site. Additionally, if content is developed specifically to enhance or expand an in-library exhibit, assessment of the usefulness and effectiveness of that content will be planned in order to weigh that against the staff time involved in development.

REFERENCES

Fabian, Carol Ann, Charles D' Aniello, Cynthia Tysick and Michael Morin. "Multiple models for library outreach initiatives." *The Reference Librarian.* 82 (2003): 39-55.
Slack, Frances, and Jennifer Rowley. "Kiosks 21: a new role for information kiosks?" *International Journal of Information Management* 22(1) (February 2002): 67-83.
Ya Ni, Anna, and Alfred Tat-Kei Ho. "Challenges in e-government development: Lessons from two information kiosk projects." *Government Information Quarterly*, 22(1) (2005); 58-74.

Copy That!
Reaping the Potential Benefits
from Incorporating a Copy Center
within Access Services

Phil Roché

INTRODUCTION

The Copy Center at Southern Utah University (SUU) is located in the Gerald R. Sherratt Library (the campus's single library facility), operating within the Access Services department structure and providing many valuable products and services to the campus. Although maintaining a copy center within Access Services is a somewhat unique situation that can present challenges outside the normal scope of typical operations, the SUU Copy Center is a prosperous, flourishing enterprise: it not only provides indispensable goods and services, it also serves as a way to attract more patrons and promote the Library's excellent services and resources. Moreover, the Copy Center works closely with the other areas of Access Services (Circulation, Interlibrary Loan, Media/Curriculum, and Serials) in training and sharing of the Library's Work-Study students, thereby creating a more unified and cross-trained pool of workers. However, prior to attaining its current robust state, the Copy Center struggled for several years in a somewhat perplexing operational mode as it attempted to function in disparate locations and without a clearly defined role. At one point university administration strongly considered closing the Copy Center and eliminating this valuable service from the campus altogether. Yet, over the past few years the Center has been revitalized through a fortuitous combination of smart resolutions and good fortune that have coalesced to create a healthy, thriving setup that is beneficial beyond simply providing copy service to the campus.

HISTORY

The SUU Copy Center has been affiliated, in one form or another, with the Sherratt Library for many years. However, it was not until the latter part of 2005 that it became a centralized enterprise within the Access Services department. Previously Copy Center functions were stretched across two campus buildings, the Sherratt Library and the Electronic Learning Center (which houses, among other things, student computer labs, a media center, and facilities for televised classes), and two departments, the Library and Information Technology. This unusual situation had its genesis in the early 1990s prior to the construction of the Sherratt Library, when all library documents and operations were located in the Electronic Learning Center and the then Copy Center included all materials and supplies for creating and duplicating.

However, due to construction limitations, appropriate square footage to accommodate a copy center could not be requested for the new library building (the future Sherratt Library), so it was decided to initially move only copy machines in to the new library and leave behind all other machinery in the Electronic Learning Center. Thus, after the Sherratt Library opened in 1996, a Copy Center (consisting of a collection of copy machines) relocated to this new library building, while a Media Center (other duplicating machinery and supplies including overhead projectors and VCRs) remained in the Electronic Learning Center. Naturally, this arrangement caused much confusion and irritation for the campus as well as some considerable administrative challenges. Additionally, various employees (some of whom were not involved in daily operations of the Copy Center or Media Center) were engaged in the ordering of materials during this time, which resulted in materials requests and purchasing being completed in an often haphazard manner. This led to an enormous accumulation of excess amounts of materials and supplies, many of which were not needed or, consequently, used (who knew there were so many shades of blue construction paper available?). In an effort to alleviate this knotty situation, some of the equipment and materials located in the Media Center were methodically shifted to the Copy Center over the course of the next several years. Despite employing 2 to 3 staff members to oversee services, as well as a dozen or more student assistants, during this time operations were muddled as the Copy Center/Media Center was not a profitable enterprise and, to make matters worse, the situation was exacerbated as this period coincided with several lean funding years due to lack of growth in student enrollments.

KEY DECISIONS AND IMPROVEMENTS

With a bleak outlook and a financially draining enterprise, as well as a frustrated customer base, university administrators were forced to take a fresh look at the Copy Center in 2005, and it was at this time that several key decisions created the momentum that has carried the SUU Copy Center to its currently successful model. First, at the behest of the Provost, all pertinent materials and services were consolidated in to the Sherratt Library's Copy Center location. Next, the decision was made to send all remaining hardware, such as VCRs and projectors, to individual departments for usage as needed. Following this, the Library Dean and Associate Director elected to add the Copy Center to the Access

Services department in order to make certain that the enterprise could be closely monitored and supervised. In addition, library administration hired a former student employee who had recently acquired a Master of Accountancy degree to administer and supervise the daily operations of the Copy Center. This employee has not only brought stability to the Copy Center, but a great deal of valuable expertise in accounting, book-keeping, and inventory control. Lastly (and perhaps most importantly), this newly hired staff member's salary recently became a part of the general library funding, thus ensuring that regular financial support for the position would not be contingent upon future Copy Center revenues. While each of these actions has greatly contributed to an improved level of service, they have also significantly reduced the confusion and ill-will that many patrons had formerly experienced concerning docu-ment reproduction services. For example, to maximize convenience and minimize confusion, the Copy Center adopted the Sherratt Library's hours of operation and assumed the same billing options offered at the Circulation Desk (cash, check, credit card, debit card, Blackboard One-card, and campus departmental accounts). Most importantly, the newfound success of the Copy Center helped to bring additional patrons in to the library, thus making the Sherratt Library an even more valued resource. An excellent example of increased traffic to the library is the near doubling of the number of copies made in the Copy Center over the course of the past two academic years (from 218,573 to 421,002).

PRODUCTS AND SERVICES

Since the changes of 2005, the revamped SUU Copy Center has been offering many products for sale. Current offerings include:

- Blue Books
- Carbonless forms (NCR 2 part, 3 part, 4 part, 5 part, and 6 part)
- Certificate paper (8.5″ × 11″)
- CD-R disks
- CD-RW disks
- Covers (clear plastic, composition, leatherette, linen, marble, sturdy grain, and windows)
- Craft Sticks
- Dividers (folder tabs)
- DVDs
- Envelopes (9″ × 12″, 11.5″ × 14.5″, legal, and letter)

- File folders (letter size)
- Index cards
- Paper including bright paper, butcher paper (36″ wide), construction paper, copy paper (8.5″ × 11″, 8.5″ × 14″, and 11″ × 17″), cover paper (heavy), graph/grid paper, index paper (pastel heavy), parch paper, penny paper, and résumé paper
- Paper sacks
- Pencils (number 2 size)
- Poster board
- Process board
- Scantrons
- Zip Disks (100MB, 250MB, and 750MB)

Some of the services now provided by the Copy Center include:

- Binding including ring binding and VeloBinding®
- Collating
- Copying and printing including black & white and color prints (8.5″ × 11″ and 11″ × 17″), microform reader/printer prints, black & white and color transparencies, and transparency frames
- Cutting including die cutting, drilling (hole drills), and pre-made die cuts and stencils
- Dry mounting
- Fax service (receiving and sending)
- Laminating (12″, 18″, and 27″) and pouch laminating (for business cards, credit cards, driver's licenses, and jumbo size)
- Lettering and numbering on forms
- Machine folding
- Padding for note pads (1″ pads)
- Perforating and scoring
- Poster printing (17″ × 22″, 20″ × 27″, 23″ × 31″, and 36″ × 45″)
- Scanning
- Shrink wrapping
- Stapling

CURRENT CHALLENGES

As with any business enterprise (successful or otherwise), the SUU Copy Center is not without challenges. For example, administration of daily functions is an ever-present concern in that a single, 30 hours per week staff member is currently employed, in the role of Copy Center Assistant, to directly manage the program. While this position, in combination with other Access Services personnel and approximately a half-dozen student assistants, has managed adequately until now, it can occasionally prove difficult to run the program taking in to account time for sick leave and vacation. Happily, this past winter the Assistant Library Secretary agreed to serve in a backup role to cover any staff shortages. However, this is not an ideal manner in which to rectify the situation as the Assistant Secretary is not necessarily always available to train and assist the program. A better model would be to gain an additional position (either half or full time) that is dedicated exclusively to Copy Center operations. Also, it would be preferable that the Copy Center Assistant position be a full time (40 hours per week) one. However this has yet to occur simply because the current Assistant has elected to remain as a 30 hour employee. Another challenge is the ongoing replacement of equipment. Copiers and other duplication machinery that are heavily utilized are normally in need of replacement every few years and this process can be very time consuming and slow the completion of work, as staff often must spend considerable amounts of time learning the details of new equipment. Yet another challenge (and one that did not even seem remotely possible just a short while ago) is that due to the recent success of the SUU Copy Center, the operating budget fund balance has grown so large that it is possible the Sherratt Library might again be asked to use Copy Center revenues to fund the Copy Center Assistant position. Although in the current climate this seems feasible, should revenues begin to suffer this could easily become an enormous burden upon the enterprise owing to the significant ongoing expense of employee salary and benefits. Finally, an aspect of the integration of the Copy Center in to Access Services that has yet to be fully exploited is the tremendous potential that could be realized via support staff (other than student employees) being cross-trained to work in a more cooperative relationship. Due to the fact that the Copy Center has slowly shifted its base of operations to the Access Services department and was not fully integrated until recently, this potential has yet to be fully realized.

FUTURE

The future of the SUU Copy Center appears very bright. It is a thriving enterprise that offers nearly all duplication and reproduction products and services required by the campus community, and this success has led to greater customer satisfaction as well as appreciation for, and increased utilization of, other library resources and services. Yet major changes to the operation are looming as the Copy Center Assistant is considering leaving the university in order to pursue a career in accounting, and continuing the momentum generated from the expertise this employee has brought to the position is absolutely critical. Looking to the future, the SUU Copy Center should continue to move forward with its current successful management and operations arrangement. In addition, to maintain the prosperity of the enterprise, it's critical that the Copy Center persist in keeping close tabs on product and service offerings as well as maintaining a flexible approach to the needs of the campus. For example, creating and maintaining a staffing and technology plan that addresses the specific needs and concerns of both the Copy Center and its patrons would go a long way towards accomplishing the continued success of this valuable campus resource. In addition, ongoing strong support from university administration is a key component of any continued success for the SUU Copy Center and it is hoped that this continues to be forthcoming. Finally, based upon anecdotal evidence of customer satisfaction, as well as large increases in the number of copies made since the reorganization, continued movement in the direction of a complete assimilation in to the Access Services department points to even greater Copy Center and Sherratt Library usage and customer satisfaction.

REFERENCES

Bond, Naomi. 2007. Interview by Phil Roché. May 14. Gerald R. Sherratt Library, Southern Utah University, Cedar City, UT.

Brown, Vik. 2007. Interview by Phil Roché. May 11. Gerald R. Sherratt Library, Southern Utah University, Cedar City, UT.

Gerald R. Sherratt Library. "10 Years of Excellence: 2005-2006 Annual Report." Gerald R. Sherratt Library. *http://www.li.suu.edu/library/Annual Report/AnnualReport2005-06. pdf.*

24-Hour Service
at Georgia Southern University:
1989-2007

Fred Smith

BEGINNINGS

When we at Georgia Southern have visitors from other libraries and we're talking about what we do that really stands out, the one thing which always raises eyebrows is when we tell them we are open twenty-four-hours a day from Sunday at noon until the following Friday at midnight.

To explain what motivated us to try this experiment, let me take you back eighteen years. In 1989 Georgia Southern was a medium-sized public senior college which had experienced tremendous growth. Our Academic Vice President, Dr. Harry Carter, told the Deans and University Librarian Julius Ariail that we were expecting one thousand more students the next Fall Quarter than the previous one. (Yes, quarters in those days, not semesters). He challenged the library and the other academic divisions to come up with creative ways to accommodate 1,000 more students which did not involve construction and the related costs.

One of the library's main concerns at the time was what to do about the crowds that came in to use the computers the last few weeks of every quarter. This was a time of transition during which the typical college paper went from being typed to being word processed. At that point all floors were open until midnight. We had only a handful of computers on our first floor and we were the only computer lab on campus open at night. Every night during the last part of each quarter there was a mad scramble for the seats at the computers and we had to practically drag people out to get the doors locked somewhere close to midnight. There was some demand for other library services late at night, but the computers, and especially the word processing, were the main thing.

We could have just extended the hours, but we had a sense that unless we extended them until well into the early morning it wouldn't be enough. And we couldn't figure out whether to hire part time people or ask people already on staff to work later. We could have just extended service for part of the quarter, but we have found that to only offer a service part of the time causes confusion and we wanted consistency. The University Librarian was aware of a gymnasium which was open 24 hours a day, and he found the idea intriguing.

There were some library classrooms and study space on that floor also. The main entrance was on the second floor, but there was a door on the first floor which we used for access to people with disabilities. It was possible to lock off the other floors and let everyone come and go from the first floor entrance. We thought about opening the whole building, but given what the demand was for, we figured that opening the first floor would suffice. The first floor contained periodicals and the Learning Resources Center (LRC), a computer lab. Patrons could use the computers, periodicals, and copiers overnight and they could study. There were quiet pockets with carrels and tables and classrooms that could be used for group study.

The University Librarian and Mary Dudman, the Circulation Librarian, realized that opening from eleven o'clock at night to eight o'clock in the morning, which was a nine-hour shift with a supper break (or breakfast or lunch depending on your orientation) would resolve the nagging problem of what time to begin service for the day. No current staff would have to work any later and the jobs would be full time with benefits and thus easier to fill. It seemed a perfect answer to Dr. Carter's challenge. So the University Librarian, Circulation Librarian, and the Department Head in charge of the Learning Resources Center met to plan the service. They decided that reference service would not be provided nor would expert help with the computer applications. The overnight staff would assist with copiers and periodicals, and provide security.

Security was the main concern of the gym model and it seemed prudent for us to consider it our top priority too. We decided that two people would be enough to staff the first floor of the library shift, one working inside the lab and the other out. The one inside the lab would report to the LRC Department Head and the one out would report to the Circulation Department Head. They would have some security work experience, would wear uniforms, and carry flashlights. We also decided that if one of the people was not able to come to work, we would not allow only one staff member to run the shift alone. On the first day of Fall Quarter 1990 we began the service. Within days we realized this was unworkable and went back to the Academic Vice President to ask for a third person. No matter how dependable people are, you can't expect them to never be out for any reason, so we realized we needed to hire a third person. We didn't think we needed any more security people, but we quickly found something for the third person to do: shelve periodicals.

OVERNIGHT STAFF DUTIES IN THE EARLY DAYS

In the beginning we called two positions "security," and the other "shelver." The shelver worked hard shelving periodicals while the security person outside the computer lab hardly ever broke a sweat. This did not seem fair or practical, so we added periodicals shelving to that security person's responsibilities. For several years there was so much shelving that sometimes the two of them would shelve the entire night. The other person spent his time at a service desk in the computer lab. His seat had a view of the door so that no one walked out with any computers.

We had to rehire the positions many times, and each time we hired a new person we had to have him/her fitted for a rented security uniform. By the third year of the program I had become Head of Circulation. Not long after becoming department head, I realized that we had never had a security type incident in the first two years. So we stopped bothering with the uniforms and de-emphasized the security aspects of the job when hiring.

In the space of a few years big changes had taken place on our first floor, as I'm sure they had all over the library environment. The number of computers for student use had increased several times and they had overflowed to the area outside the lab room. Those outside had networked CD-ROM periodical indexes for patrons to use. Help in using them was provided mostly from a group of student assistants who worked until midnight, but after midnight students were on their own. As was the case with the applications inside the lab students did not like to be told that there was no one to help them. Students could easily forgive the staff if they tried to help and couldn't find what they were looking for, but they pitched a fit when a staff member told them they were not going to at least try to help them. So I instructed the two staff members who reported to me to go ahead and try to help when it came up, but to explain to the users that they were not trained on this and that more knowledgeable people would be available in the morning. We also tried to point late night users to the many brochures and manuals available.

FOOD AND DRINK ISSUE

One request that seemed to come up, over and over again, through our suggestion system, was to allow the late night customers to bring in food and drink to the facility. And since so few places in Statesboro were open that late they asked if we would consider putting in vending machines. At first the idea seemed anathema as it is in most libraries. But we wanted to be responsive to patron needs so we decided to try it. The name of the library is the Zach S. Henderson Library and we named our small vending area on the first floor "Zach's Snacks." We have had few serious problems with allowing food and drink and the goodwill this created has been more than worth it. The food and drink issue is just one example of the twenty-four-hour service influencing a decision about the whole library.

EVOLUTION OF OVERNIGHT SERVICE

We had a major organizational change that began when the department head in charge of the LRC left the library. We had long thought we needed to provide reference service on the first floor and Laura Davidson, the new Head of Reference, had a background in computer applications. The University Librarian decided to put all of the public service aspects of computing–whether applications or information searching–under the Reference Department and rename it Information Services. At the same time, my title became Head of Access Services and all three of the late night staff began reporting to me. In time we had computers for Internet access outside the lab, which meant email, chat, discussion groups, gophers, bulletin boards, MUDs, games, and music. The Web, Netscape, Explorer, and GALILEO had come along. We had moved the older half of our periodicals collection to a storage room on the fourth floor to make room for more computers. We still had about 100 computers that we mostly used for applications in the lab room, now called the Microcomputer Applications Area or MAA. We put about 40 older, slower machines outside the MAA for students to use for email and chat, and we got another hundred new, top-end computers for information searching and applications. We put applications on these machines too, hoping to blur the distinction between what students could and could not do inside the MAA and outside the MAA. But old habits die hard and most people still went inside the MAA for applications and outside for informational searching.

By this time we had many databases that contained full text articles. Printing was free. As you would imagine, there were still some periodicals to shelve, but the overnight crew spent less and less time shelving periodicals.

MORE SPACE, MORE STAFF

When we added the last batch of computers we also took away a large chunk of the seating space on the first floor, which was still the only floor open for overnight service. We had added a projection system to the two classrooms. The equipment was so expensive that we decided we would have to stop using the rooms for group study for fear of vandalism. An unwanted side effect of these two changes was that we had little space left for those who just wanted a quiet place to study. And we began hearing about it. We thought of allowing students to go up to the fourth floor to study, but we were concerned about providing security for those areas. Another complication was that there were only certain times during the quarter when the students asked about more study space.

From time-to-time the University Librarian had mentioned opening all four floors for twenty-four-hours, but we had thought it would take at least five people to have enough staff patrolling the upper floors to have a real security presence. This seemed like a lot of personnel money to spend on a service that wouldn't be used throughout the entire quarter. During Spring Quarter 1997 a candidate for a student government position announced that one of his campaign platforms was to open all four floors of the library for study and for checking out books. The student newspaper wrote an editorial asking for the same services. We were aware of the study problem, but we had not had many requests for book checkout overnight. We had also not had many requests for reserves service, but more so than book checkout. We realized it would be nice to be able to tell faculty that their reserves would be available all night so that students could never say they didn't have time to use them.

The Academic VP and University Librarian got together and decided they would love to be able to say yes to the students. From the point of view of the Academic VP, it would take only a tiny piece of the budget to create good will with the Student Government Association, student newspaper, and student body as a whole. So we decided to hire one more person and open the second floor, which includes the Circulation Desk and the A-V/Reserves Desk, which were separate service desks at that time. The main entrance on the second floor remained the entrance all day and night–we didn't change it to the first floor at midnight anymore. We decided to actively staff those two desks until 2:00 a.m. and then staff them as needed. The staff went to the upstairs stacks to retrieve books for students all night and assisted students with reserves as requested. One staff member provided circulation and reserves service all night. All of the staff members carried walkie-talkies so the person at the Circulation Desk could summon others as needed. In this way we could offer around-the-clock service for those two areas, raising the security. Students would also have access to the reference collection and the browsing book collection all hours.

When the Student Government Association and the student newspaper first brought up the idea of opening the upper floors, we were surprised. We wished they had talked to us before writing editorials and using the idea as a campaign plank. But we soon realized we had been given a huge compliment. We saw it as an affirmation of the value of the twenty-four hour service.

OVERNIGHT SERVICE IN RECENT YEARS

Overnight service rocked along for a few more years with no changes. As was the case in most of the library world our hard copy periodicals and printed materials in general were being used less and less. So there were fewer periodicals to shelve. Assistance with computer issues, especially printing, became a large part of the overnight service routine. We continued to offer all circulation and reserve services. We now send most of our notices by e-mail, but for those who still receive paper notices we utilize the overnight crew to print and fold the notices. Toward the end of the shift the overnight staff always helped the day shift by filling all printers and photocopiers with paper and putting up the signs which we use to schedule and reserve our classrooms.

After many years of being the overnight supervisor, one of the overnight crew wanted to join the day shift. He had performed well for many years and we wanted to accommodate him so we looked at the possibilities. We were not going to be given a new position to replace him and we had no vacant positions open in the day shifts. We mulled over using part-time staff, casual labor, or student assistants. Dr. Carter, the long time VP for Academic Affairs, to whom the library reported for many years, had a rule that students could not work past midnight. After he left Georgia Southern we decided to reconsider that option.

We had conducted counts of the users in the building since the first days of the service and we knew that the number dropped substantially between 2:00 a.m. and 3:00 a.m. With any team that works at a time when there is no back up allowances must be made for sickness, emergencies, and lunch breaks. But with three full staff members, we thought that if we had a student assistant from midnight until 4:00 a.m. we would have all the bases covered.

We had not been staffing the overnight service with this arrangement long when the economy turned sour. For two years in a row the state of Georgia took big budget hits and the University System of Georgia was part of the massacre. After much discussion, the Henderson Library decided to absorb most of its part of the budget reduction by cutting the student assistant budget.

In order to cut the student assistant budget, we cut hours for some services and we substituted staff for student assistants. Since enrollment drops substantially summer semesters we decided to close at midnight during summer semesters. The staff who had been working overnight began working days and evenings so we were able to manage with very few student assistants during the summer semester.

Part of the scheme for substituting staff for student assistants had to do with the evening shift. For years, the busiest time in the library was weekday evenings. There was only one staff person available in Access Services during this time. We had merged the Circulation and A-V/Reserves Desks so there was only one service point. We had an ample number of student assistants, but she was the only staff person and we require a staff person to be available at the Circulation/Reserve Desk at all times. If she was ill or needed to take a day off work unexpectedly for any reason it was a bit messy. She had long called for another staff member to work at night. If we had a staff member on her shift it would free up student budget money. Again going back to the fact that he heaviest usage occurs before two o'clock we came up with a plan to have one of the staff members work a schedule of 5:00 p.m. to 2:00 a.m. The remaining two staff members were asked to take all breaks before 2:00 am so that there would be at least one staff member on each floor.

This staffing arrangement addressed some issues, but in time a new one arose. The person who worked the 5:00 p.m. to 2:00 a.m. schedule had one supervisor for the first part of her shift and another for the second, and this caused problems. So we decided to ask her to work 3:00 p.m. to midnight and hired a second student assistant to work the overnight shift. That remains the current arrangement.

Several years ago now we introduced electronic reserves. Few library services we have introduced have been more immediately successful. No matter how many resources we threw at e-reserves the demand stayed ahead of our efforts, especially at the beginning of each semester. The usage pattern with the overnight service is the opposite of reserves; there are very few late night users the first few weeks of each semester when reserves processing is at its most intense. To accommodate this pattern, one of the overnight team began scanning e-reserves for part of his shift thereby helping us keep up with that demand.

This past fall we moved into an addition to the library while the old library building is renovated. In this building we have an Automated Retrieval Collection or ARC. This is a large room full of metal storage bins filled with library materials. When an item stored in the ARC is needed, a machine delivers the bin for retrieval. In most cases, the items stored here are returned to the bins after uses. There were many new workflows with the integration of the ARC, but who would return the materials to the ARC and was a sticky one. By now you can probably guess who was selected.

SECURITY ISSUES

We have had very few true security incidents since we began the service. Exceptions would include the time someone tried to throw a fire extinguisher through the front of a television monitor and an altercation between students. The University Police were called and they came immediately and nothing more came of it.

One of our early concerns was that we might attract the homeless, and we are probably one of the very few libraries which have a sleeping policy. Ours is sort of like the old billiards rule: you can sleep in a chair so long as you have one foot on the ground. We do not allow people to bring pillows or sleeping bags or other sleeping equipment into the building.

An under-utilized service on our campus is the Escort Service. From midnight on, University Police can be summoned to escort students to their cars or dorms. The parking lots are nearby and they are lighted, but the lighting is a soft, amber light that doesn't provide a feeling of safety to everyone.

There have been what I'll call quasi security problems. Patrons seem to prefer late nights to download music–possibly illegally–but I believe that's just because there are fewer other users around. It does happen other times. We have had a few hard drives stolen, but were never able to pin down when it happened. Our guess was that it was during the late night because it would be easier when few patrons or staff are around, but we never knew for sure.

For a number of years we had a dummy security camera in place in front of the largest room of computers. The "camera" looked just like a real security camera; it had a red light which blinked menacingly throughout the day and night. After a security incident in another part of the building at eleven o'clock in the morning we installed real cameras. We have signs at the entrance declaring that there are security cameras around. It's hard to say whether this has helped, but it couldn't hurt!

We ask that our overnight workers wear a blue vest or name tag for two related reasons. One is to make it clear that she/he is a library employee so that patrons can ask the person for general assistance. The other is that if there were an emergency and a patron were in an agitated state it would be easy to quickly pick out the person working for the library. This is not as important for persons behind service desks, but it may not be obvious that students and staff who are shelving periodicals or performing other duties are employees.

One precaution we take is that we have only a small amount of money available at the Circulation Reserve Desk for giving change. All large sums and other valuables are kept in the safe and the overnight crew is not given the combination. This protects them as well. We have a policy copied from other businesses and institutions that says that whenever there is only one person on duty that person does not have access to the safe.

USE PATTERNS

The patterns of use are predictable. You can be certain there will be few people in the building during the wee hours the first couple of weeks of each semester. Usage usually begins picking up about the third week and continues to grow until the last weeks of the semester. The week of finals use drops off considerably and what we're left with are students studying for finals and some surfers and game players. The use patterns each night are predictable too. There is a lot of activity until two o'clock or so. Between 2:00 a.m. and 3:00 a.m. the numbers drop off sharply. Between 7:00 p.m. and 8:00 a.m. students start to come in before class.

COMMUNICATION

Communicating with the overnight workgroup is very important. I see everybody briefly when I come in the morning and we discuss anything unusual that may have happened. We depend on e-mail a lot. The overnight crew must plan vacations as far in advance as possible. If one finds at the last minute that she or he can't come in, she/he is instructed to call the night supervisor at the Circulation/Reserve Desk. The night supervisor only calls me if more than one person is expected to be out.

HIRING

A drawback to the service is that while we have had no trouble finding people to fill the jobs, keeping the positions filled is another matter altogether. Many of the applicants are students. They tend to know a lot about using the library, but they want to take off at inconvenient times for us. No matter how many times we preach to them that this is a staff position, many seem to retain a student mentality. For instance, they will inform us at a busy time that they must study for a big test the next day and won't be working their shift. When we say, "Whoa! Sorry about the test, but you can't have tonight off" they are shocked and affronted. When we remind them about the expectations of a staff position they still don't get it.

There are benefits to hiring people who are used to staying up late and like it, and there are benefits to hiring people with knowledge of the Web and computer applications. But we have to be careful not to hire someone who is going to want to play on the computers all night long. Dependability is by far the most important characteristic we look for. There is no real backup if you find at 10:30 p.m. that both of your people can't come in. Despite the scarcity of security incidents we look for people with cool heads and good judgment.

All who have worked in public service know the way students sometimes come in to the library, just starting on a paper due within a few hours. They expect everything to work out exactly as they planned and if materials aren't on the shelf or printers aren't working or there is no one on duty who knows how to show them how to do something, and it's two o'clock in the morning, they get frustrated. Not only do they want expert help in finding the information, they want to write it using word processing software and they want to be taught the word processing software from scratch, too. So the staff must have cool heads and must be good with the public. The cool head helps too if they have to lead an evacuation for any reason. Actually, the way these jobs have evolved through the years, the people in these positions are some of the most versatile and capable people in the library.

Hiring both staff and student assistants can be a challenge. We have had at least one staff person say she simply could not handle the schedule. And we have had numerous student assistants say the same. As you might imagine, we often find we cannot be too picky in filling these positions. What qualifications we want and what qualifications the applicants bring to the job may not match well. But one thing we always look for is whether they have at some time in the past worked a similar shift successfully. In the case of student assistants, we sometimes interview those whom our late night crew see in the library during their shift, since we know they are already used to the late night schedule.

HIRING STUDENTS VS. STAFF

The advantages and disadvantages of hiring students versus staff to work the shift share similarities with any shift. I believe it is necessary to have at least one staff person on duty for security reasons and there are circulation functions only staff are allowed to do. Student employees are notorious for turning up "sick" during the busiest times. Sometimes they quit their jobs without giving any real notice. Of course paying them minimum wage with no benefits is a lot cheaper.

Given that there are only two staff members on duty it is imperative that they have a clear understanding of each other's job. The person who works mostly in the computer lab must be thoroughly familiar with all circulation policies and procedures. The person who works the Circulation/Reserve Desk must know how to release print jobs, charge for printing, and understand what printing is free and what isn't. They must know how to handle printing for patrons who aren't Georgia Southern students, and how to add toner and paper to all the various printers, photocopiers, and microfilm copiers.

ADVANTAGES OF 24-HOUR SCHEDULE

The main benefit is that the students really like the library for providing 24-hour service. It's a good selling point for the library and the university. It stretches your resources. By extending the hours you allow maximum use of your facility. From a circulation or access services department head's point of view it has the added benefit of letting us get the majority of our periodicals shelving and shelf reading done by staff and frees the student assistants for book shelving. The notices which aren't sent by email are printed and mailed by the overnight crew.

Because they work at what are often slow times the overnight crew gets other thankless jobs from time to time, both from me and the Dean's Office. Do you ever have jobs which are too disruptive to do during normal business hours? If you run this shift, you can get them done at five o'clock in the morning, and very few people will be disturbed by them. Once we wanted to switch all the chairs from one floor to another. The late shift was perfect for that job. Sometimes when ILL is in a pinch the late night team pulls and copies or scans articles during overnight service hours. They do periodical shift and book shifts. At one point one of the crew was trained on processing instructor's reserves and this was particularly helpful at the beginning of each semester.

Once you get used to the idea that you have this workforce, other ideas along these lines will begin occurring to you. We are very appreciative of the extra help the overnight staff give us on all kinds of things.

Sometimes what we ask them to do probably makes as much sense to them as counting the holes in the ceiling tiles, but they do it. Counting the ceiling tiles holes is an inside joke here. We frequently ask them to help us gather statistics by counting various things which they can't imagine why we think need to be counted.

There is no closing the library, so that sometimes onerous duty is avoided altogether. The overnight crew at the Henderson Library also fill the copiers and printers with paper and toner and put reservation signs on the classrooms. If furniture has been dragged to places where it doesn't belong, the overnight crew drags it back.

During the intersessions, night staff can be handy. We don't stay open overnight during the intersession, so we have to offer them other hours and other duties. As is the case with all public service people, we encourage them to take vacations then. We always try to be flexible in what schedule they want to work during the breaks; after all, we are asking them to disrupt their regular sleeping pattern. They know circ and reserve routines and can pinch-hit for other people taking leave. They can pull and copy or scan ILL materials. While many academic libraries close at 5:00 p.m. on intersession weekdays, we close at 8:00 p.m. and the overnight crew is a big help in staffing that 5:00 p.m.-to-8:00 p.m. period. They are great to have when we are doing a major shift, a major shelf reading, or other building project. But when we have no major project going on, we must find them something beneficial to do. A number of times through the years they have helped the upper administration of the library and other people outside my department with special projects.

DISADVANTAGES

The program does what we hoped it would do all those years ago. The students are quite pleased about it except for one thing: until midnight the students get help from a reference librarian and staff and student assistants trained in the use of applications software. After midnight we can't deliver much more than help with printing and very basic software and reference. The students do not like being told that there is no one there to help them.

Twenty-four-hour service can present some unusual personnel issues. If there are disputes between members of the shift, it's hard to understand all sides of an issue and come to a resolution since you only see the staff briefly at the beginning of each day. Annual evaluations for overnight staff are difficult, since day supervisors have so little chance to observe and interact with them.

There is considerable time spent hiring employees. Occasionally you will get lucky and find someone who thrives on working the overnight shift, but much more often the people will apply for the day position that comes open in your library after they have been hired for an evening position.

Another problem has to do with the Circulation/Reserve Desk. For the first several years we didn't allow access to the floor it's on. Once we allowed access we had to train staff on circulation and reserve procedures. As any circulation person will tell you there are a zillion details to remember about circulation work. The Circulation/Reserve Desk is not busy at night, and this means that anything somewhat out of the ordinary will be hard for the overnight staff to deal with. Mistakes may be made, which can lead to friction between members of different shifts.

At the Henderson Library at Georgia Southern we have twice used the LIBQUAL program to assess our effectiveness. A library with our hours of operation is going to score great on that part of the survey, right? Nope. LIBQUAL measures how your patron groups perceive your services and compares their perceptions to their expectations. It seems that we have been open twenty-four-hours for so long that our students are no longer impressed; it's what they *expect* from us.

OVERNIGHT SERVICE AND OUR FUTURE

Interlibrary loan service is part of the Access Services Department at Georgia Southern and this summer we plan to begin allowing faculty to request articles from materials we own. The plan is to scan the articles and link them on a server using the ILLiad software. Faculty members will be able to access the articles with an accession number. We may use some of the overnight staff time to do some of the scanning or we may use an overnight student assistant if we can find qualified students.

In 2008, the renovation of the original building will be complete and we will occupy both the addition and the existing building again. For years we have had a serious noise problem in the library. Individuals wanting to study quietly have a hard time finding a suitable spot even on our "quiet floors." During the day, this isn't much of a problem, but as evening falls noisy groups file in and the place is just louder generally. With the extra size of the building we anticipate the problem getting worse. So the Dean of the Library, Bede Mitchell, has started the ball rolling on getting a new staff position, a professional "shusher" of sorts. In addition to trying to ride herd on the noise, the person will see that the stacks are neat, help with printer problems, scan for document delivery, and serve as backup for several positions. We envision the person working from 6:00 p.m. to 3:00 a.m., which will mean that the person will have two supervisors during the course of the night. We are hoping our previous experience will help us head off trouble of that sort this time.

When we open the new/old building the Information Services Department (ISD) intends to include a Learning Commons. This will be an area with flexible seating arrangements. We will offer a combination of software, audiovisual media, and computer help as well as regular reference service. The ISD and student assistants have done a certain amount of this for years and it has always been part of a larger customer service problem for us. Patrons do not like to be told that they must go elsewhere for a service or that a service is only available at certain times. If we are open, they think any employee they approach should have the answers. When the Learning Commons is operational with a wider array of services, will the problem be magnified? What kind of fallout will that have for us in Access Services?

But for now, the twenty-four-hour service is a real point of pride for the whole campus community. The librarians are quick to mention it to other librarians at conferences or when they visit. It is a drawing card for prospective students. The Georgia Southern community would say that twenty-four-hour-a-day library service is not an experiment, but a permanent fixture of campus life.

ALI–
A Digital Archive of DAISY Books

Åsa Forsberg

INTRODUCTION

Project ALI, which aims to create and launch a digital archive of DAISY books, runs between April 2006 and September 2007. DAISY stands for Digital Accessible Information System and is a standard for Digital Talking Book (DTB). With DAISY printed text can be adapted to structured talking books in which the reader can navigate between pages, chapters, sections etc.

Project ALI is directed by the Library Head Office at Lund University, in collaboration with librarians and co-ordinators for students with reading disabilities at other universities and with the Swedish Library of Talking Books and Braille (TPB). It is financed by the Department for National Co-operation at the National Library of Sweden. Originally the project group consisted of Lund University, Karlstad University and Växjö University. Today the group also includes the universities of Södertörn and Växjö.

BACKGROUND

Students with reading disabilities in Swedish higher education have the right to have mandatory course literature adapted. Printed books can be adapted in different ways, but in this paper only the adaptation of print to talking books will be discussed.

According to the Swedish Copyright Law, paragraph 17, libraries and organisations which have obtained permission from the government are allowed to produce phonograms of literature and lend them to users, in this case of university libraries to students with reading disabilities.

TPB produces talking books from published literature having more than 100 pages. In Swedish higher education course syllabi quite often also include journal articles, book sections or chapters and texts written by course teachers. Shorter texts are often compiled in course packs which are sold to the students. All of these shorter texts are transformed to talking books locally by the participating universities for their students with reading disabilities.

Sweden has 42 universities and university colleges, all of which must produce talking books from mandatory course literature whenever they have students with reading disabilities enrolled in a course or a programme. In 2005, the Library Head Office at Lund University and the Library of Malmö University made a pilot study to investigate the needs and possibilities to develop an archive of locally produced talking books. Included in the pilot study was an inventory of how universities are currently producing and managing talking books for their students. With very few exceptions talking books are still produced as analogue tape recordings, with little possibility of archiving or reusing them. Every time a student needs a text it is produced as a new talking book, even if has been recorded before.

THE ALI PROJECT

The project consists of several interconnected activities, all on a national level:

a) To promote and facilitate the implementation of new digital production techniques to produce talking books at the universities.

The project has purchased licences for the production tool Plextalk Recording Software for further distribution to participating universities. The project has also, in collaboration with the Swedish DAISY Consortium, organised two training sessions for the narrators employed to produce the talking books.

Furthermore, the project has produced a user manual for the production tool and offers ongoing support.

b) To promote and facilitate the implementation of new routines for a rational and efficient handling of the production of talking books and the distribution to end users.

The project has analysed the different activities involved in the production of talking books at the participating universities and assigned more well-defined roles to the participants involved in this production.

The student contacts the librarian to discuss the syllabus. The librarian identifies and locates all course literature in order to find out which of the following applies:

- A text is already available as a talking book, in which case it naturally will not be produced as a talking book again; or,
- A text is already available in digital version, in which case the student can read it on a computer equipped with a speech synthesizer, and thus does not need to be produced as a talking book.

After this control the librarian orders the necessary production of talking books, either from TPB (books of 100 pages or more) or through the co-ordinator for students with disabilities.

This process demands some effort from the librarian in charge but saves both time and money since producing a talking book takes quite a long time and is also quite expensive.

The co-ordinator for students with disabilities has the economical responsibility for all support to students, including production of talking books. The advisor also co-ordinates supporting activities for individual students and administrates the students' access to databases such as the TPB catalogue and ALI.

c) *To develop a digital archive including an administration tool for libraries and a user interface for students.*

The project group's first effort was to specify the requirements in collaboration with the technical developer, who is based at the Library Head Office at Lund University. During the specification phase, and also during the development phase, the developer and the project leader have had thorough discussions and consultations with the very experienced technical developers at TPB in order to learn and also to create a solution compatible with the TPB digital library.

The beta version of the archive ALI was launched in January 2007. It has since then been tested by librarians, co-ordinators and students. The developed version 1 of ALI will be up and running in September 2007, but the project group is already planning for version 2, with more advanced and developed features.

A detailed description of ALI and its functions can be found below.

d) *To investigate the possibilities of the copyright law and how it can be interpreted in relation to the talking books in the digital archive and in relation to the very well defined user group, i.e., students with reading disabilities.*

The right to produce literature as talking books is regulated by the paragraph 17 in the Swedish Copyright Law, according to which libraries with talking book permission may produce talking books and distribute them to persons with reading disabilities. Our project to store talking books in a national digital archive is a new phenomenon which must be tested against the law and its possible interpretations. Through this process the project group gains knowledge and experience for further engaging in the production and dissemination of talking books to students with reading disabilities.

e) To market the archive towards librarians and end users.

The project and the resulting archive, ALI, have been presented at several Swedish and International conferences for librarians and co-ordinators for students with disabilities. The launching of the beta version in January 2007 is also part of the marketing. The project aims to include new participants during the project period, and two universities have joined the project group since the start. Training for librarians, co-ordinators and students is part of this process and has already taken place.

DAISY BOOKS

All books in ALI are produced with DAISY technique and are DAISY books. DAISY stands for Digital Accessible Information System and is a standard for Digital Talking Book (DTB). DAISY makes it possible to structure the text and to mark up for instance headings, subheadings and page numbers. The reader can navigate between headings and other text elements, jump back and forward in the text and skip parts if she or he wishes (Kerscher 2002; Morgan 2003). So far, the generally used version is DAISY 2.02 (DAISY 2.02 Specification 2001), which is built on xhtml and smil, the latter a standard to synchronise sound and text. There are several different types of DAISY. The two most commonly used in Sweden are DAISY sound and DAISY text and sound. The software the project uses can only produce DAISY sound, so the DAISY books in ALI will be of this type.

ALI–A DIGITAL ARCHIVE OF DAISY BOOKS

ALI is a digital archive which is published on the Internet. Today the archive contains around 100 DAISY books, produced by five Swedish universities (Lund, Karlstad, Växjö, Södertörn and Jönköping). The aim of the project is that all Swedish universities having students with reading disabilities enrolled produce DAISY books and upload them in the archive.

The content of ALI is made up of journal articles, book chapters, reports and texts written by course teachers. All documents are in the standardised DTB-format DAISY and can be produced either by a human narrator or with a speech synthesizer. Each text in a so-called course pack will be produced and archived as an individual DAISY book. Thus every single article, book chapter and other text will be searchable in the archive.

ALI consists of an administration tool and a user interface. The administration tool is the working space for the librarian. It is here the documents are registered and uploaded. The co-ordinators also use the administration tool to register the end as well. Since the production of DAISY books is regulated by paragraph 17 in the Swedish Copyright Law it is very important that only students with reading disabilities can access the material. The user interface is public but only students having an account can log in to download or order DAISY books.

The ambition is that ALI will be available in connection to the catalogue of TPB, to make it optimally visible and to offer one gateway to all DAISY literature to students. In the future a cross search in both systems is planned, as well as a spelling tool for the search engine.

WHAT WE WILL ACHIEVE WITH ALI

ALI will contain all DAISY books produced by Swedish universities and make them available in one single system, in connection to the TPB catalogue which contains published books in DAISY format. A cross search with spelling help will be available.

- Students, teachers, librarians and co-ordinators can search all literature in DAISY format in one place.
- ALI will allow faster access to already produced DAISY books.
- ALI can give support to teachers looking for alternatives for mandatory course literature.
- Each text will only be recorded once and can be reused as many times as needed.
- ALI offers a possibility for libraries to handle non-text material.

INFORMATION LITERACY AND LEARNING

During their academic education students are supposed to develop information literacy. An increasing number of courses and educational programmes use student active teaching methods, like problem based learning, where students are trained to take responsibility for their learning, and to search, evaluate and use information.

In Sweden, students with reading disabilities have only the right to have mandatory literature produced as DAISY books. In addition they have access to all DAISY literature in the TPB catalogue, consisting of published books. They have also access to the very large collections of electronic journal articles licensed to the universities, which can be read with a speech synthesiser, under the condition that the students have access to a computer equipped with speech synthesiser.

Through the ALI project, students and teachers at participating institutions will eventually have access to a substantial collection of DAISY books, such as scientific journal articles in many subject areas. This means that the students will have the opportunity to train their capability to search for relevant scientific information and this training is necessary if the students are to develop capabilities such as information literacy (Bowden 2004).

CONCLUSION

The ALI project has proved to be more complex and contains more dimensions than we had anticipated before the project started. Besides building the actual archive, we have had to consider different aspects involved in creating DAISY books as well as copyright and policy issues. The creation of a national digital archive of DAISY books produced by universities has not been done previously in Sweden and we are constantly walking along untrodden paths, testing new situations and acquiring new knowledge and new experiences.

So far, the project has been successful and the archive and number of users have grown faster than expected. In order to continue developing ALI and involve more universities we have received financing for a second project period between October 2007 and December 2008. The major activity during this period will be to ensure that ALI is compatible with the catalogue of TPB, so that the two collections can be made available on a common platform by the end of 2008. In order to comply with the digital library TPB is right now developing, we must develop and implement technical solutions such as streaming and cross searching. To provide our end users with as direct and seamless access as possible to all available DAISY collections we must also further explore and agree on policy and copyright issues, in close collaboration with the TPB staff.

REFERENCES

Bowden, John. (2004). Capabilities-driven curriculum design. In *Effective Learning and Teaching in Engineering*, edited by C. Baillie and I. Moore. London: Routledge-Falmer.

DAISY 2.02 Specification. (2007). DAISY Consortium 2001 [cited 10/5/2007]. Available from http://www.daisy.org/z3986/specifications/daisy_202.html.

Kerscher, George. (2002). DAISY is. Paper read at United Nations, at Bangkok.

Morgan, Greg. (2003). "A word in your ear: library services for print disabled readers in the digital age." *The Electronic Library*, 21 (3), 234-239.

STAFF DEVELOPMENT

Retraining is Draining:
Motivating Student Employees
to High Performance and Longevity

Nancy Lichten Alder

INTRODUCTION

At Brigham Young University we have an unusually high ratio [86:17] of student employees to regular staff employees when compared to other college or university libraries. Because the majority of our staff is student employees primarily interested in the completion of their own academic responsibilities, we have had to develop ways to encourage interest in and commitment to the job. Our philosophy is that if the student employees are happy in their job they will stay with us until they graduate. Cutting down on the hiring and training merry-go-round is high on our list of priorities. Clearly, motivated employees are more productive and more likely to stay with the organization. We aim to limit staff turnover and encourage growth in expertise and efficiency to maximize our employees' value to our organization while promoting their job satisfaction.

THE SCIENCE OF MOTIVATION

In developing methods of motivating our student staff, we turned first to the research affirming a hierarchy of human needs. Maslow indicates that when the basic needs for safety and physiological well-being are satisfied, the need for belongingness emerges, followed by the need for self esteem and then self-actualization. We sought to identify ways we could address and fulfill these needs within the work environment. We needed to go beyond the basics of providing a safe, comfortable environment and meeting survival needs though we found some success in what we call 'nacho motivation': providing food treats to reward and energize our student employees.

We found that there were clearly things we could put in place to help meet our student staff's desires in the areas of social satisfaction, increased self esteem, and self actualization even though their library jobs are temporary and peripheral to these employees' central life concerns.

THE ART OF MOTIVATION

Our process of semester-end student staff evaluations provides an opportunity to identify what our employees themselves want from their jobs. Because their part-time jobs are secondary to their main goal of successfully meeting class requirements, we had to look beyond the typical job-related aspirations for advancement in the organization. We asked questions such as, *"What would you like to see improve in your job? More interesting work? More say and participation? Greater recognition? More challenge? Better opportunity for skills development?"* We used their responses to develop ways to spur them to increased effort and foster greater job satisfaction.

We addressed general areas within the hierarchy of needs individually, identifying broad ideas of how these needs could be fulfilled within the workplace and then specific ways to fulfill each area. It broke down as follows:

- social needs: providing opportunities for team work, including shared fun activities, encouraging pleasant and non-superficial interpersonal relationships,
- self esteem needs: offering rewards for excellence, public praise and recognition,
- self-actualization needs: providing promotion possibilities and skills enhancement.

PLAYING WELL WITH OTHERS

One desire that came up again and again in discussions with our student employees was the feeling that their study responsibilities and stresses needed relief. They wanted to focus some energy and time on relaxation and fun, but the need to work along with taking a full class load and doing homework and projects did not leave much time for that. They expressed a desire to enjoy the time spent with coworkers and to develop friendships within the workplace.

Accepting their desire for a less-formal work environment, we incorporate playful methods of training and task completion where possible. We needed to keep a professional air in the office as patrons and other library staff moved in and out, but we were eager to loosen up a bit in any ways that did not compromise that professional atmosphere.

Our first efforts went to helping the employees get to know each other and their supervisors and managers, emphasizing personalities and interests and subverting the separations caused by job assignments and departmental divisions. We identified opportunities for purely social interactions such as parties and 'fun' meetings. Thus, the Borrowing unit started each weekly meeting with a Question of the Week. They went around the group in turn asking and answering such questions as "What is your favorite Christmas memory" or "Tell about an embarrassing moment."

We kicked off our Fall Semester Opening Meeting with a *Jeopardy*-inspired game. The object was to match a statement of a little-known-fact or interest with the supervisor it describes. We created a power point presentation and each student was given a clicker to signal when they had the answer. Frivolous statements such as:

- *attended the opening of JAWS with Donny and Marie Osmond,*
- *refuses to eat refined sugar,*

are just for fun, but designed to give a truthful glimpse into the real people with whom they work. At this meeting we also introduced the students to our policies and the perks we offer. We took care to emphasize that, while we plan to 'squeeze them dry' using all they have to offer in skills and talents, we encouraged them to find ways to incorporate artistic gifts or communication skills or a flair for writing into improving their work.

We identified opportunities for purely social interactions such as parties or group activities held outside work. The annual Circ Department Halloween Party was a real hit with our student staff. Supervisors and full-time staff provided a simple menu (this year it was chili and chips) and organized activities. The Palm Reader is always a favorite. Gag gifts were given as prizes for the group games we played. Each December we have an Access Services Christmas Party with food, music, movies and games, and each summer a barbeque is held in a nearby park. Some supervisors have organized weekend hikes or 'field trips' with their student staff. The emphasis is always on interaction and not just a hit-and-run for a free meal.

We also added a 'just for fun' component to training meetings and task requirements. Our Lending Unit's Supervisor, regularly holds Olympics where her student workers adopt a country to represent and compete in various timed work activities. Because we use Ariel and ILLiad, the tracking of request processing times is easy. The supervisor employs a stopwatch in the competition to pack items for shipping and again in the competition to retrieve a requested item submitted with a vague citation. Small prizes are handed out at the end of the competition.

Each semester our Borrowing unit plays the *Bertie Bott's Every Flavor Beans* game. Using a box of the famous Harry Potter candy for reward and punishment, the supervisor asks the students questions about the work process. A wrong answer means they have to eat one of the nasty tasting beans. We've found that linking a taste of earwax, dirt, or black pepper to the question reminds them not to make THAT mistake again. Believe it or not, this game is one of the students' favorites.

Occasionally at the end of Faculty Delivery Service unit weekly meetings the student workers are sent off to find an intentionally mis-shelved book. The first one to return with the correct answer of where it was found gets a candy bar.

At Brigham Young we make great use of our library's Wiki. Each unit of Access Services has its own Wiki page to which any employee can add. To keep student employees connected on a personal level, we have a section for posting wedding announcements, pictures, notice of sport or cultural events in which they are performing, and a recounting of the forehead-smacking gaffes that happen in the course of the job. This idea works well with permanent staff as well.

One of the most successful methods for ensuring student employee 'buy in' when projects have to be assigned is the Project Auction. The auction is prefaced with a survey where 50 or so points are awarded for silly 'accomplishments':

- ate breakfast this morning,
- socks match,
- has 9 or more letters in first name,
- has pierced ears,
- ate peanut butter last week.

The student worker can then use the accumulated points as currency for bidding on projects that would normally just be randomly assigned. Each can choose to blow all of his or her points on a single big project or bid on several smaller ones. Projects vary from routine housekeeping, such as reviewing and updating portions of the training manual, to one-time jobs such as designing a promotional flyer or bookmark or even shooting a training video.

We have found that adding an element of fun makes the 'medicine' of having to do a project at all go down easier. The students are able to choose a project that holds some interest for them and this often leads to a more conscientious effort and timely completion of the job. It's a win-win situation!

PICKING THEIR BRAINS–
TAPPING THEIR CREATIVITY

We use several methods to encourage our student staff to make suggestions for improving service and tweaking processes and tasks. Soliciting suggestions from the bottom up serves a dual purpose: it gives employees a voice in the processes of the department, engendering a feeling of empowerment, and it improves the work flow and the processes themselves. It is just good practice to solicit input from those on the 'front lines' who see glitches and stalls in the workflow most clearly. Often students bring their talents and interests to the table in addressing ways to improve things. We find that having a new student employee take a look at our procedures in light of their own experiences often yields a fresh take on how things can be done.

In keeping with the 'fun' aspect of our endeavors we periodically have our student employees submit a list of five 'Things That Must Go.' These may be things they just don't like, such as *Dismantle the copier that jams every few sheets* or substantial suggestions for change, such as *Let's change to an electronic log of daily pick-ups and do away with the paper copies*. We read the lists out loud in a meeting, enjoying a laugh at the funny ones and brainstorming on how to best implement those that are good ideas for improvements.

The Wiki comes into play, again, as an ideal venue for encouraging deeper thinking in regard to discrete work processes. Students are encouraged to write articles or create power point presentations on aspects of the job at which they excel. Sharing their expertise polishes the way the job gets done and the Wiki gets the word out department-wide. All employees have expressed interest in learning new skills from one another and in sharing their own expertise.

Student employees that have expertise with computer applications are truly valued and, I might say, even exploited. We have had students use time during slower request periods designing Flash presentations, interactive training modules and such. Students with demonstrated competence with Access have designed and run reports. We see that workers who take on these more challenging tasks that lie outside the proscribed workflow are typically more engaged in their jobs and more satisfied overall.

We have had a few student workers with artistic skill and interest. We enlist their help in creating bookmarks, flyers, brochures and other items to promote our Faculty Delivery Services to good result. We use their help in making the posters and displays that highlight accomplishments of our other student employees as well.

NON-TANGIBLE REWARDS

Certainly our employee's satisfaction with their jobs grows as they come to see that they are truly heard and that their input is valued regardless of where they stand on the organizational ladder. We demonstrate that suggestions for change or ideas for improvements are welcomed and appreciated by providing a forum for these suggestions to be presented. We find ways to shine a light on our student employees' creative gifts.

The library's Wiki can be viewed by those outside our own department as well as within. Seeing a process you have developed or polished presented in print for others to salute and implement is a powerful boost to self esteem.

Library-wide Town Meetings are a place where excellence is acknowledged to the larger organization. Mention of academic honors, the awarding of ORCA grants, and participation in University-wide projects or events are made there as well.

Department-wide meetings offer a chance to encourage the interaction between segments of Access Services. We use our department-wide meetings as an opportunity to offer public praise and recognition for benchmarks met or advanced in regard to customer service, accuracy, turnaround time and the like. These are also a venue for the presentation of ideas for policy or procedure improvements, especially those that straddle departmental units. Suggestions for streamlining communication between Circulation and Interlibrary Loan, for example, serve to solidify the joint commitment to customer service shared by different parts of Access Services. Recognition that a student employee's idea for improvements is accepted for consideration beyond the bounds of his own job can do much to raise confidence that his or her voice is being heard. It signals to all a student employee's worth to the organization as a whole. It can be heady stuff to have one's input sought and accepted by those outside the immediate work sphere and by those who are in positions of management.

TANGIBLE REWARDS

Perhaps the most ubiquitous method of motivating staff is the use of various tangible rewards to acknowledge excellence. These take a number of typical forms such as raises, bonuses and recognition awards. We operate on the bonus system, utilizing a complex formula of points reflecting and rewarding above-average performance and extraordinary talents or skills. We factor in longevity as well, rewarding the student employee who chooses to stay with our department rather than job-hop as so many temporary workers do. We provide a way for the student worker to advance to higher pay levels as they embrace additional tasks and demonstrate increased ability. These are not in the nature of raises but are rather advancement to a different job description within the organization.

Our excellence-recognition award, The Golden Bagel, is awarded based upon the nomination of their peers. We have a little ceremony each semester where the recipient is given an award–suitable for framing–that reiterates the positive comments given by coworkers and an accolade by their supervisor. A poster is also mounted for the semester with the employee's photograph and a blurb highlighting comments made in support of the nomination. Refreshments are served and the recipient is given two movie theater discount tickets as an added prize. An award of $15 is added to their bonus amount given at the semester's job evaluation meeting.

At Brigham Young University we also provide occasional perks such as the aforementioned food treats. Homemade goodies are the most appreciated, perhaps because they bring in the Mom factor, but the students never turn down a chance to dive into bags of chips or candy either. We acknowledge and celebrate the birthdays that fall within each month with cards and cake.

We also provide limited free scanning and electronic delivery or photo copying of papers, reports and projects. This is a real boon to students with little time and money.

CONCLUSION

Our experience has been that once attention is paid to where our employees find true job satisfaction, methods of motivation can be found that don't call for any great investment of training or money. Making the workplace pleasant and relatively stress-free, encouraging individual commitment to the vision and setting the stage for improving competence all benefit both the individual employee and the organization. Here at the Harold B. Lee Library, we determined that our Access Services student employees remain for an average of seven semesters in comparison to the three semesters worked in other library departments. Many of our student employees work in our department through their whole time at Brigham Young University. For us, the fact that student employee job satisfaction translates into longevity on the job and an active interest in the work processes is well worth our efforts to motivate and reward.

Improving Circulation Services Through Staff Involvement

Cynthia M. Kisby
Marcus D. Kilman

OPPORTUNITIES FOR IMPROVEMENT

Upon becoming the Department Head for the Circulation Services at the University of Central Florida's main library in September, 2004 the new leader was advised by the Associate Director of Public Services that there were some areas of service and other employee issues within the department in need of attention. Those areas needing improvement impacted not just quality of service at the Circulation Desks, but also staff morale and attitude, and, in turn staff attendance and tardiness. In fact, at that time the normal staffing level of ten permanent full time employees was down to five permanent and one temporary employee. It should be pointed out that most of these problems were not related to staff capability or desire.

At that time the Circulation Department included four units; circulation, reserves, stacks, and bills and fines. In addition, the circulation unit consists of two shifts, those working Monday through Friday days and those working evenings/weekends. Another significant factor was a lack of communication or a sense of team unity between these different groups. Other than coordinating their overlapping shifts to ensure complete coverage at the public service desks, there was little cooperation between the different units and shifts. The units did not share any common projects or goals and did not get involved in the work of each other's units.

DEVELOPING A PLAN FOR CHANGE

In order to bring about positive change in employee attitudes and improve morale in the department, and as a result, improve services to patrons it seemed that several items were critical to success. These included:

1. communication
2. training
3. empowerment
4. buy-in
5. commitment

The highest level of success, in this case the best possible patron service, could only be accomplished through the involvement, commitment, and direct actions of the staff. In order to get that sort of commitment the staff must buy in to the idea of accomplishing common goals. Buy-in requires a staff that is empowered to make decisions and take ownership of objectives. The ability to make the best decisions comes from proper training and the knowledge that their input, concerns, or suggestions are listened to, evaluated fairly, and acted upon. Empowerment of staff also means giving up some control as department head. A supervisor can become more comfortable with empowerment and delegation by being very clear about expected outcomes and deadlines, scheduling regular feedback and progress checks, and asking the employee to paraphrase back his understanding of the assignment. Responsibility should not be given to someone unless he/she is also given the authority required to succeed. The combination of authority with responsibility enhances buy-in, attitudes, and morale.

Communication

We embarked on this road to change with a series of department meetings where the goals of improving customer service were laid out as well as the belief that it could only be through staff ideas and actions that we could succeed. It was important that staff felt free to express their views and concerns and to also know that the "open door" policy was just that. While some changes that directly affected public service at the desks were made immediately as an initial step, working groups from the department staff were formed to look at modifying the department's student assistant guidelines, with the clear understanding that everyone would be held to a higher standard than the student assistants. Regular department meetings to solicit input and suggestions for positive change followed up by emails for clarification and discussion, plus encouraging staff to take advantage of the "open door" policy allowed plans for improvement to develop and mature. Specific ideas for improvement would then be finalized by consensus of the department as a whole at regular department meetings. As staff became more accustom to having the power to make positive change, their willingness and desire to assume even more responsibility and "ownership" of the department naturally increased.

Training

With the assistance of the Human Resources Librarian, a series of monthly training sessions was also implemented. The emphasis of these training sessions was customer service, dealing with change, and team-building. One of the more interesting training sessions was the Mystery Shopper program arranged through the UCF Human Resources Office. After meeting with Human Resources trainers to coach them on some more "difficult" circulation questions and patron issues, the HR staff made trips to the library or called in with questions, with the goal of being a "problem" patron. Staff was not made aware of the Mystery Shopper program until the results were presented to the staff by Human Resources at one of our regularly scheduled training sessions. Responsibility for responding to and making changes based upon the Mystery Shopper program was assumed by and successfully accomplished by the staff.

The Circulation Department Head also asked that Human Resources provide the Myers-Briggs Type Indicator survey, believing that understanding the strengths and weaknesses of different basic personality types would help staff be more understanding of each other and our patrons and thus help in providing better service. To assist staff in providing better patron service during library hours when the reference desk is not staffed by librarians, several of the staff asked if the reference librarians would be willing to provide some instruction on searching several of the more commonly used databases. Two very beneficial training sessions were planned and conducted, as a result of this suggestion staff was better able to respond to patron questions on how to search library databases during hours the reference desk is closed.

Buy-In and More

Once the group was well into the training sessions, it was decided to tackle a complete revision of the department's policies and procedures manual as well as development of a departmental mission statement and goals. Again, working groups within the department were set up, with each group responsible for developing some particular portion(s) of the revisions. In follow-up sessions, the draft revisions were discussed as a whole, modified as necessary, and implemented. The department's mission statement and goals have been posted on the web and are available at the public service desks.

As a direct result of the successful implementation of the improvement plans, and more importantly the dedication and efforts of staff, many changes within the department have been successfully implemented. Customer service is much better, staff morale is higher and instances of tardiness and absences have decreased. There are other examples where staff suggestions and initiatives resulting from this new direction in leadership have made significant contributions to both the department and the library.

IMPROVEMENTS AND BENEFITS

One of the most visible improvements is a reorganization of the layout of the stacks on the third floor of the library where the "flow" of the materials by call number range was confusing to patrons. As patrons followed the ranges of shelves by call number, when they would leave the HX call number range and walk straight across an open area to the closest range of books, they would find themselves in the M call number range. The K call numbered books were at the opposite corner of the building. This resulted in many complaints about not being able to locate materials on this floor. The stacks staff approached the department head with the idea of reorganizing the third floor to create a more logical call number "flow" of the collection. They also proposed adding some additional shelving in the HC–HX call number range at the same time by constructing new shelving in some available spaces and narrowing some aisles. The staff was asked why they wanted to take on this project and if they fully realized the significance of the effort involved. Their response to the "why" was that they wanted to make it easier for students to find materials on the third floor. They had also worked out a proposal that included the estimated numbers of staff and student hours required and a time-frame to complete the project. It is important to note that currently our stacks are estimated to be 98 percent filled to capacity and this shift involved almost twelve thousand shelves of books. Once completed, over 550 critically needed new shelves were added to the floor and, due to the near-capacity status of the stacks, each book was shifted at lease twice, so roughly 500,000 books were shifted. Staff from the other Circulation units and even other library departments volunteered to help out, so it was truly a team effort. The layout of the third floor is now much more logical, resulting in less confusion for patrons and far fewer complaints.

There are other examples of staff initiative and motivation. Staff from the circulation and stacks units initiated and proposed to the library administration a plan to consolidate the entire bound collection of periodicals to the third floor of the library, where the current issues and microfilm/fiche issues are housed. Currently, the bound periodicals are integrated with the general collection, on the other four floors of the library with a portion of the general collection being on the third floor. Moving the general collection materials from the third floor to the other floors and then consolidating the bound periodical from the other four floors onto the third would require the shifting of almost 55,000 shelves of materials. When presenting this proposal to the library's administration, circulation staff clearly stated their goal, and thus their motivation, was to make it easier for patrons to locate and use the periodical collection. In preparing for their proposal to library administration, staff had successfully completed a literature search to determine what was published regarding this issue of segregated or integrated bound periodical collections and had even conducted a user survey of students and faculty to determine patron preferences. This proposal is currently under consideration for possible inclusion within a plan to renovate the main floor of the library.

Circulation staff members have also initiated, developed, and implemented new and improved methods for training and evaluating departmental student assistants. The lost and found procedures were updated and revised at the initiative of the staff. Many of these departmental initiatives have been collaboratively developed by members of different units or shifts and all are a tribute to the dedication and commitment of the outstanding members of the Circulation Department team.

MOTIVATION THEORIES BEHIND THE CHANGES

If this experience demonstrates a best practice in staff empowerment, one might wonder if this transition could be replicated in other libraries. During this evolution a key question was, "can we motivate our employees?" Current theories tell us that individuals cannot motivate others; people can only motivate themselves. However, managers and supervisors can indeed use many strategies to create a satisfying work environment that could motivate individuals to commit and contribute. The difference is worth investigating.

The exploration of motivation leads down a psychological and philosophical path that many prefer not to follow. It is common for librarians to believe that, "We're all professionals and we shouldn't have to stand over people and tell them what to do." It is also common for supervisors to conclude that motivating others is just too personal and complex, and therefore not a good use of time. What follows is an attempt to summarize, simplify, and make practical some of the motivation theories.

The Pleasure/Pain Principle

Many philosophers, going as far back as Aristotle, have concluded that people will seek pleasure and avoid pain. This is a time-tested principle that holds true in most cases. Managers could accept this basic assumption and extrapolate it to mean that employees will do what makes them happy. The next hurdle for a manager intending to motivate people would be to discover what makes each employee happy. This is challenging since everyone has different values, needs, and wants. Fortunately, there is an abundance of research that has surveyed work satisfaction and peak performance.

Flow

The work of Hungarian psychologist Mihaly Csikszentmihalyi (pronounced "chick-sent-me-high-ee") on peak performance provides a manageable framework for considering motivational factors. His research identifies a "flow" experience, a type of effortless action that stands out for individuals as the best performance of their lives. This is such a positive experience that people willingly seek to recreate it. Fortunately, the factors related to "flow" can easily be replicated to create a pleasant experience in the work environment. Then, involvement in the work itself intrinsically motivates employees to do more of the same, producing a type of commitment.

Of the eight factors identified in this research, the four that can be controlled to some degree by most library managers are the following: clear goals, immediate feedback, balanced challenge and skill level, and being in control. The other four factors are more a result of being in the "flow" state, not necessarily contributing to achieving the state: concentration deepens, only the present matters, loss of ego, and lost sense of time.

Clear goals about library tasks give meaning and relevance to the work and make it easier to buy in to a project. This is why it is helpful for new employees to be oriented to the functions of all other departments and to understand how their work impacts the whole. The goal is made clearer when the reason for doing it is explained. An example of the second "flow" factor, immediate feedback, was studied in computer games where the player develops skills and advances or fails in a real-time environment. The gamer does not have to wait for a weekly meeting or an annual evaluation to judge his progress on a project. Motivation is enhanced when an employee has a clear set of expectations to measure against and regular feedback from a supervisor. This theory was applied at UCF in the form of increased communication in the Circulation Department.

A critical factor in the "flow" experience, and in developing commitment or the intrinsic motivation to persist, is achieving a good balance between an employee's skill level and the challenges of the work assignment. If the work opportunity is too easy, the employee will be bored or apathetic. If the challenges of work are too difficult, the employee will become frustrated or anxious. This finding emphasizes that an important task for managers is to assess employee abilities and provide appropriate training opportunities. The Circulation Department Head involved both library and campus Human Resources in helping staff develop skills to meet new challenges.

The fourth flow factor is the sense of being in control, or empowered. When the skill set is matched to the challenges of the job, the employee has a sense of being able to cope with the situation and this contributes to a feeling of control. Other ways to offer control to employees include allowing them to decide how the process gets done as long as the result is acceptable. Flexibility in scheduling the order of tasks and personal work time can enhance worker satisfaction. If the situation allows, controlling one's own environment can also contribute to a sense of control and therefore motivation. As previously described, the Circulation staff members were given appropriate authority to manage their proposed projects.

Other Motivation Theories

All of the "flow" factors are compatible with other research on motivation. For example, Frederick Herzberg identified the following factors that lead to job satisfaction: achievement, recognition, the work itself, responsibility, advancement, growth. A sense of achievement comes with knowing what the goals are. An employee could be achieving goals on a daily basis but if it is not clear that that is what he is doing, he will have no sense of achievement. Recognition is positive feedback. The work itself as identified by Herzberg is the same concept as Csikszentmihalyi's whole "flow" experience. The work is motivating when the skill level and challenges are well balanced. Herzberg's factor of responsibility is comparable to having a sense of control. Increasing control over the work is similar to increasing responsibility. The "flow" research suggests that managers encourage an environment where an employee is advanced for developing skills and growing, both satisfiers that Herzberg identified. It is comforting to see research in this area that is not contradictory and can be practiced in the field.

The "flow" research is primarily about how work itself can be intrinsically rewarding. Other individual values that drive behavior can encompass a wide variety of needs as categorized by a pioneer in motivation, Abraham Maslow. Maslow describes a hierarchy of needs that progresses from survival, safety, interpersonal, and esteem up to self-actualization needs. The discussion of commitment to the work itself as a motivator could be considered a fairly high level need and is most likely at the top of Maslow's pyramid. If an individual is able to use his unique skills and abilities to contribute to a greater good, that person has to some extent fulfilled his highest self-actualization need according to Maslow. The esteem need is comparable to recognition and positive feedback. The interpersonal, social, or belonging needs represent other values that some employees may seek to fulfill in the work environment. Survival and security needs such as food, housing, and insurance are generally met by salary. A supervisor who is aware of the level and type of needs of his employees can attempt to create an environment that fulfills those needs.

INTEGRATING THEORY AND PRACTICE

Can the theories of motivation described above explain the actual, successful changes at the University of Central Florida's Circulation Department? As the departmental changes were being implemented, some clear goals were established and staff was presented with the opportunity to get involved and to affect the direction of the department and how those goals were implemented. Staff members could have chosen to take the more "painful" course of resisting or fighting the changes, but when given the chance to directly impact the changes and to have control, participating in creating changes more to their own liking made the path of cooperation the more pleasurable route. Because staff members were being asked to modify procedures around their own position descriptions in order to improve customer service, they were able to maintain a comfortable skill level. Once the changes were being incorporated and staff was receiving the recognition for their achievements from the library's administrators and their peers, they responded with their own initiatives for improvements. Staff members were fueled by their own sense of accomplishments and self-satisfaction in the realization that it was within their power to shape and make significant changes for the betterment of the Library.

CONCLUSIONS: WHAT OTHER LIBRARIES CAN DO

The experiences described here offer evidence that sharing or delegating leadership responsibilities and building consensus have a positive impact on employee buy-in and morale and ultimately customer service. Consider the basic assumption that employees will naturally seek pleasure as they define it. In order to achieve library goals, i.e. enhance services, managers might link institutional goals to employee satisfaction. This could be achieved by making the workplace as pleasant and attractive as possible, imbuing the job with meaning and value by clarifying common goals, providing training so that employees have the skills required to meet daily challenges, allowing as much control and authority as appropriate, and rewarding positive behavior through regular communication and praise for a job well done.

REFERENCES

Csikszentmihalyi, M. (1997). *Finding Flow: The Psychology of Engagement with Everyday Life*, New York, NY: Basic Books/Harper Collins.
Csikszentmihalyi, M. (2003). *Good Business: Leadership, Flow, and the Making of Meaning,* New York, NY: Viking.
Herzberg, F. (2003). "One more time: How do you motivate employees?," *Harvard Business Review*, January, p 87-96 (reprint from January-February 1968).
Rooks, D. C. (1988). *Motivating Today's Library Staff*, Phoenix, AZ: Oryx Press.

Great Service Pays:
A Model for Service Delivery
in an Academic Music Library

Andrew M. Wilson

Delivering good patron service should be important to any library, but why is superior service so vital to music libraries, in particular? Music libraries hold a great variety of materials, in many different formats, that may or may not circulate to different user populations. The multitude of formats (book, score, microform, sound recording, videorecording, etc.) and languages can complicate navigation in the OPAC, slowing patrons from obtaining what they really need. Further, collections may have different classifications and/or call number systems, based on format (including differences between materials housed in open and closed stacks). There are also the usual difficulties with equipment needed for music library access: listening stations, video rooms, microform readers, copiers/scanners, and the like, which often require staff assistance. And, finally, music libraries employ the language of music (and foreign-language equivalents) that may not be familiar to many users. Faced with these hurdles, music libraries need to concentrate on providing the best possible service, to ensure that patrons see the music library as a useful resource, and a positive experience.

Ten years ago, the Eda Kuhn Loeb Music Library of the Harvard College Library was very casual about its attitude toward serving its patrons, a holdover from quieter times. A single student assistant was assigned to sit at the Circulation Desk, but when there was no student available, or the student was needed for shelving, the Public Services Librarian was responsible for covering Circulation. Often, this meant that the Public Services Librarian sat in an adjacent office waiting for patrons to approach the Circulation Desk, which looked, under these circumstances, like no one was home. If the Public Services Librarian (who was an extremely capable librarian and reference provider) was particularly busy in his office, he would place a bell on the Circulation Desk and ask patrons to "ring for service." A full-time support-staff person supervised the library during afternoon and evening hours, while a succession of part-timers staffed the facility over the weekend. Because the Public Services Librarian was the sole professional staff for access services, his attention was frequently diverted from providing meaningful service to patrons if a reference question happened to pique his interest. This situation was eventually deemed unacceptable, and with the retirement of this worthy gentleman, a new model was soon called for by the head of the library.

With the arrival of a new Public Services Librarian, improving circulation services and patron access to the collections became the top priority. The first step toward rebuilding the provision of patron service was to change the staffing model. Clearly, times had changed from the era when a single professional librarian could manage circulation, reference, reserves, bills and fines, stacks maintenance, and student assistants in a busy, well-used research library. A second layer of supervision was required so that student assistants could carry out the day-to-day work of circulation and stacks maintenance under the eye of an on-site supervisor, but not necessarily the Public Services Librarian. The solution to this situation was to place a support-staff-level Circulation Supervisor "on duty" during all open hours (60 hours per week, later increased to 65). This required an addition to the staff of one new FTE (certainly, no small achievement in today's environment), whose hiring spoke to the importance placed on improving service in the library. One full-time Circulation Supervisor staffed the Circulation Desk on weekdays from 9:00 a.m.-5:00 p.m., while another covered weekday afternoon/evening hours, and a part-timer continued to hold down the weekend responsibilities. All three had significant additional responsibilities in their job descriptions (course reserves, ILL, material transfer to offsite storage, etc.), so they could turn their attention to these tasks when the students were able to run the Circulation Desk without immediate assistance. The additional tasks located with the support staff permitted the library to upgrade the competence and productivity of the Public Services unit, in that it freed the library to participate more widely in new services and initiatives that patrons had come to expect in other libraries across campus. A computer terminal was installed at the Circulation Desk for the use of the supervisors, though they could also continue to use their own desks in the immediately-adjacent Public Services office. The pool of student staff was beefed up so that two students could work simultaneously during weekday business hours; a single student working was deemed adequate for nights and weekends. This allowed for one student to handle circulation and reception while the other could reshelve and perform other stacks maintenance tasks. The Public Services student roster ultimately grew to 18-20 student workers.

By having a supervisor on hand at all times, the students could be trained to handle most circulation, reception, directional, and other lower-level tasks, while the supervisor was available to take care of some reference questions, more complex circulation tasks, billing inquiries, and administer library patron policies (such as guest admission). In turn, the Public Services Librarian was then available to work on many of the other important duties incumbent to the position. After this model had been in place for a few years, front-of-house operations became far more self-sufficient (while still under the guidance of the Public Services Librarian), and the Circulation Supervisors turned their attention to standardizing student training and procedures. With the system running smoothly, the next opportunity to fill the Public Services Librarian position allowed for a reconfiguration of duties and a new title, Reference and Research Services Librarian, since the daily management of access service operations was no longer necessary.

The result of this staffing model is that patrons receive fast and attentive service at the desk, and when there is a line, both the student and the supervisor can serve patrons, speeding up circulation. Having a supervisor always at the student's side also means that the patron service is consistent, without variances based on the individual student's mastery of library policies. A patron can receive personalized assistance from the supervisor while circulation tasks continue uninterrupted. Stacks maintenance and shelving need not be deferred when things get busy at the desk, so patrons have quicker access to newly-returned library materials. The Research and Reference Services Librarian can concentrate on providing reference services from a dedicated service point elsewhere in the library, removing patron congestion from the circulation area (where reference services had been provided, previously). Over time, the success of this staffing model has meant that the library has earned recognition (including awards from the central library administration for superior service, and public acknowledgments for contributions to faculty publications) across campus for efficient, friendly, and helpful service. While surveys to quantify this improvement have not been conducted, we see evidence of our efforts every day, such as when faculty tell us how much the library *and its staff* mean to their work.

Public Services staff are the "public face" of the library, coming into contact with patrons (and in the academic setting, this frequently means faculty) on a daily basis. By putting forward a friendly, welcoming face to the world, library staff can move their users into a more sophisticated relationship with the library, which goes a long way toward encouraging library use. While bigger circulation numbers, reference statistics, and foot traffic will raise the stature of any unit in an academic library system (and our numbers all trended sharply upward after implementation of the new staffing plan), satisfied patrons are an extremely important measure all too often overlooked, and good word-of-mouth will enhance the reputation of the library among its most important constituencies, faculty and administrators. When a library starts to win awards and grants based on competence and usefulness, the central library administration cannot help but to think that something special is going on there.

This staffing model, as proposed, does require a commitment of funding for staff (student and support staff) as well as sustained management attention. It is particularly well-suited to the larger academic institution, but its main concepts are still translatable to smaller libraries. The model also provides positions in the library that can foster the development of future librarians, in that the responsibilities gained as Circulation Supervisors can greatly enhance their professional career paths. The approach to service, however, is universal, and can be implemented successfully in any size library. Where the improved staffing model increases the efficiency of patron service, the fundamental *attitude* toward service goes toward defining a positive relationship between the library and its users.

Here are some service pointers which may, on the surface, seem obvious, but if followed consistently, can lead to satisfied users, a professional-acting student staff, and an enhanced reputation on campus:

- How many times have you entered a library, and felt invisible when passing the first library staff you encounter? By requesting Circulation Desk and reference staff to look up and greet people (even in the most minimal way) as they enter the facility, patrons immediately feel welcome, and will be more likely to ask for assistance when needed. It cannot be overemphasized how much having a policy of being pleasant and helpful will enhance a library's local reputation. Further, by making the attempt to open the conversation between staff and patron right from the point of entry, inherent problems in the specific library (poor floorplan, confusing call number systems, clumsy OPAC navigation, etc.) can be explained *before* the patron has a chance to get frustrated.
- Along similar lines, by keeping a sharp lookout for patrons who may appear a bit lost, or are experiencing visible difficulty with the OPAC, library staff can seize the initiative to offer help, relieving the patron from the burden of asking. Users are particularly reluctant to "bother" library staff, thinking that they are somehow being disturbed from more important work, but this impression can be immediately dispelled if library staff make the effort to offer assistance first.
- While this can be a delicate subject among some library workers, for Public Services staff, professional appearance can raise the atmosphere of professionalism with little additional effort. As a former Public Services Librarian once remarked, "When people want help in the library, the first person they look for is the guy in the

tie." Ignoring the gender-specificity of his remark, Public Services staff should be visible to patrons, so that there is no confusion as to who they are, particularly when approaching users to offer their assistance.

- Think "retail." Public Services staff should always be thinking about providing service to their users with the goal of satisfied "customers." Simple enough, but try to treat patrons how you would want to be treated. As librarians, we want people to return to our library again and again, and when people feel that they were well-treated on their last visit, they will have good feelings about coming back, which might overcome other, more traditional reasons to avoid going to the library.
- If the library has failed a patron in some way, apologize for the failure. Patrons are far more forgiving of a lapse in service, a billing error, or the inability to access an item immediately, if the staff offer unqualified apologies for the let-down. A simple apology can diffuse a patron's anger or disappointment, and patrons are more likely to leave the library with the impression that the staff did the best they could. There should be no loss in stature among library professionals for honestly addressing minor service failures, then taking steps toward correcting them.
- Keep the facility neat and orderly. Push chairs up to the tables, clear return shelves frequently, remove any waste materials from public areas as quickly as possible, and reset computers to default displays. These little maintenance chores do take a few minutes out of each day, but patrons appreciate a library that appears ready for their use, not worn out after someone else's.
- Despite the investment required for support-staff-level FTE in this staffing model, it is still highly dependent on student assistants. Employment of Federal Work Study students is an obvious means by which student staff availability can be enhanced at little additional cost, but don't overlook other sources of student payroll support that may be available to an academic library, such as city-sponsored summer youth job programs, union-sponsored training programs, and internships. Interestingly, students need not be music majors, or otherwise from a serious musical background, in order to be successful and effective in the music library setting; over time, they become fluent, which reinforces the desirability of low student turnover. Familiarity with the music vernacular is probably the most helpful experience students can bring to their

employment, but it is not necessary to limit student hiring to students enrolled in the local music program on campus.

- Lead student staff by example. This goes beyond the basic notion of not assigning any tasks to others that one wouldn't do oneself; if students see courteous, attentive, friendly, and professional library staff, it *will* rub off on them. Students are usually impressed by the response library staff receive from patrons when they are addressed in a helpful manner, with respect and a smile. They learn that this is how a good service organization succeeds.

- Invest in the student assistants. Students who come to identify with a campus job well done tend to return year after year. Reducing turnover cuts down on the aggregate amount of training that needs to be done each year, as well as provides the operation with more highly-skilled assistants. Thank them for their work on a daily basis, throw them that end-of-the-school-year pizza party, and otherwise make them feel as though they are part of the organization's success. It is also worthwhile to retain a large enough pool of student assistants, so that when the inevitable illnesses and schedule conflicts arise, the library is not left short-handed. This does not end up costing very much more, because the result is more students working fewer hours each, and student schedule flexibility can be facilitated by a system of requiring subs to cover shifts. Today's busy student can rarely work more than 6-8 hours per week, no matter how desirous of the hours they may be. They are less likely to blow off a shift if they are, in turn, invested in their relationship with the library job. In addition, having an adequate number of students from which to draw can reduce the tension between students and supervisors, in that the inevitable absences cease to be as big of a hardship on supervisors.

- Since the Circulation Supervisors are "on duty" during all open hours, and supervisor absences can become difficult to manage, consider some extra effort in training a handful student assistants to be "substitute supervisors," with added responsibilities and a higher pay rate. Circulation Supervisors will appreciate the work-schedule flexibility this can provide, which, in the long run, enhances the staffing model by helping to reducing supervisor turnover.

Having worked to implement these ideas into our own provision of service, we have seen, over time, a steady rise in our reputation on campus. While a good reputation for service and friendly staff seem, anecdotally, to translate to increased use of the library, it can also result in another beneficial effect, on a more pragmatic level: becoming more highly thought of by the larger library administration at the University level. Further, if the faculty are pleased with the service they receive, they can become extremely valuable advocates on behalf of the library, advocates upon whom we depend at every opportunity. A professional front-of-house operation compliments other aspects of the library's endeavors, completing a picture of a well-run organization, and as a result of this, we feel that we may get a more favorable hearing when it comes time to make funding requests, ask for equipment and facility improvements, or propose increases or additions to our programs. In part, because of the positive reaction we get from our user community, we may be treated more favorably by the administration in many of the ways we think are most important. The return on our "investment" has been successful and gratifying, and the increase in professionalism at every level of our staff, from the students to the senior management, has made the library a more satisfying place to work.

ALOHA to New Learning: Uniting Student and Career Staff Through Training

Lynn N. Baird

INTRODUCTION

"Libraries are people, services, and stuff," declared Joe Janes, Associate Dean for Academics of University of Washington's Information School, at the *2020 Vision: Idaho Libraries Future Conference*. He's right; in library budgets, personnel and information resources are the primary expenditures. Library budgets are constrained by funding commitments to serial subscriptions and personnel costs. Discretionary spending available is then considered fair game to be used to develop our services, leaving us to choose among our programs such as instruction, interlibrary loan, and what to emphasize in cataloging priorities. One way we translate this spending into service is through the development of our human resource capacity. Through ongoing education and training, a library creates and develops its attitudes and values about service. This is a means of reinvigorating a library's organizational culture, building upon existing values and assumptions and clarifying a vision of service.

In academic libraries, educational opportunities are offered to library faculty and career staff. Funding is committed to developing careers of employees who have permanent positions because these are employees who are invested in carrying out the mission of the library. Another significant and important part of the library's labor pool, however, is part-time student employees. These individuals require a different orientation to the workplace. Their training is often minimal and directed from the trainer (top-down), feeding them skills that serve the library's need. Students are recruited at the beginning of the academic year and are given rudimentary skills so they can begin performing basic tasks. Some training consists of computer-based instruction programs on how to shelve books with the Library of Congress Classification system, orientations to the facility, and fundamental library policies. This minimalist approach is justified because of the high rate of turnover, the costs of training, and the reluctance to give priority to training over other library work (Kathman & Kathman, 2000).

This article examines training from a different perspective, as a means of transmitting organizational culture to student employees through closer communication between career and part-time student employees. An academic library sponsored joint student/career staff training to improve library services in a team-building event conducted by outside facilitators, and this article examines how participants viewed the event. The students and staff comprise multiple generations, spanning the Millenials through Baby Boomers, with different cultural assumptions about technology, social relationships, and approaches to public service. The concept of bringing student workers together with career staff in training is not commonly done, if the literature is a reflection of practice. The cost of this investment may be a deterrent, evidenced by the previously mentioned factors, and student contributions to the workplace are typically discounted because they are not perceived as being connected to the long-term objectives of the organization. Yet becoming part of an organizational culture can be a powerful motivator for an employee (Tovey, 2001). And students contribute to the professional passion of long-term employees as well; connecting career staff to principles of service that originally attracted them to their positions (Bell, 2003). To develop an understanding of how students and career staff perceived the value of this event, participant responses were solicited by a survey.

SETTING THE STAGE

An organization is characterized by how institutional information is treated. In traditional hierarchical organizations, information is power and is to be controlled. By contrast, information is 'nourishment' (Wheatley, 1999, p. 101) in a learning organization, something necessary for organizational life. The concept of a learning organization is founded upon humanistic principles, where each individual staff member is valued for the experience they bring to the workforce, learning they create with other employees in their work, and for contributing to the direction of work through a shaping of the organization's vision. Peter Senge (1990) suggests a learning organization is characterized by the principles of personal mastery (where employees are given the support and education to be expert in their sphere of work), mental models (worldviews created by individuals through their previous experiences and beliefs), team learning, shared vision, and systems thinking. Such organizations encourage the flow of information as a source of energy and vitality; opening these conduits requires commitment and support from leadership (Garvin, 2000). Watkins (2005, p. 415) suggests, "A learning organization is an organization that has an enhanced capacity to learn and to change." This learning is necessary to position an organization in different modes of thinking about how it relates to the external environment.

The library where this study is situated has been challenged to become more agile within its home institution because it has been cut off from administrative information through recent reorganizations. Under a previous administration, the library was merged into a new unit with the university's information technology services. When the vice-provost administering this unit left, the university restructured the units and the former communication lines were not re-established. During this time of administrative isolation, the library internally strengthened communications to become more responsive, recognizing that librarians will be more productive and confident in the directions the university is taking if they are better informed. Thus, as an entity, this library has become more open to exploring alternative ways of communicating and learning.

Leaders of organizations that find themselves in tumultuous change might look to the literature of organization development (OD) for guidance. While there is no single definition of OD, French and Bell offer this:

> Organization development is a long-term effort, led and supported by top management, to improve an organization's visioning, empowerment, learning, and problem-solving processes, through an ongoing, collaborative management of organization culture-with special emphasis on the culture of intact work teams and other team configurations-using the consultant-facilitator role and the theory and technology of applied behavioral science, including action research. (1999, p. 25-26)

This definition expands on the concept of the learning organization, including the long-term commitment to examining the organization's culture and processes. Carnevale (2003) provides more clarity for organizations operating in the public sector, noting that there is no "bottom line." "Public OD is a more difficult undertaking. The operational domain of public institutions are structured so that change demands the involvement of multiple actors. Politics, not economics, run the show" (p. 24). The commitment for change must come from the leadership; the results will be demonstrated in the culture.

Who are citizens of this culture? Mojab and Gorman (2003) criticized the learning organization concept on the basis that it gives further privilege to the full-time employees of larger organizations, marginalizing the part-time employees. "The most at-risk workers are the ones who receive the lowest investment in employer-provided skill training and learning" (p. 233). If the learning organization, indeed, results in tiered employment as these authors suggest, then the part-time employees are not included in the continuous learning. Student employees additionally have more challenges to gain access to the library's culture. Their first priority is school; work is much less important in their values system and is squeezed into their hectic schedules. As such, ". . . permanent employees have much more time to acclimate to an organization's culture on their own, while interns do not" (Tovey, p. 236).

Student employees add to the workplace and the workplace adds to the students' college experience. Reports from assessment tools on student engagement clearly show that the college experience for students who have both academic and non-academic forms of connecting with school are more successful in their college careers (Pascarella & Terenzini, 2005). This connection to the workplace can last well beyond graduation. It is because of this connection and my commitment to providing this opportunity to student development that I felt a need to include the student employees in the training with career staff.

ALOHA IN IDAHO

The ALOHA training, an Idaho State Library program, is designed to promote "exceptional customer service" (*Idaho State Library Newsletter*, 5/05). State Library consultants work with individual libraries to create an educational opportunity that incorporates local issues with other learning opportunities that help libraries build their capacity for providing excellent public service. For our library, it was the first training designed to bridge organizational boundaries in that it invited participation from all segments of library work, from frontline service desk to those employees who do not usually work directly with the public. The timing of the event was based on a number of factors: workload (Friday nights are typically the least busy due to the early closing of the library-based computer labs), availability of trainers, and travel schedules. The choices available were either a Friday night or a Saturday morning, and since it seemed obvious that students would not participate in an 8:00 a.m. training session on Saturday for any amount of money, Friday evening was selected.

The training is a fast-paced, activity-filled unit that builds a sense of team through scenarios, videos, and small group activities. The facilitators request that the host library organize seating at the tables to ensure maximum interaction and provide themed items to help create a climate of openness and sharing. We asked several career staff to be the table hosts and mixed up each table so there were student employees and career staff from different work groups in each group. We decorated the room with paper palm trees, scattered squeezable fish on each table, and turned up the volume of the Beach Boys. By changing the climate and the mood, we made a new space for learning.

RESEARCHER AS INSTRUMENT

I am intensely curious about this new space for learning as I have just recently moved into an administrative position. From my graduate studies in adult and organizational learning, I have examined how communications contribute to effectiveness in organizations. I see that building trust and relationships can change organizational culture and provide more confident and productive employees who feel that they have support in taking risks and making change. As a tenured faculty member, I am committed to contributing to the success of the library and the university; I've enjoyed the support of the institution as I've built my career and desire to support others in the same manner.

Personal experience has shown me that some of the most fruitful conversations I've had with my colleagues have occurred at conferences. My knowledge has deepened through these discussions and I am convinced that training extends beyond the planned learning, which has been noted in the literature (Marsick & Watkins, 2003). Daily routines are disrupted and conversations are encouraged to flourish.

My library career began when I was a student employee. In every stage of my career, I have sought opportunities to share my ideas with administrators, to provide them with the perspective of how the library was operating from the ground floor view. Administrators who listen to the heartbeat of the organization and are open to the voices of the many levels of employees will be better informed in practice, from my perspective. These views are consistent with constructivist philosophy that sees learning is contextual and connected. In these ways, my thoughts are congruent with fundamental principles of leading a learning organization: I support others in developing their skills and understanding as well as team learning, and expect contributions to creating shared visions.

METHOD

I initiated this study of the ALOHA training to understand how the career and student employees perceived the value of training. Using qualitative inquiry methods to study a phenomenon, I created a survey that could be completed online. I wanted to create a space for "real talk" (Belenky et al., 1986), where I could carefully "listen" to the words of the participants without having the barrier of power to stifle the conversation. This online survey served the purpose of removing the power issues that could arise from having employees respond to inquiries from their supervisor. I have worked with developing and revising training programs for student employees in this library for over ten years in my previous position and have felt that these programs do more than teach job related skills. Academic libraries that employ students as pages or desk workers are providing basic work skills as well as library procedures (Baird, 2003). Communication skills are the foundation upon which we build additional learning.

Thirty-three participants attended the program, sixteen career staff members and seventeen student employees. The participants completed the trainers' evaluation forms the night of the event to provide feedback about what they found to be helpful and how they would change the training to be more effective. About a month later, the participants were asked to perform a second evaluation that was more open-ended, to see how individuals perceived the training. This period of time was structured to provide the participants time to work with the information that they discovered during the training and to learn more about their reflections on the experience. Certain themes emerged from both surveys that could help inform the organization about the value of this activity.

The first survey from the trainers consisted of three questions: what participants found to be the most useful part of the training, suggestions they had for improving the training, and what other educational opportunities would they like to see. Of the three questions, the first yielded the most substantive and specific responses about content. The training design gave participants a chance to learn through discussion and group work and the social learning aspect of this was highly valued. In terms of suggestions for the future, the overwhelming majority reflected how difficult it is to be engaged on Friday nights, wishing for a shorter or different time frame. It is to the training team's credit that this was the only serious suggestion for improvement.

The researcher's survey was conducted in an anonymous setting. A web survey tool was used that protected the identities of participants, which was particularly important given the role of the researcher as employer. Participants were notified that a study was to be conducted in an initial email. The purpose of the research and the procedures for the research were outlined in this communication. An invitation to participate was issued shortly following this notification letter. Near the end of the survey period, they were reminded to participate. Because the privacy of all participants was protected, the surveyor had no means for following up with the few who did not participate. Out of the 33 participants, 27 surveys were returned. Again, three questions were asked: briefly describe your understanding of the purpose of the ALOHA training, in what ways could the ALOHA training influence your relationship with co-workers/supervisor, and if another ALOHA training was organized, what would you like to see addressed?

SERVICE, TEAMWORK, AND CLIMATE

These questions yielded different perspectives and provided more insight into how this training was valued. The participants discussed three primary themes in response to the question of purpose: to improve customer service, to build teamwork, and to be more self-aware of how our actions influence the climate of the organization. These three themes were universal with nearly every participant addressing more than one theme in their response. Customer service (26 responses) was the most popular theme but both teamwork and climate were nearly as popular, with 16 and 15 responses each. Participants viewed the results with comments such as, "to improve the way we interact [with patrons] while providing a better environment for the patrons to study and learn in as well as a more positive environment for the workers at the library" and "to make us more aware of our actions and how they affect the patrons we help" and "to boost morale and increase interaction among staff members who might otherwise never meet" (survey results, 11/1/05). The question about further topics for training yielded the least amount of information, which might raise questions for future discussion.

RELATIONSHIPS, WORK PERCEPTIONS, CLIMATE

The responses to the question about how the training could influence relationships yielded a variety of responses that were grouped into themes of relationship building, perspectives on work, and organizational climate. The most popular responses were grouped into the comments about building relationships with co-workers and provided some insights about work and space: "For me personally, I didn't know many of the people that work in the library because I don't work down on the first floor where most of the other people work. So it definitely made it so I at least met some of them and had an experience shared with them. It definitely had the potential to create many relationships as we were all thrown into that situation together and were encouraged to communicate and talk to the people around us" (survey results, 11/1/05). Others found value in discovering their supervisors were people, "Help you see your superiors as more than superiors. See them and your co-workers as people you can count on and be good friends with" and "It helps to see them as people, instead of only 'bosses' or coworkers" and "it would also make us feel more comfortable talking to our supervisor about issues that arise and talking with our co-workers when problem solving issues arise" (survey results, 11/1/05).

Feelings about work were expressed most often through comments about shared understanding. "It could give us more respect for each other", "It helped me respect the job they [the student workers] do as they balance their commitment to both work and study", and "It was eye-opening to hear what other co-workers' jobs entailed with regards to the patrons. I have more respect for people in positions that I thought were pretty easy/non-challenging jobs" (survey results, 11/1/05).

Other comments regarding organizational climate provided information that leadership should be cautioned to note, such as the comment about close relationships. "It has allowed me to see that there are groups of us that are closer than others. Especially with the older employees who have been here longer, there are 'cliques' that have formed that the new workers are not in" (survey results, 11/1/05). Another participant noted, in a comment about supervisors, "They are not just there to make life harder, they have a job to do as well, and sometimes they have bad days or difficulties too" (survey results, 11/1/05). Overall, with these comments in the extreme minority, it is easier to keep them in perspective as common elements in workplaces, but awareness is part of solutions.

MORE QUESTIONS

Looking at the responses to these questions led me to consider some additional threads of inquiry, such as the difference of work perceptions between career and part-time employees. Is it possible for part-time employees to commit to creating a learning organization? As one participant noted, "I would not like to see another ALOHA training. I am a part-time temporary employee. I do take pride in my work [. . .] but I think it was a waste of my time" (survey results, 11/1/05). Regardless of how the employer might feel, the part-time student employee might not wish to invest in this involvement.

It should additionally be noted that this mix of employees included adult learners and not-yet-adult learners, as half of them are experiencing the world of work perhaps for the first time. These undergraduate students are not yet fully mature, nor are they necessarily committed to the future of the organization. That they dedicated the time and energy to participate in both the training and the survey is a comment on their character, for they are experiencing life with work being but a minute portion of their interest. Fenwick (1998) notes that the workplace is one of the many components of the employees' lives and that not all knowledge learned contributes to the growth of the organization.

After over a decade of developing training programs for beginning workers, I have learned how to meet learners' objectives and match them with organizational goals. This concern for improving communication between student and staff employees has been of especial interest to me. As I note elsewhere, "The adolescent employee can be characterized as someone who has little opportunity for communicating with adults in a work relationship" (Baird, p. 13). Developing bonds that permit more open communication is critical to any staff development program, and putting work into context enables staff to gain a broader perspective on their role within the organization. This survey showed that nearly all employees seek to find meaning in their work and need to have that larger view to make this possible. Additionally, this survey helped me understand how important it is for career employees to have opportunities to work with the part-time student employees so that they can remain in closer contact with the many pressures these students have on their time. I think this develops the understanding necessary to schedule work tasks and to enhance service to the library users.

NEXT STEPS

In opening the conversation to gain an understanding of how students and career staff viewed this training, I sought to discover if there are perceptions about work that can help us create opportunities for improved service. Additionally, I wanted to understand how relationships between career and student employees are perceived. These perspectives might be considered initial steps towards one library's cultural development, moving towards a concept of the learning organization that values the contributions of both career and temporary employees. By listening to the comments made by the participants, I seek to show that employees are more alike than different in their perceptions about the workplace.

The vast majority of the responses from these employees indicated an interest to belong to the organizational unit in a broader capacity than is currently provided. It is interesting to note that comments were not identified as being from part-time student or career employees, yet the themes of building relationships and learning more about the workplace were universal. Questions related to current practice and policy can only be addressed if individuals feel that they can approach others to gain understanding. While a single experience does not create a learning organization, it has helped contribute to a more open level of communications through the construction of new relationships and understanding the roles that individuals play in the organization. The continued exploration of such opportunities to bring individuals together from all units will help inform all participants about the service goals of the library and it is this new administrator's role to ensure these activities occur.

REFERENCES

Baird, Lynn N. "Student employees in academic libraries: training for work, educating for life," *PNLA Quarterly, 67* (2003): 13, 23.

Belenky, Mary F., Clinchy, Blythe M., Tarule, Jill M., and Goldberger, Nancy R. *Women's Way of Knowing.* New York: Basic Books, 1986.

Bell, Steven J. "A passion for academic librarianship: find it, keep it, sustain it-a reflective inquiry," *portal: Libraries and the Academy, 3* (2003): 633-642. http://muse.jhu.edu/journals/portal_libraries_and_the_academy/v003/3.4bell.html.

Carnevale, David G. *Organizational Development in the Public Sector.* Boulder, CO: Westview Press, 2003.

Fenwick, Tara. "Questioning the concept of the learning organization," in *Learning for Life: Canadian Readings in Adult Education,* edited by S. Scott, B. Spencer, and A. Thomas, Toronto: Thompson Educational Publishing, (1998): 140-152.

French, Wendell L. and Bell, Cecil H. *Organization Development: Behavioral Science Interventions for Organization Improvement.* 6th ed. New Jersey: Prentice Hall, 1999.

Garvin, David A. *Learning in Action.* Boston: Harvard Business School Press, 2000.

Idaho State Library Newsletter "ALOHA ready to rip" (*http://www.lili.org/isl/pubs/news/news5-05.pdf*).(2005).

Kathman, Jane M. and Kathman, Michael D. "Training student employees for quality Service," *Journal of Academic Librarianship, 26* (2000): 176-182.

Marsick, Victoria J. and Watkins, Karen E. "Demonstrating the value of an organization's learning culture: the dimensions of the learning organization questionnaire," *Advances in Developing Human Resources, 5* (2003): 132-151.

Mojab, Shahrzad and Gorman, Rachel. "Women and consciousness in the 'learning organization': Emancipation or exploitation," *Adult Education Quarterly, 53* (2003): 228-241.

Owenby, Phillip H. "Organizational learning communities and the dark side of the learning organization," *New Directions for Adult and Continuing Education, 95* (2002): 51-60.

Pascarella, Ernest T. and Terenzini, Patrick T. *How College Affects Students: A Third Decade of Research.* 2nd ed. San Francisco: Jossey-Bass, 2005.

Senge, Peter M. *Fifth Discipline.* New York: Doubleday, 1990.

Tovey, Janice. "Building connections between industry and university: Implementing an internship program at a regional university," *Technical Communication Quarterly, 10* (2001): 225-239.

Watkins, Karen E. "What would be different if higher educational institutions were learning organizations?" *Advances in Developing Human Resources, 7* (2005): 414-421.

Wheatley, Margaret. *Leadership and the New Science.* San Francisco: Barrett Kohler, 1999.

Student Workers:
Cross Training
in the Academic Environment

Lani Hall Draper
Tina A. Oswald
Margie Renfro

STUDENT WORKERS:
CROSS TRAINING IN THE ACADEMIC ENVIRONMENT

The area with the biggest number of student workers is often the Access Services/Circulation Department. Libraries are always looking for helpful, smiling faces for desk duty. Training these smiling faces is important. At Stephen F. Austin State University in Nacogdoches, TX, we realize the importance and found that cross training desk attendants to shelve and work several of the library's public service stations, help them know more about the library, and give better service. It also benefits the library by making more students available to staff these different areas.

BACKGROUND

In the beginning, most student workers in libraries were trained to do one job–shelving. Though the life of a shelver is not glamorous, library jobs were seen as the better jobs, at least to the students. It is an inside job. The library is usually a nice and comfortable building–maybe a little quiet. It is better than any job in food service! There is an opportunity to listen to music while doing the job, using an iPOD or portable CD player. There is not too much interaction with the public. While the students are looking for all the positive aspects, the Library, as the employer, is looking for a worker who is conscientious and pays attention to detail. If a book, a periodical, or a piece of microfiche is not placed in the correct area, then it may never be found again, and therefore will not, and can not, be used.

There are student workers in every academic library worldwide. Such is the case at SFA. There are students working in just about every department. The jobs that they are doing at the present encompass more than what they did in the past. They can include everything from answering the phone, to keeping a public service area staffed, to graphic design and web development. It all depends on where they have been hired to work.

There are twenty students in the Steen Library that concentrate on getting the materials back to their correct places on the shelves and in the cabinets, so that they are available for use. They are responsible for collecting the materials, putting them in call number order on a cart, and placing them in that same call number order on the shelves. In the Steen Library, there are three classification systems used: Library of Congress classification system, the Dewey classification system, and the Superintendent of Documents classification system. Therefore, the student workers are trained to shelve in at least the LC and Dewey classification systems. When they are not shelving, they are assigned other duties: shelf reading, filing, etc. Other students are hired to assist in staffing the Circulation Desk, and still others to staff the first floor Information Desk.

All of that changed a year ago when the staffing and scheduling of the Information Desk was transferred to the person in Access Services who hired and trained all the shelvers. She immediately realized the benefits of cross training and decided that instead of having one group to shelve and another group to staff the desk areas, these two groups of student workers should be combined into one group and be cross-trained to be able to handle all those jobs. So, the students are available to work in three different arenas, and they can use more of their talents. As a bonus, there are extra people to call upon for staffing a particular area, if needed.

The Information Desk itself was an issue. It began many years ago as a form of exit control as patrons left the building. It was staffed by a Circulation Desk student and was also a place where books could be dropped off or checked out. As exit control became less of an issue, the desk was still there–in between the main doors into and out of the building. So, the idea was posed that the desk be transformed and made a more viable part of the Library. Could it become an all-encompassing information area, not just for library information, but for the entire university and community? This is what was accomplished. First, the desk itself was rebuilt in a hexagon shape. It was also raised to be high, so that people would be comfortable with walk-up type questions, but not so comfortable as to stay around and block the entrance/exit area. The questions that are asked at the Information Desk can range from: "What are the Library's hours today?" and "Can you transfer me to the Registrar's Office?" to "What is happening downtown this weekend?" and "Can you help me locate a research article about diabetes in adult males?" The students are told, and constantly reminded, to refer any questions that are lengthy or of a research nature to the Librarian that is on duty during that time. When the Information Desk first opened, there were actually librarians scheduled to be there during the weekdays. This was stopped when librarians began to staff a separate Reference Desk on the first floor. Still, the librarians try and maintain relationships with the Information Desk student workers, so that the students are comfortable in referring questions to the Librarian.

TRAINING THE STUDENTS

Students that are hired to work a public service desk have to be a certain kind of person. There is a personality type that is better suited for this type of work and there are certain personal skills that cannot be acquired. They need to have a positive demeanor and look approachable, but they must also maintain an air of professionalism at the Information Desk. They must be outgoing and friendly. They are expected to look up and acknowledge each individual who comes in the doors. At the front entrance, they are "the face of the Steen Library." The only contact that patron may have with anyone in the building, may be that initial contact from the Information Desk or Circulation Desk. That contact should be positive.

In order to be able to cope with any question that comes up, they must be extensively trained. To achieve this training, many online tutorials are used and are required viewing for these student workers. The most critical is the Library Tutorial that was created using TILT as the model. This tutorial gives the students some background information so that that can provide answers for simple research questions especially if the Librarian is unavailable. The tutorial has a "final exam" that the student workers are required to take. The exam is automatically e-mailed to the student worker's supervisor. This allows the supervisor to check the progress of the student's training and their understanding of using Library resources. Since the student worker will not always be the one sitting at the Information Desk, they are also trained to shelve using LCEasy. Before these students were cross trained, the librarians frequently heard student workers saying that they did not know where things were located, and some had never gotten farther in the Library than the first floor. In some libraries this is not a huge concern, but most of the Steen Library holdings are located on the second, third, and fourth floors. Since this training has been instituted, the students now know where things are and can aid others in finding materials.

Once a student has done the tutorials, they are scheduled to work at the Information Desk with another student who is proficient at working that desk. They also maintain contact with the Librarian on call who can provide additional training as necessary. Most daytime hours, the Information Desk and Circulation Desk workers can physically see the librarian at the Reference Desk. This close proximity makes it easier for the students to refer questions.

Scheduling can be something of a nightmare! Both desks are open all the hours that the Steen Library is open which is 105 hours a week.

There are always two students scheduled to work as students are notorious for running late, or calling in sick, or having car trouble, etc. If there are two students scheduled for each hour, then if someone does not show up, the desk is not left unattended. One thing that makes it easier is having shelvers on hand that know how to work a desk. Then, if a student worker does call in sick, or calls to say they are running late, the supervisor can pull someone shelving on another floor down to staff a desk.

CONCLUSION

Because of the cross training, students do not get bored with their jobs and the library has a bigger pool of students to choose from when having to schedule a public service desk. As information technology has evolved, the role of the library student worker has changed. The student workers must understand and be able to utilize the resources, especially the electronic resources that the Library provides. Still, there is something to be said for the personal touch of a real person who answers the phone, or a real person who greets you as you enter a campus building. These student workers are able to do both with the training that is in place. Their contributions to the overall success of an academic library should not be underestimated.

Stacks Tour Project Presents Staff Development Opportunity

Barbara M. Coopey
David Nicastro

INTRODUCTION

Oftentimes, a staff member encounters a student in the stacks of Pattee Library who, with a panicked look states he/she can't find the way out. The overwhelming complexity of a huge university library can be daunting to an undergraduate student. The Penn State Pattee Library and Paterno Library complex is comprised of the Pattee, West Pattee and Paterno interconnected buildings occupying more than thirty linear miles of collections. Paterno Library is the newer section with spacious stacks areas, whereas Pattee Library has older, smaller areas and compresses seven levels of stacks into three stories with dim lighting and narrow passages. Creating successful approaches for staff to introduce incoming students to the Libraries' extensive layout can be a challenge.

One way the University Libraries are meeting this challenge is by inviting incoming students to a party-themed Open House that focuses on fun, play, and personal interaction to reduce students' fear of the library.[1] Access Services staff participate in Open House activities, promoting the services Access Services offers and help reduce "stacks anxiety" by giving students a tour of Central Pattee Stacks, a gloomy section of the library. Both students and staff benefit from Open House. Students become acquainted with librarians and staff, they are reassured the library is a friendly environment where one can get help with their study or research needs, and they learn the layout of the library.

The Access Services staff are involved in the Open House planning, and activities have staff development opportunities. They improve teamwork, communication and collaboration skills, and utilize others not required in their daily duties to creatively share their expertise with students. Through this, they gain a broader knowledge of and a sense of belonging to both Access Services and the Penn State Libraries. One example of a staff development opportunity from Open House is a pilot project which grew out of the Open House Stacks Tour.

The Stacks Tour Pilot Project was initiated by a Collection Maintenance Stacks Unit staff member on the Open House Committee. Inspired by the student-centered goal of the Open House and the success of the tour during Open House, he sensed a need to offer this service more often. He proposed, designed, implemented and evaluated the results of the project and made recommendations about the continuation of the tour. This project helped Access Services define the best ways to reach undergraduates about the stacks. The bonus was its success as an excellent staff development experience.

LITERATURE REVIEW

Library literature reveals many approaches to training and staff development. The more skills and abilities a staff member acquires, the more valuable he or she becomes to the library. The goal of a staff development program is to acquire needed technical and communication skills and to gain a broader understanding of how 'my job' contributes to the library's organization. It increases self assurance and contributes to morale. While much has been written about library tours, their merit and format, the literature reveals little or nothing about the resulting benefits to the staff members who implement or conduct library tours. For this paper, literature on both library tours and on staff development was examined.

Library Tours

Today's users can become familiar with a library's layout without entering the building. Ashmore (2005) stated that recent literature on guided tours emphasizes using technology, such as virtual tours where a user can tour a library at any time from anywhere and become familiar with the layout. [2] The California State University at Fullerton, Hickok (2002) found that guided tours were not well attended due to a variety of reasons–lack of publicity, perceived unimportance, student unavailability during touring time–and developed an interactive web tour.[3] Nonetheless, as Mosley (1997) asserts, "Though it may not teach in-depth research skills, a guided tour service may be critical in making an overwhelmed freshman more comfortable entering the library."[4] Moreover, Oling states that according to a 2000 Association for Research Libraries (ARL) survey, guided tours remain the most popular type of tour compared to self-guided, audio, video, or virtual, although librarians have mixed views on their effectiveness.[5] Weighing the user's benefits of taking a tour with the required staff resources remains a discussion topic for libraries.

Penn State Pattee Library and Paterno Library

At Penn State many students are reluctant to venture into the Pattee Central stacks. They see the stacks as stepping into the past. Narrow passages, unexpected turns, dim lights, the occasional broken tile, the ticking of light timers or burnt out light does not inspire a student with confidence. In a new and unfamiliar area during a new and unfamiliar time in their lives some students tend to focus on the negative. A student generally gives his or her exposure to the central stacks too little time to notice the research potential of direct access to such a large collection. The computers on every floor and the quiet study areas are overlooked in favor of a gated elevator that students view as a curious and possibly dangerous relic, despite the prominent inspection sticker dated for the current year. The University Libraries Marketing Steering Committee conducted focus groups with undergraduate students in Fall 2005 to obtain perceptions about the University Libraries and found that both freshman and sophomore students perceived the stacks in Central Pattee Library as "scary and uncomfortable." The students also noted the lack of directional signs.[6] Penn State Libraries offer online maps;[7] a virtual tour;[8] regularly scheduled and pre-arranged tours; as well as tours accompanying library instruction classes. Although the Gateway Library staff mentions the stacks in their regularly scheduled general tours of the Pattee Library and Paterno Library complex, there is not enough time to take participants into the stacks area.[9]

Staff Development

Effective staff development is essential within both the Penn State Libraries and the University. The University Libraries Strategic Plan 05/2006-07/2008 states as one of its ongoing goals: "Recruit, develop, and retain a diverse and qualified faculty and staff with expertise and skills to provide services and collections expected of a technologically advanced, nationally ranked research library."[10] Penn State's Staff Review Development Plan defines staff development as "the improvement of an employee's knowledge, performance or career."[11] Staff development is a continuous practice resulting in important benefits for the employee, the supervisor, and the organization. In his introductory letter in the Penn State Mastering Supervision Program handbook, our university president links staff development to Penn State's vision, "This vision calls for an approach to supervision that places a premium on helping others to achieve their best in whatever they do–as individuals, as a team, and as an institution."[12] Trotta (1995) states "[staff development] keeps people from "burning out," and it helps them become aware of how their behavior affects the overall library operation.[13] Staff development possibilities progressing beyond technical and procedural training into job-relevant, interesting, stimulating, and rewarding opportunities can be found. Jurow (2001) states, "Adults want to use their knowledge to accomplish something. Adults expect what they learn to be relevant to their needs."[14] Laverty and Burton (2003) observe that "adults prefer a problem-centered orientation to learning that draws on real-life applications rather than hypothetical situations and draw on their own life experiences as a resource for learning."[15] The Stacks Tour Pilot Project provided a job-relevant, real-life learning experience.

BACKGROUND

Access Services

The Access Services Department at Penn State University Park Pattee and Paterno Libraries is comprised of fifty-two full-time staff, including two librarians. The units in Access Services are Collection Maintenance, Course Reserves, Interlibrary Loan, Lending Services, and Library Services for Persons with Disabilities. The retention rate of the full-time staff is high, with eleven years as the average length of service and many staff spending most or all of their years in Access Services. Providing development opportunities is essential to a well-trained workforce. Staff need to be familiar with the Libraries' mission and values. They need a customer service focus and a variety of skills to meet constant challenges and increasing user expectations. It was found that Open House Committee members developed a broader understanding of the Libraries and discovered ways to use their talents and skills not primarily used in their daily jobs. They increased communication skills and improved skills such as goal setting, creative thinking, cooperation, time management, problem solving, and customer service. They felt a sense of accomplishment and developed a department camaraderie that extended into everyday work life.

Libraries' Open House

At the beginning of Fall Semester each year, Penn State University Libraries at University Park campus offer an Open House targeting incoming freshman. Attendance at the event has grown yearly, totaling 5,000 students in 2006. Each subject library and unit within the Libraries develops activities centered on their subject area or expertise. The Access Services Units are responsible for two of the nineteen Open House activity stops, one in Lending Services and one in Course Reserves. At these two stops students learn how to view their library account on-line, find an item on reserve for a class, and order books from another Penn State campus. They become aware of the Libraries Lending Code and learn how to read a LC call number. An additional activity is a Stacks Tour, an activity that evolved over several Open Houses. The stacks are in the older section of the Pattee Library and Paterno Library complex. The area has low ceilings, is somewhat dingy in appearance and has shelves winding through a smaller core section out into a larger area. With seven floors of stacks bunched into three stories of Pattee, some of the stacks floors do not have a direct exit to library service areas. Following call numbers as they snake through the sections is confusing. For several Open Houses, an activity challenged students to go into the stacks area to find a prize. We surmised this activity failed because few students were willing to venture into the stacks area by themselves. Therefore, the Access Services Open House Committee felt it was very important for students to feel comfortable going into the stacks to find a book, but knew the activity needed to be revamped to make it successful. One member of the Committee, a Collection Maintenance staff member, initiated the idea that we may need to take them into the stacks–a stacks tour. The first year (2005) the Open House Stacks Tour was offered it was attended by approximately 1,200 students during the two-day Open House. For the 2006 Open House 1,300 students participated in the Stacks Tour. Because of this success, the staff member suggested perhaps a tour was needed throughout the year. He volunteered to develop a Stacks Tour Pilot Project.

The tour's objective was two-fold. It could help reduce student's stacks anxiety. The tour would also give staff in the stacks unit a chance to share their expertise as the stacks' maintenance managers and develop skills such as customer service, communication, self-management, and teamwork. Under the direction of the Assistant Head of Access Services, the project coordinator developed a Stacks Tour proposal. The proposal is described in the next section.

PILOT PROJECT: PROPOSAL

The goal of the Project was to help new users become oriented to the physical layout of the Central Stacks and to alleviate some of the apprehension that students feel upon entering the dismal stacks. The ultimate goal was to make new users feel more comfortable and informed when using the library. The Stacks Tours were half hour tours introducing the patron to the Central Stacks of the Pattee Library. They emphasized how to find one's way into and out of the stacks, in addition to the best ways to become familiar with everything the facility has to offer.

Tour Format and Schedule

The Stacks Tours were held from January 15, 2006 to March 1, 2006. We decided the best time to add the Stacks Tour would be at the end of the existing tours already offered by the Gateway Library in Pattee and Paterno Libraries.
Our reasons included:

- Save the costs and time involved in publicity
- Tap into an already existing group of students who are interested in learning about the Libraries
- Benchmark results with an established tour
- Develop a cross departmental relationship.

To follow the Gateway Tours, the Stacks Tours took place on Tuesdays at 3:00 p.m., Wednesdays at 4:00 p.m., and Sundays at 4pm. The Project lasted until spring break in March for two reasons. It was determined that patron interest may be higher in the beginning of the semester and the tours could end before the heavy workload staff in the stacks unit experiences at the end of the semester.

Resources Required

For materials, handouts were created using the stacks unit's paper, copier and printer. As for staff resources, the tours had minimal impact on the daily operations of the unit. Some of the Project's preparations, such as outlining the tour route had already been completed for the Open House activity. It was estimated that the project would require around 20.5 staff hours each semester, with the work shared by five or six staff members volunteering as tour guides. Estimated time would include 10.5 hours for the tours (thirty minutes for each tour), five hours for training (ten staff) and five hours for statistics compellation. A minimum of three staff members were needed to cover the proposed times and provide a backup tour guide, based on a three tours per week schedule. The estimated staff time also included preparation time for up to ten staff; the time used to produce materials and time to log statistics. Each Stacks staff member had a thirty minute tour guide training session, covering the format of the tour and recording statistics. The projected staff hours were based on all of the Stacks Tours having participants.

Tour Promotion

The Stacks Tours promotion made use of the established Gateway Library Tours' publicity since the Stacks Tours were immediately following the Gateway Library tours. Some flyers and a Stacks Tour advertisement were created.

Statistics

The following statistics were kept to assess planning and tour format, progress, and if users' expectations and needs were met:

- Date/Time
- Number of patrons on the Gateway tour
- Number of patrons on our tour
- Questions asked.

Anticipated Benefits of a Stacks Tour

Several benefits were anticipated:

- Help patrons learn how to find a book in the stacks
- Reinforce the idea that the stacks area is a useful and safe area in the building
- Help patrons become more comfortable using the stacks for study space
- Reduce number of patrons getting frustrated by being lost in the stacks
- Inform international students, many of whom believe that the stacks are closed, they can browse the collection
- Better collection maintenance since tour reminds patrons not to re-shelve books
- Promote a cross-department relationship with the Gateway Library
- Provide a professional development opportunity for Stacks staff wishing to focus on the following job performance factors: job knowledge, communication, customer service and teamwork.

Continual Assessment

The tours were appraised throughout the project and altered when necessary. One concern was that patrons might not have 90 minutes free in their schedules to take the Gateway Library Tour and the Stacks Tour back-to-back. The tours could be shortened if it appeared patrons were not willing to spend additional time taking a Stacks Tour after the Gateway Tours. A shorter tour though abridged and less preferred, would still convey the information about the stacks to the patron.

Measuring Success

It was anticipated that the tours could produce a variety of positive effects that might be difficult to quantify. One measure of success was the benefits previously mentioned under "Anticipated Benefits of a Stacks Tour." Patron feedback indicating satisfaction with the tours and a willingness to learn about the stacks was another. One of the indications that the Open House tours were successful was the high volume of positive comments received from patrons. One of the most visual indications of success would be attendance. Assuming the Gateway Library Tours are successful, a high percentage retention rate transitioning from that tour to the Stacks Tour would be a measurement of success, indicating patrons see the Stacks Tour as a valuable use of their time.

Discussion of the Pilot Project versus an Ongoing Program

If statistics and analysis merit an ongoing program, slight changes to the daily times and frequency would be necessary. The Pilot Project was designed to confirm the value of a Stacks Tour and observe patron interest. An ongoing service would need to be structured to accommodate both patrons' interest and needs and the stacks unit's workload.

Tour Guide Instructions

Instructions for the staff giving the Stacks Tour included a checklist of areas to mention or show the patrons.
Checklist:

- Meet by the 1st Central Pattee Floor stacks entrance
- Show library map outside the central room
- Show Core (central room) elevator and computers
- Walk to main stacks area
- Show main elevator
- Inform patrons how to use that elevator as an orientation point

- Show stacks map near the main elevator, rangefinders and over-sized collection
- Show and explain study carrels
- Inform patrons they do not need to re-shelve their own books
- Demonstrate light timers (which turn on additional lighting)
- Show Diversity Reading Room and explain this is another way to exit the stacks
- Exit near Reserves and explain Course Reserves services
- Show West Pattee stairs
- Walk to West elevator and explain elevator access is available for all floors
- Get off at 3rd floor West Pattee
- Walk from 3rd floor West Pattee to 3rd floor Central Pattee
- Walk to 2nd floor West Pattee and across to 2nd floor Central Pattee
- Show copiers and Arts & Humanities Library Service Desk on 2nd floor
- Walk down to 1st floor Central Pattee
- Exit and take questions while ending at the tour's starting point
- Give LC call number handouts
- Fill out statistics sheet.

PILOT PROJECT: IMPLEMENTATION

Once the proposal was accepted by the Head of Access Services, we met with the Gateway Library Supervisor to review the proposal. The Stacks Tours would occur immediately after the library tours conducted by the Gateway staff. The Pilot Project would have three tours a week between January 15 and March 1, 2006. A poster and flyers about the tour were designed and reviewed by the Libraries Public Relations and Marketing Department but were not developed in time to have any promotional effect. We relied, instead, on the Stacks Tour sign and referrals from Gateway Library.

PILOT PROJECT: RESULTS

Statistics and the questions students asked were kept and tallied for each tour. Out of the twenty-one tours offered, eight were attended with an average of three students each. There were eight people who took the

Stacks Tour following the Gateway Library Tours. The other eighteen were in the library at the time, noticed the Stacks Tour sign temporarily posted where the Stacks Tour began and decided to take it. Table 1 lists the day of the week and the number of students who took the tour.

Most of the students were underclassmen. Nineteen were 'traditional-age' students and seven were returning adult students, is seen in Table 2.

There were 113 questions asked during the tour, is seen in Table 3).

PILOT PROJECT: EVALUATION

Students commented that the tour was worthwhile and informative. We made several observations about the tours.

1. Tour participants did not come to the library specifically for the tour, but were already in the building for other services or needs. Students think they are too busy to come to the library for a single reason unless it is required for a class.

TABLE 1. Days of Week and Number of Students Who Took the Tour

Day of the week	# students
Sunday	16
Tuesday	2
Wednesday	8
Total	26

TABLE 2. School Year of Tour Participants

School Year	# students
First Year	16
Second Year	8
Third Year	2

TABLE 3. Questions and Number of Times Asked

Question	# Times Asked
Is there a reading room or quiet study areas?	17
Where is the popular fiction?	16
How many books can I check out? What is the loan period, fines?	10
Where are the new magazines?	10
Why are the new fiction books not together?	9
Is there a list of which subjects go with the call numbers?	9
Where are the books on Course Reserves?	6
What are the library's hours?	5
Where are the movies and music? Where can I watch the movie for class?	5
How many books does the library have?	5
Why are the new magazines not together?	4
Where am I allowed to eat in the library?	4
Is there anywhere my children can go while I study?	4
How do I get a study carrel?	3
Are the stacks safe? Are they patrolled?	2
Is the old elevator safe?	2
Is it true someone died here?[16]	2

2. Giving the Stacks Tours immediately after the Gateway Library was handy for those patrons who were already focusing on the library. However, having a tour after the Gateway tour involved more time than some patrons wanted to devote to a library tour.
3. Having a tour guide familiar with the stacks helped students feel more comfortable and secure in the facility.
4. Students were interested in how the library could serve as a place to rest or get away from class. Most of the questions centered on study areas or location of leisure reading material.

In comparing the Pilot Project to the Stacks Tours offered during Open House in 2005 and 2006, data, feedback and observations from the Project revealed that the Open House tours were more effective. Open House is held at the beginning of Fall Semester when students are acclimating to the university and are more responsive to a tour invitation. As most students are required to attend Open House for a class, this captive audience of over 4,000 are focused on learning about the library and are eager to participate in the Stacks Tour and give feedback and suggestions. Most of the participants in the Stacks Tour Pilot Project happened upon the tours, were appreciative of the experience, but would not make an effort to attend otherwise. During the Project we reached twenty-six students over the twenty-one tours offered. Even though there were no participants in thirteen of the tours, there was staff time invested in preparation and waiting. During Open House we had a continuing stream of students ready for the tour and reached 1,300 students in two days. Table 4 compares the number of staff hours invested and the number of student tour participants.

If we would continue with the three tours on a weekly basis as in the Pilot Project, the staff time-to-participant ratio would be higher as fewer patrons are interested in tours during certain times of the year. We thought about offering the Stacks Tours at different times throughout the year, for example in the beginning of each semester, but decided this inconsistency may be confusing for Public Services library staff referring patrons. The ideal situation would be to have the tours on a regular schedule, like Gateway Library. However, an advantage the Gateway Library Tour has over the Stacks Tour is that Gateway staff start their tour at the Gateway service desk where the staff member can continue to work while waiting for participants. Stacks staff work throughout the library and have no service desk where interested participants can meet. For the Stacks Tour, the staff member needed to leave his or her duties

TABLE 4. Staff Hours Invested Comparison

Tour	Staff hours invested	Total # Students
Pilot Project	18	26
Open House	28	1300

to walk to the area where the tour began. This was poor use of time, especially when there were no participants.

In conclusion, we decided to discontinue the three Stacks Tours per week schedule. We will definitely continue the Open House Stacks Tours each Fall Semester. The Open House participants are the incoming undergraduates we believe need the tour the most and we can reach a large number of students during this time. It is well worth the time invested to focus on getting the Open House participants to take the tour. Since the participants during the Pilot Project commented the tour was useful, we will continue to look for specific tours with pre-arranged times. For example, tours for new library faculty and staff, or part of a library orientation for graduate students, international students, or honor students, during Parents Weekends and other special events in coordination with Public Services. We will continue to collaborate with Gateway Library staff on possible pre-arranged tours.

THE STAFF DEVELOPMENT SIDE OF THE TOUR PROJECT

The Tour Project proved to be a win/win arrangement for both our patrons and the staff members involved. We found ways to effectively reach and teach students about the stacks, the library, the collection, and the LC call number system. We also found an excellent development opportunity for the Collection Maintenance Stacks staff member. From the beginning, the Pilot Project posed a number of challenges. Below is what we learned.

Coordinating Resources and Needs of the Stacks Unit and Tour Project

As the project coordinator was writing the proposal, he met with his unit's supervisors to review the staffing and resources needed for the project. They discussed how to execute the project without negatively impacting the unit's core duties. Since we wanted to extend the opportunity to all full time Collection Maintenance stacks staff to participate in being a tour guide, some modifications to tour times were made to best utilize unit personnel and synchronize the peak work times of the stacks unit. He endeavored to create a Pilot Project that:

- Gave all stacks staff the opportunity to be involved
- Would not add undo stress to the stacks unit workload
- Would achieve both the Project and the unit's goals.

Communication

To increase the chances of success and to be sure he had unit support, the project coordinator updated the stacks unit supervisors on the project's progress. Monitoring the project was important in order to make adjustments in case it began to have an unexpected drain on the unit's resources. One could not assume that everything would go according to plan and continue as if the project was self contained. The project needed stacks staff involvement and would turn out best if everyone was invested in the outcome. He found that communication and collaboration are necessary and must be effective for a successful project.

Coordinating Tour Guides

The project coordinator invited all Stacks staff to have a development opportunity by being a tour guide. Because of this, he learned how to incorporate the additional tour schedule into the regularly scheduled unit duties, thus increasing his organizational and time management skills.

Learning Signageand Publicity Policies

The project coordinator learned about the Libraries' signage and publicity policies and discovered they were more complex than anticipated. Even though each library unit may have different signage needs, there is a standard process to follow. He learned that Penn State Libraries are not a collection of disassociated units, but a library of many units working together to achieve the same goal.

Developing Cross Departmental Relationships

The Collection Maintenance stacks unit is not under Public Services as is Gateway Library. We recognized that all units in the library in a sense provide customer service, with some more specialized with that focus. As a strategy to promote this new service we capitalized on the existing Gateway Library tours by adding the in-depth Stacks Tours to the end of their tour. We collaborated with the Gateway Library personnel to coordinate staff and tour times, as well as to discuss the overall project goals. Learning the importance of other departmental cooperation and collaboration developed through this arrangement.

Learning How to Initiate and Implement a Project

The project coordinator discovered initiating and implementing a project requires organization skills, communication, an understanding of the Libraries' mission, the unit's and his personal goals, and an understanding of the established parameters. Equipped with the resources available, the cooperation and support from other units, signage, volunteers, and his supervisor's support, he reviewed the project proposal for adjustments and presented it again to his supervisors. His aim was to balance the project's parameters with its purpose and goals to fully utilize available resources, resulting in an excellent exercise in increasing job knowledge and self management skills.

Presenting the Project

The project coordinator was aware that the project would not be successful if it did not involve input from others. He was able to present his ideas for the project on several occasions. He presented the Tour Project during several stacks unit meetings; he sought suggestions and evaluations from colleagues during and after the Project's completion. He met with staff from the Gateway Library several times to review and comment on the project and tour schedule. He presented the project's results and his evaluation of the Tour Pilot Project for the Access Services Department seventeen unit supervisors during one of their monthly meetings.

Gathering Statistics

Sometimes the hardest part of a project is deciding what statistical data should be recorded to gauge success. The question is whether success is measured simply in numbers that relate to the current project or whether a project is successful if what you learn also benefits a wide range of unit concernscurrently unrelated to the project. The project coordinator deduced that the latter would be more constructive. So he tried to gather the information in a way that also benefits currently unrelated or future projects that need to know about the needs and attitudes of our patrons. He counted the people in each tour, tallied the patron status, and recorded the questions asked. This would provide a picture of who the participants were, what they wanted to know, and what types of services they would like in the library. Such information could be used in the future for any project that needed a base understanding of what our patrons were like and the services they desired.

CONCLUSION

The project coordinator wanted to learn more from the project than "if a tour is available, patrons will take it." He wanted to see how the data gathered could be used in relation to the Libraries' mission. Understanding the Libraries' mission and its focus on educating students, he wanted to measure success by the participant's interest in the tour, what we learned about patrons needs, and how we can apply the knowledge gained from the project to better serve our patrons. The project was successful for several reasons. We received information about how we can better serve our patrons, we were able to gauge the interest level in ongoing separate tours, we were able to quantify what we learned, and he developed skills enhancing his job responsibilities.

One outstanding accomplishment was the project coordinator's ability to objectively evaluate the tour project. He analyzed the results, considered alternatives and assessed effective use of time. He was confident in his commitment of providing the best service that he was able to recognize that success is based on an objective evaluation of the data collected, not on recommending that the tours continue because it was his idea and there were tour participants.

The project proved to be an enriching staff development experience. According to the project coordinator:

> It can be difficult in a job that has many repetitious duties to see how daily, weekly and monthly tasks fit into the overall mission statement or strategic plan of a library. The successful implementation of a single idea required me to gain a deeper understanding of

such diverse factors as chain of command, publicity, scheduling concerns and patron needs. Although I had a surface understanding, the work for the project brought me to a functional understanding and participation in these issues. The overall effect on my organizational, communication,presentation and customer service skills has enabled me to better perform my daily duties. I have a better understanding of our patron needs and have improved the skills necessary for me work more productively with supervisors and fellow staff. Now, far more than before, I can see how the different departments and skill sets work together toward achieving mission statements and strategic plans. I think the development of these skills has led to a deeper personal investment from me in every facet of my job as well as the library's overall goal. (Nicastro, 2007)

To have the opportunity to extend beyond one's normal routine to develop a job-related, self-initiated learning project, to interact with different staff in the Libraries, and to discover a sense of accomplishment, not just personally, but for the Libraries as a whole proved very rewarding for the project coordinator. Through this experience, he progressed toward a greater awareness of the Libraries as an integrated organization and how he and his unit play a valuable role. What began as a suggestion within our Access Services Open House committee blossomed into a full-scale project launching a staff member into a valuable staff development venture. His appreciation of the Libraries mission, his desire to educate students about the library, his recognizing that Collection Maintenance stacks staff have an expertise to share, and his desire to learn and improve both his job environment and himself melded into a successful project. This education will prove to be beneficial for both him and the Libraries in future endeavors. The tours will continue, we will continue toward our goal of educating students about the library and we have a more informed, creative, valuable employee.

NOTES

1. Cahoy, Ellysa S. and Rebecca M. Bichel. "A Luau in the Library?" *College & Undergraduate Libraries* 11, no. 1 (2004): 49-60.

2. Ashmore, Beth, Jill E. Grogg, and "Library virtual tours: A case study." *Research Strategies* 20 (2005): 77-88.

3. Hickok, John. "Web Library Tours: Using Streaming Video and Interactive Quizzes." *Reference Services Review* 30, no. 2 (2002): 99-111.

4. Mosley, Pixey Anne. "Assessing the Comfort Level Impact and Per eptual Value of Library Tours." *Research Strategies* 15, no. 4 (1997): 261-270.

5. Oling, Lori and Michelle Mach. "Tour Trends in Academic ARL Libraries." *College & Research Libraries* 63, no 1 January (2002): 13-23.

6. Penn State University Libraries Marketing Steering Team, see "Final Report of Committee." *http://www.libraries.psu.edu/adminladup/spec1proj/marketing/* (accessed 4/05/07).

7. Maps of Penn State University Libraries. *http://www.psu.edu/pubinfo/ libmaps.html* (accessed 4/05/07).

8. Gateway Library's Virtual Tour of Penn State University Libraries. *http:// www.libraries.psu.edu/gateway/vtour/index.html* (accessed 4/05/07).

9. "Pattee Library and Paterno Library Tours" web poster. *http://www.libraries. psu.edu/news/tours/* (accessed 4/05/07).

10. "University Libraries Strategic Plan 05/06-07/08." 2005. *http://www.libraries. psu.edu/pubinfo/stratplan2005/* (accessed 4/05/07).

11. "Staff Review and Development Plan," Office of Human Resources, Penn State University. *http://www.ohr.psu.edu/SRDP/nsrdpm.cfm* (accessed 4/05/07).

12. "Putting the 'D' Back in the SRDP: a Toolkit for University Libraries Supervisors." 2004. *http://www.libraries.psu.edu/humanresources/SupervisorManual/Evaluations/ SRDP.htm* See under section "SRDP Resources for Supervisors:" (accessed 4/05/07).

13. Trotta, Marcia. *Successful Staff Development. How-To-Do-It Manualsfor Librarians.* 55, New York: Neal-Schuman, 1995.

14. Jurow, Susan. "How People Learn," in *Staff Development,* 3rd ed. (Chicago: American Lib. Assn, 2001),6-9.

15. Laverty, Corinne and Melody Burton. "Building a Learning Culturefor the Common Good." *Reference Librarian* 83/84 (2003): 71-81.

16. Boyer, Lauren. "Penn State legends uncovered", *The Daily Collegian Online* (8/ 912006), *http://www.collegian.psu.edu/archive/2006/08/08-09-06freshl08-09-06dnews-01.asp* (accessed 4/0512007).

REFERENCES

Ashmore, Beth, and Jill E. Grogg. "Library Virtual Tours: A Case Study." *Research Strategies, 20* (2005): 77-88.

Boyer, Lauren. "Penn State Legends Uncovered", *The Daily Collegian Online* (8/9/2006), http://www.collegian.psu.edu/archive/2006/08/08-09-06fresh/08-09-06dnews-01.asp (accessed 4/05/2007).

Cahoy, Ellysa S. and Rebecca M. Bichel. "A Luau in the Library?" *College & Undergraduate Libraries, 11,* no. 1 (2004): 49-60.

Hickok, John. "Web Library Tours: Using Streaming Video and Interactive Quizzes." *Reference Services Review 30,* no. 2 (2002): 99-111.

Jurow, Susan. "How People Learn," in *Staff Development,* 3rd ed. Chicago: American Library Association (2001), 6-9.

Laverty, Corinne and Melody Burton. "Building a Learning Culture for the Common Good." *Reference Librarian, 83/84* (2003): 71-81.

Mosley, Pixey Anne. "Assessing the Comfort Level Impact and Perceptual Value of Library Tours." *Research Strategies, 15,* no. 4 (1997): 261-270.

Oling, Lori and Michelle Mach. "Tour Trends in Academic ARL Libraries." *College & Research Libraries,* 63, no 1 January (2002): 13-23.

Penn State University Libraries.

–Marketing Steering Team, see "Final Report of Committee." *http://www.libraries. psu.edu/admin/adup/speclproj/marketing/* (accessed 4/05/07).

–Maps of Penn State University Libraries. *http://www.libraries.psu.edu/pubinfo/ libmaps.html* (accessed 4/05/07).

–Gateway Library's Virtual Tour of Penn State University Libraries. *http://www. libraries.psu.edu/gateway/vtour/index.htm* (accessed 4/05/07).

–"Pattee Library and Paterno Library Tours" web poster. *http://www.libraries. psu.edu/news/tours/* (accessed 4/05/07).

–"University Libraries Strategic Plan 05/06-07/08." 2005. *http://www.libraries. psu.edu/pubinfo/stratplan2005/* (accessed 4/05/07).

–"Staff Review and Development Plan," Office of Human Resources, Penn State University. *http://www.ohr.psu.edu/SRDP/nsrdpm.cfm* (accessed 4/05/07).

–"Putting the 'D' Back in the SRDP: a Toolkit for University Libraries Supervisors." 2004. *http://www.libraries.psu.edu/humanresources/Supervisor_Manual/ Evaluations/SRDP.htm* See under section "SRDP Resources for Supervisors:" (accessed 4/05/07).

Trotta, Marcia. *Successful Staff Development. How-To-Do-It Manuals for Librarians.* 55, New York: Neal-Schuman, 1995.

Lean Thinking in Libraries:
A Case Study
on Improving Shelving Turnaround

Nancy J. Kress

INTRODUCTION

The University of Chicago's Joseph Regenstein Library Bookstacks Department has used a number of management techniques to successfully improve operations. Since 2003, the department has used process mapping to improve many aspects of the operations. Past projects include reducing department payroll processing time and automating submission of search requests from the library catalog. We have also reduced the time needed to perform daily shelving operations, making materials available more quickly and accurately for users. Continuous process improvement allows us to resolve issues as they arise. Far from perfection, the Bookstacks Department continues to search for ways to improve. In examining other businesses for best practices, we began to focus on Lean manufacturing, an initiative centered on eliminating all waste in manufacturing processes. These principles are increasingly being applied in service organizations, which face many of the same challenges that manufacturers face. Among these is the need to improve speed and quality while reducing costs, as improving quality can significantly reduce customer complaints. Lean manufacturing promises dramatic changes in a short period of time. This article will present a case study using Lean principles to improve shelving turnaround time during the high volume due dates.

LITERATURE REVIEW

Lean thinking principles have origins in automobile-manufacturing, specifically in the Toyota production system. Lean is a management philosophy focused on creating value when delivering a product or service to customers while reducing unnecessary steps. By increasing the rapidity of operations, libraries can respond to user demands to have library material available when they want it and where they expect to find it.

A book commonly recommended as an informative and easy introduction to Lean is "The Goal" (Goldratt & Cox, 1992). While not written specifically to describe Lean principles, the book simplifies many of the concepts in the form of a novel. This book primarily concerns the theory of constraints, describing basic cause and effect towards achieving a business objective or goal. Many of the techniques directly related to Lean principles are illustrated, making the ideas easy to assimilate. "Lean Thinking" (Womack & Jones, 2003) outlines the five principles of the Lean system: (1) defining value for each product/service, (2) eliminating all unnecessary steps in each value stream, (3) making value flow to the customer, (4) knowing that the customer pulls all activities, product and service, and (5) pursuing perfection continuously. This book clearly demonstrates the principles using case studies from industry, and how to apply Lean thinking to any product or service. "Creating Level Pull" (Smalley, 2004) led to resolving the problem of high volume book returns. This workbook outlines the implementation of a system to control situations when processes–in our case high volume returns–operate faster than the resources necessary to handle them. This book was instrumental in managing the surge in books coming into the department, by deciding which books to hold as "inventory" and which books to return quickly back to the shelf.

In a survey of library literature, two journal articles were found that present cases in which Lean principles have been used to improve library operations. The first is "Implementing Process Improvement into Electronic Reserves: A Case Study" (Tuai, 2006). In this case study the goal was to improve processing of electronic reserves. The change was initiated through an internal project leader who learned about Lean techniques from "Lean Thinking" (Womack & Jones, 2003). While not citing specific measurable results, the author summarizes that Lean thinking can produce significant improvements in a short period of time. "The Impact of an Accelerated Improvement Workshop on Ordering and Receiving" (Alexander & Williams, 2005) presents a case study from Wichita State University. The article describes a workshop project to improve processing time for new library materials. Getting new material to library users faster was identified as valuable, based on the knowledge that these items accounted for a higher percentage of collection use. Using Lean management theory with the training and coaching of a Lean consultant from Boeing, they reduced processing time from

25 to 15 days by eliminating waste and focusing resources on what customer's value.

Lean places a high value on people and their contributions. In both articles, the authors note the importance of involving staff directly doing the work in the improvement. Collaboration between individuals and teams at every organizational level is an important component of any Lean strategy.

DEFINING THE PROBLEM

The Internet allows library users to obtain information quickly, almost instantaneously. This often leads to an expectation that all library material regardless of format should be promptly available. In the University of Chicago Library's Strategic Planning report from 2004, the Current Situation Analysis describes the expectations of users concerning collections: "materials listed in the catalog will be where they are supposed to be." Users expect books with the item status of "not checked out" to be on the appropriate shelf in the bookstacks, in correct call number order. Based on evidence from search request results, it is known that books are not always where they should be.

Among academic research libraries, Regenstein houses one of the largest circulating collections under one roof, numbering close to 4 million volumes. Over the past five years the department processed an average of 750,000 items annually. Many academic libraries experience peaks in re-shelving volume at the end of academic terms. Variability can be reduced somewhat by introducing rolling due dates or by adjusting due dates depending on borrower type. Regardless of how the library tries to even the flow of material, library users control much of the situation surrounding when materials are removed from the shelf and returned to the library.

To understand the problem defined in the case study, some context should be provided. The Bookstacks Department used process mapping beginning in 2003 to progressively reduce re-shelving turnaround from an average of fourteen days to two. While the total turnaround time had been lowered, during some weeks of the academic quarter turnaround remained high. In particular, we continued to struggle with the increased volume of books coming into the department following the due date. Most libraries face a similar situation at end of semesters, when student employees are scarce. Turnaround greatly increases at these times of year simply because there are more books to shelve and fewer people to shelve them. A typical pattern of items processed is illustrated in Figure 1, using data from one academic quarter of 2005.

BEYOND THE PROBLEM: THE CRISIS

Each year the Bookstacks Department selects two to three major improvement goals. In fiscal year 2006/2007 we aimed to improve shelving turnaround to 24-hours during all weeks of the year with the exception of end of quarter peak return periods. The prior fiscal year our non-peak turnaround averaged two days, while the peak turnaround averaged ten days. The 2006/2007 goal was to improve turnaround during peak return periods to four days. In addition to the high volume of returns, the department is responsible for re-shelving the 5,000 to 6,000 items that have been shelved in Reserve collections each academic quarter. There is an urgency to perform this work in the week between the end of one quarter and the beginning of the next as the amount of Reserve shelving is extremely limited. During these weeks between quarters, at worst books were piled up in no order on the countertop and books could sit in the Bookstacks Department for five to six weeks before being shelved. An internal frustration bordering on panic was created as every empty shelf and book truck would fill to the point of spilling over. Finding best practices for bookstacks within other aca-

FIGURE 1. Numbers of Returns Processed Per Week

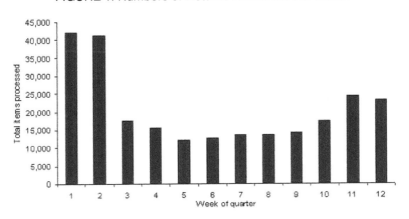

demic libraries yielded a few ideas, but not a solution that we could apply. We needed a breakthrough.

During staff brainstorming sessions, staff had difficulty coming up with organizations to look at for best practices. As the department manager, I took on the work of examining what kinds of organizations outside libraries that also had customers controlling the workflow. The nearest models were large mail, package and materials handling operations. We found a reactive operation similar to our own when we learned that Heckman, our library binder had significantly reduced turnaround time for binding shipments. Using Lean manufacturing principles they were able to reliably turnaround shipments regardless of volume and they were handling books, not mail or packages. I contacted them to inquire if a plant tour was feasible. I discovered that they had implemented Lean manufacturing principles in 2003. Using Lean, they were able to offer better service and guarantee complete shipments. My staff was unsure of what they would learn. They didn't expect that watching library books going through the binding process would help us much; however the Heckman staff were very positive about sharing their success so I felt it was worth the trip. I hoped to learn some best practices which could be applied to solve our peak return problem.

HECKMAN TOUR

The six University of Chicago Bookstacks staff who visited the North Manchester Indiana plant in August 2005 included me (the department head), four clerical staff and one student employee. It is important to note that in any process improvement effort, the people who work directly in the process should be part of the team. Employees responsible for actual improvement are less skeptical to change and often provide the best solutions. Heckman staff created a customized tour for our group. Our goal was to see how Lean manufacturing improved the movement of materials through the binding process, and how we could apply what we learned to improve efficiencies at Regenstein. Before we entered the binding plant, Heckman management shared with us the value stream maps of the binding processes illustrating the before and after situation analysis. Charting work processes is a useful way of recording the essential features of a work situation, allowing everyone to examine the process clearly. The Regenstein staff, who have been through prior process mapping, were familiar with the concept. Some of the symbols were different but everyone agreed that seeing the process on paper was one of the most valuable experiences in any process improvement. As we began the tour, Heckman staff explained one of the core principles of Lean: cut waste, not staff. Waste is defined as any actions that are involved in the creation and delivery of a product or service, that do not add value as perceived by the customer.

As we walked through the plant, Heckman staff illustrated where they used Lean principles to affect workflow improvements. They stressed limiting the number of times a book was handled and moved from place to place. Throughout our tour we observed cases in which employees doing the work were responsible for the improvements. I heard my staff correlating how what they were seeing at Heckman could be applied in the department. By the end of the plant tour the Regenstein staff was clearly excited about what might be possible. Afterward, we convened with staff from Heckman for lunch and to discuss what we had seen. We learned more about their experience with Lean thinking, and they gave us some ideas of how to solve our high volume peak periods. Something that made an impression of all of us was how Heckman had eliminated much of the rolling track that had previously snaked through the plant. They achieved this by blocking off large sections of track using yellow caution tape and urging staff to find a shorter route. We also learned tangible ways to reduce the number of times a book is touched. From my beginnings in bookstacks maintenance, this was the admonishment I heard over and over: every time you touch a book, it increases the time it takes to process it. It was my job to figure out how to solve this and I had found a breakthrough.

OUR PATH TO KAIZEN

Womack and Jones recommend a specific sequence of steps to produce the best results. Looking back at the department's own Lean transformation after our Heckman visit we had followed the same progression of steps. They write: "The most difficult step is simply to get started by overcoming the inertia present" (Womack & Jones, 2003, p. 247). We were eager to reduce the number of days it took to re-shelve materials during end of quarter peak return periods so this was an easy step to take. After this, a change agent is needed, plus some knowledge of Lean. Next in order is to identify a crisis to create an opportunity for change. Mapping out the process follows. Finally, start improving a specific activity as soon as possible.

The change agent in our case was me, and successes from previous process mapping projects had staff convinced that continued improvement was possible. Our next step was to become knowledgeable in Lean. Heckman managers advised us to read "The Goal" (Goldratt, 1992) as an introduction to Lean concepts. The following week, I started reading while the staff started to experiment with ideas from the site visit. As I encountered concepts in the literature that would help solve our turnaround problem, I sent emails, stopped employees in the hall and held impromptu meetings. But book knowledge can only go so far; we learned the most about Lean by applying the principles one by one to our crisis. This is an important point for anyone wanting to understand how Lean works. Womack and Jones write: "The only way to gain this understanding is by participating in improvement activities, hands-on, to a point where Lean techniques can be taught confidently to others." (2003, p. 250).

Our crisis has been identified earlier in this article. For those who are not comfortable using the term "crisis," simply identify what work in the organization really needs to be done. Most organizations are not in crisis, but there will likely be at least one process that could benefit from an improvement. For the Bookstacks Department, our crisis can be further illustrated through comments from the 2004 LibQual+ survey:

> "One area where the library could stand to improve: the amount of time for turnover from returned to reshelved books. It sometimes takes a week during the term, which is a pain."

> "I would request much quicker turnaround in getting books back on the shelves. Sometimes there are 20 carts of unshelved books, and I can't access what I need."

> "Books should be re-shelved every day. I have been told that it can take up to 3-4 days for books taken off the shelves to find their way back to their correct location–why is this not being addressed?"

When it came time to map the process, we revisited the process maps we had created during prior improvement projects. This time we began to look at the process from the library user's point of view, questioning how they determined value. "The critical starting point for Lean thinking is value. Value can only be defined by the ultimate customer. And it's only meaningful when expressed in terms of a specific product (a good or a service, and often both at once), which meets the customer's needs at a specific price at a specific time" (Womack & Jones, 2003, p.16). Thus, we identified the value of the work performed by the Bookstacks Department as shelving items in the Regenstein bookstacks in exact Library of Congress classification in under 24-hours.

In the weeks following our site visit, we started to brainstorm around two elements of what we had seen that were relevant for everyone. Throughout our tour Heckman staff reiterated the importance of doing away with bottlenecks. They also described how they had eliminated much of the rolling track that had previously snaked through the plant floor. Visually observing how they had improved these elements helped the Regenstein staff to understand and apply two principles of Lean: flow and pull.

FLOW

Regenstein staff remembered Heckman personnel advising us to reduce or eliminate bottlenecks. We learned during the site visit that any time work is allowed to pile up, a bottleneck is created. Bottlenecks limit the speed of everything in the process and once they develop, all work behind one stops. The larger it becomes, the longer it takes to work past it. The Lean principle that addresses eliminating bottlenecks is *flow*. Continuous flow refers to processing one piece at a time, with no delay between the beginning and end of the process. We had identified the beginning and end of the shelving process as the moment a book enters the Bookstacks Department to shelving the book in the stacks. Staff reasoned that the work of the department was to process the books, not to store them. The open bookstacks were where users expected the books to be stored, not behind the closed doors of our department or a book truck waiting to be shelved. Every time we allowed books to fill any shelving unit we created bottlenecks. The book trucks and pre-shelving areas were identified as places we were storing the books, delaying their return to the shelf. Now that we could see where the books should flow, we had to work on pull.

PULL

During the tour we were collectively impressed with how Heckman had taken out much of the rolling track that books previously traversed. Steve Heckman noted: "We had conveyor track everywhere, throughout the entire facility with people pushing materials around. Through Lean we've learned to pull, not push" (Monroe, 2003). Regenstein staff reasoned that in our case, the book trucks and pre-shelving areas correlated to the conveyer track where books would sit until the next step in the process. The Lean principle of *pull* means that within a process, a product or service should not proceed until the next step is ready for it. In our old process, the books were pushed (literally and in the Lean sense) to floors in the library bookstacks, where they would wait until a student employee was available to shelve them. Just two weeks after our visit, the formal and informal meetings, emails and hallway conversations culminated in the moment that my lead staff person excitedly came into my office and said: "We are doing immediate shelving." Staff had created a process to work towards shelving books immediately from check-in to the shelf. The pivotal realization was that the books did not have to be in exact call number order until they were shelved. Finally we had a tangible ways to reduce the number of times a book is touched, in our case by two. We eliminated putting books in exact call number order until the end of the process, as this is only valued at the point of shelving. In addition, we eliminated building book trucks in advance of shelving, as student employees now pull books directly from pre-shelving prior to immediate shelving. Now we just had to coordinate the amount of work to the time available to complete it.

REDUCE BATCH SIZE

Batch sizes are integral to flow and pull. I clearly recall that the first thing we were told at the beginning of our tour: don't put a book through a process unless it can move through the entire process from beginning to end with no delay. We had to synchronize the number of books shelved to the amount of time it took to shelve them. From prior benchmarking we knew that shelving one row of items on a book truck averaged thirty minutes, yet it would take four hours or longer to empty out a full six shelf book truck. The worst features of a full book truck were the total number of books, which were too many to shelve in an average work shift, and the time consuming and burdensome task of bending to reach books on the bottom shelf. Many book trucks were unable to be completely shelved in one work shift, which was frustrating to student employees. When asked what would improve this, they reported that completing a book truck from start to finish brought on a feeling of accomplishment. Once we began to match the rate of production with the employee hours, our cycle time leveled out and the books began to flow. The crucial data for designing continuous flow is to determine how many employees are available, how much work to distribute and how often to achieve the end result, which in our case is 24-hour turnaround.

SOLVING THE CRISIS

During the middle of the academic quarter our new pull-based system generated a 24-hour turnaround. But flow was not enough to overcome the 100% increase in during the due date weeks. "Creating Level Pull" offered the solution. Smalley writes: "inventory in the right place is a powerful tool to buffer against surges in external demand as well as internal process instability" (Smalley, 2004). This characterized our situation: surges of books, demand for places to put them when we had filled all available book trucks and holding shelves, while struggling with the instability of student employee availability. When I realized that a planned inventory could help the department control large swings in book returns I excitedly set up a brainstorming session to determine which staff would fill the different roles required. Smalley's workbook presents several questions that we answered as part of the step-by-step implementation process. First, we identified which books to shelve immediately. The books that were in less demand from patrons would be stored (in pre-shelving and on book trucks) as *inventory*. Finally, we had to select a *pacemaker* who would be responsible for monitoring and establishing the point at which we changed our process. The clerical employee responsible for the circulation check-in area of our department volunteered to be the pacemaker. Once again we had to determine value, specifically which books were in demand and hence most important to be on the shelf as quickly as possible. Books coming off course reserve were the books that had to get to the shelf the fastest. We knew which books were in highest demand from internal reporting and search request history. Using circulation data we identified other high use collections by call number. Prior to this understanding, we treated all books in the same manner in our centralized process. Because the student employees did not yet understand Lean principles, the clerical staff who had been on the Heckman tour conducted the training for the peak return process. The new process was ready just in time for the next high volume return period, just six months from our induction to Lean.

EVIDENCE OF SUCCESS

On the Monday following the end of academic term due date, I walked into the department and expected to find every shelving area filled, as had been during prior peak return periods. Instead, I was surprised to find the pre-shelving areas half empty, and the emergency shelving area, which in the past would have been filled to 100%, empty. In actual outcomes, the time to shelve Reserve items has been reduced from four days to two. One data point that can be tracked backward is the percentage of items found in pre-shelving areas (which includes book trucks). We can extrapolate from this data that a greater percentage of books are on the shelf, where the user expects to find them. This is shown in Figure 2.

The conversion of the Bookstacks Department from a reactive model to Lean thinking has produced some dramatic performance improvements but measuring value is a challenge in the service environment. Libraries seldom report shelving speed and accuracy statistics, and the Bookstacks Department only reports totals for the number of items processed annually. Defining and collecting the data concerning how well we meet the users' definitions of value proves difficult and we are still developing performance benchmarks.

FIGURE 2. Reduction in Percentage of Searches Found in Pre-Shelving Areas

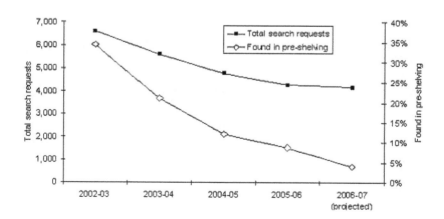

CONCLUSION

This case study illustrates that Lean principles, even when isolated to one process can produce significant improvements in speed and quality. More than a change methodology, it is a philosophy that can create dramatic improvements in an organization. Vice Chairman Fujio Cho of Toyota offers three keys to Lean leadership that have been the essence of our Lean journey: "Go See, Ask Why, and Show Respect" (Womack and Shook, 1996, slide 39). "Go See" refers to a key principle of Lean which is the ability for everyone involved in the work to see it happen, in our case by visually mapping the process. "Ask Why" is a technique to determine the root cause of a problem, by asking "why" repeatedly rather than jump to a conclusion or solution. Asking why puts focus on the work and the problem at hand, avoiding finger-pointing and blame. Finally, "Show Respect" means that leaders respect their employees. We could not have achieved our goal without teamwork. Throughout our continuous improvement journey we have collectively as a department defined value, and the waste that detracts from the flow of value. Lean promises a way to do more with less, while coming closer to providing customers with exactly what they want. For library patrons, the solution has come just in time.

REFERENCES

Alexander, G., and Williams, J. H. (2005). The Impact of an Accelerated Improvement Workshop on Ordering and Receiving. *Library Collections, Acquisitions, and Technical Services, 29*(3).

Goldratt, E. M., and Cox, J. (1992). *The Goal: A Process of Ongoing Improvement.* (2nd rev. ed.). Great Barrington, MA: North River Press.

Monroe, J. (January 2003). Cover to Cover. *The Manufacturer.* Retrieved February 5, 2007 from http://www.themanufacturer.com.

Smalley, A. (2004). *Creating Level Pull: a Lean Production System Improvement Guide for Production-Control, Operations, and Engineering Professionals.* Brookline, MA: Lean Enterprises Institute.

Tuai, C. K. (2006). Implementing Process Improvement into Electronic Reserves: A Case Study. *Journal of Interlibrary Loan, Document Delivery & Electronic Reserve, 16*(4).

Womack, J. P., and Jones, D. T. (1997). *Lean Thinking: Banish Waste and Create Wealth in Your Corporation.* London: Touchstone.

Womack, J. P., and Shook, J. (October, 2006). *Lean Management and the Role of Lean Leadership*. Presented on October 19, 2006. http://www.lean.org/images/october_webinar_project_slides.PDF.

Phantom Use:
Quantifying In-Library Browsing of Circulating Materials

Victoria H. Wagner

CONCEPT

We know our materials are being used. We find books abandoned on tables, at the end of stacks, piled and rejected in carrels and study rooms. These items have been pulled from the shelves, thumbed through, skimmed or read, and left behind. We collect, organize, and re-shelve them. At a certain point we had to ask: why not count this anonymous use of our collection?

INTRODUCTION

The Cheng Library houses a collection of over 350,000 volumes and the Lending Services department is responsible for the circulation and stacks maintenance related to the use of this collection. An ongoing goal of the Lending Services department is to assess the many services provided by our staff. Our department has the largest overall staff: one librarian, one professional staff member, four full-time support staff members, eight part-time staff workers, and between ten and fifteen financial aid/student assistant workers. We track most of our major responsibilities in traditional ways, such as our monthly and annual statistics where we report on the circulation of materials, financial statements, and gate count. By taking samples of some of the routine responsibilities we do not usually "count," we can collect information that reflects a fuller picture of the department and the breadth and depth of our contribution to the Library.

Historically, our annual statistics only report data concerning the materials actually borrowed by our patrons. Lending Services staff members sort and shelve materials whether they are returned to the circulation desk by our patrons or collected during nightly pick-ups of browsed books on the second floor of our library, which houses our circulating collection. Recognizing the active movement of materials throughout the building, we realize that our circulation statistics only capture half of the department workflow and do not account for collecting and sorting materials used within our walls. This previously unreported use of the building and its materials has important repercussions for our stacks maintenance staffing. Additionally, information about resources used but not borrowed by our patrons should inform our collection development policies and procedures.

METHODOLOGY

We are an Endeavor Library, and one major disadvantage of the Voyager system is that it does not record date or time information after an item is discharged when it is not currently charged to a patron. Unfortunately, transaction data is only maintained in an item's record as it pertains to circulation history, however, the system does mark the record with a "browse" count when it is discharged in these instances. For the purposes of our project, we ran Access queries written against our Voyager database and created an item level report constrained to the circulating locations. This Circulation Browse Statistics report reviews all items with counts in the historical browse field and provides us with the cumulative total of browses. In order to obtain a more granular view of this information, we took this report a step further by querying our cumulative total so that the browses would display by Library of Congress call number. The data in this report became the baseline for comparison once our pilot project ended.

We conducted a two week sample period of in-library use of circulating materials. These two weeks were during our busiest time of the year, late October, but, intentionally, we did not sample during mid-terms when we see a spike, or an overall increase, in use of our facility and its resources. Each night, a student worker gathered abandoned materials throughout the second floor from the stacks, study rooms, carrels, book drops, and tables. Using the circulation module, a student worker discharged these collected materials, thus marking each item's record with a browse count. At the end of the sampling period, we once again ran the Circulation Browse Statistics report with a Library of Congress view.

We created an Excel spreadsheet to manage the sampling data. Simple subtraction of the baseline data from the post-sample data provides the number of in-house uses during our sampling period (see Figure 1). We would prefer that our system would stamp each browse with a date and time, but with a little effort, we can gather enough information to make our case: Lending Services staff members shelve and process as many browsed as circulated books, and the areas with the heaviest circulation also have high in-house use statistics.

STAFFING

Our student workers contributed significantly to this project. They followed their normal evening assignments of collecting pick-ups with

FIGURE 1. By subtracting the October baseline snapshot data from the post-sample November snapshot data, we are able to determine the number of in-house uses during our sample period. This figure shows the grand total of browses as well as examples of use by Library of Congress call number break-down.

	Totals	Call #: E	Call #: HQ	Call #: RC
Historical browses as of November	34,814	1686	1874	1195
Historical browses as of October	33,320	1640	1806	1141
Browses during sample period	1,494	46	68	54

the additional workflow of discharging each item in order to process the in-house counts each night. After the sampling period, we considered adjusting our routine to include discharging pick-ups. We determined, after careful consideration, that this additional work was potentially time consuming and removes student workers from more immediate duties such as assisting library users or covering the public service desks.

SAMPLE

During the two week sampling period, Lending Services staff members collected and discharged 1,494 "abandoned" books from the circulating collection. The call numbers with the highest in-house use were: HQ, RT, RC, ML, PS & HV. (See Figure 2). During this same time period, patrons borrowed 1,582 books from the circulating collection, and the call numbers with the highest circulation were: BF, HV, LB, PS, HQ & RC (See Figure 3). Accounting for in-house use allows us to see that the workflow for Lending Services is actually twice as much as we claim in our traditional circulation statistics. Indeed, over 3,000 books were used by our patrons during the sampling period (See Figures 4 & 5).

CONCLUSIONS

This pilot shed light upon the research practices of our library users. In-house use is another significant measure of how our collections are

FIGURE 2. In-house Use During Sample Period Displayed with Library of Congress Call Number Breakdown

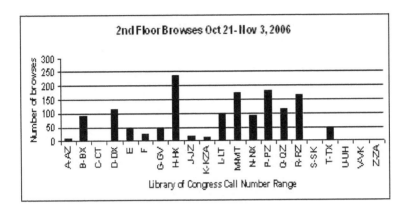

FIGURE 3. Circulated Materials During Sample Period Displayed with Library of Congress Call Number Breakdown

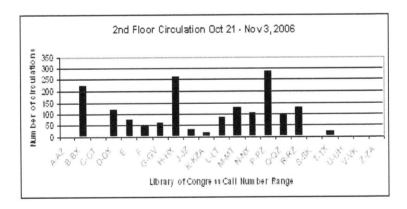

used, perhaps reflecting the serendipity of locating materials on the shelf which may not be exactly what a patron is seeking. Indeed, an essential component of research is the phenomenon of encountered materials, that is, reviewing related materials shelved near a specific title of interest. Certainly part of the research process involves the exclusion of materials, and determining what is important for the topic at hand. The pick-ups collected by Lending Services staff are reminders of this process of review, elimination, and in-house selection by our patrons.

FIGURE 4. Browsed vs. Circulated Materials During Sample Period Displayed with Library of Congress Call Number Breakdown

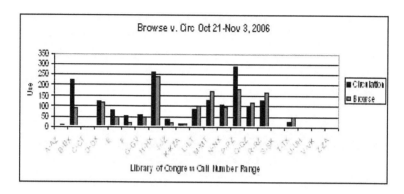

FIGURE 5. Total Use, Circulated and Browsed Materials During Sample Period Displayed with Library of Congress Call Number Breakdown

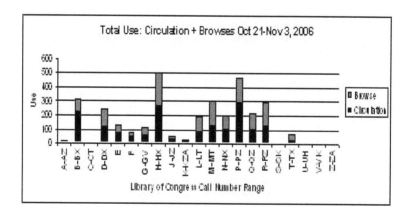

Anecdotally, Lending Services staff members felt that books in certain subject areas had extremely high in-library use, to the extent that night after night certain titles would be picked up in our normal collection rounds. In subject areas such as nursing, where the books are oversized and heavy, it seems that students prefer to use materials in-house rather than carry them around. This impression was demonstrated to be true, and books in the Library of Congress call number range R (medicine) had one of the highest browse numbers in our sample.

This sampling project was eye-opening for the Library staff. Quantifying the amount of anonymously used items that we re-shelve gave us pause for thought. While the browsed books are in the call number ranges with the heaviest circulation, ultimately these data informed us that staff members need to pay even more attention to these stack areas in terms of shelf-reading, frequency of shelving, and general straightening. These are the locations where our patrons are and these are the materials that they use.

We focused on the circulating collection but discovered that this project may have meaningful implications for our reference, non-circulating collection. Librarians and students use our reference books whenever the Library is open. The Reference department maintains shelving statistics concerning how many books are re-shelved without noting which books are re-shelved, and thus, there is no information about use of specific items or within specific subject areas. We will propose that the Reference department consider a similar project.

Counting the circulation of materials captures only one aspect of patron/book interaction. The in-house use statistics provide information to support the notion that our materials are used despite a decline in traditional circulation. Additionally, this jibes with the increased activity in our other patron-initiated services such as online book renewal. Many students prefer the unmediated experience, finding and using materials within the building independently.

In summary, this sample reinforces our belief that the Lending Services department plays a vital role in upholding the customer service philosophy of the Library. Indeed, our focus is to understand how the patrons in our building access and use the resources available to them and to make that experience a positive one. The prompt re-shelving of browsed materials is one way that we can satisfy our patrons since they use materials within the building as often as they borrow them.

We are happy to see that our contributions continue to be quite significant. This pilot uncovers meaningful data which reflect not only the department's routine tasks but also the "invisible" use of our collection. We informed library selectors about this project and the information we uncovered about the popular areas for circulation and in-house use. As a result of this pilot, the Lending Services department will continue to conduct annual sample counts of in-house use which can provide a significant snapshot of how our Library collections are used.

Managing Lost and Missing Books

Bethany Badgett Sewell
Andrew Jonathan Miller

INTRODUCTION

The Access Services department at the University of Denver has undergone a great deal of change both in terms of reporting lines and procedures in the last three years to manage the print collection of a mid-sized academic library with approximately 3 million volumes. Access Services is officially charged with directing the operations of circulation, reserves, and interlibrary loan. In July 2004, turnaround times on returned volumes measured nearly 5 days and accuracy was poor. Among other issues, there was one staff member who had been intentionally mis-shelving since April of that year with no response or action taken until Andrew Miller became the Stacks Supervisor in July.

On average, missing book complaints came to either the Circulation Desk or the Reference Desk at a rate of six per day with no immediate resolution except for marking the item record to reflect the items missing status, thus enabling the patron to request from either a consortial source or via ILL. In the authors' experiences, both in public and academic libraries, this is generally the extent of missing book maintenance. While our example is rather extreme, our solutions to managing the stacks and missing items offer the appropriate immediacy that excellent service connotes in today's proactive service environments, while providing the proverbial 'bread-crumb' trail when initial efforts fail.

Our innovation and success have been driven by standardizing procedures, streamlining responsibilities, and are decidedly low-tech. While our approach continues to evolve, a commitment of a small amount of space on public floors, training, and initial outlay for supplies (which for us includes a negligible amount of colored paper), is a simple physical method for marking the spot of a missing item in the stacks [we use Brodart's "Shelf Markers"], and a commitment to a higher service level is all that is required.

We will discuss some technological innovations we have added but even those were kept well under $500. When you consider the amount of time your staff spends searching for books either in response to ILL requests or patron requests, maintaining the stacks is more than worth it fiscally. However, we also know either anecdotally or from face-to-face confrontation what poorly maintained stacks can mean for our patrons and for our staff.

We believe it is not enough to mark our missing items as "unavailable" in the catalog. We both actively and passively pursue the wayward books for our patrons and the results have had a profound impact on the efficiency and satisfaction levels throughout the library and its users. After a review of the literature, and postings on the CIRCPLUS listerv, it became clear that stacks maintenance is a service point of great concern; however, tested solutions were difficult to come by. In an effort to present as complete and concise a piece on this topic, we offer a Literature Review, a brief introduction to the problems first addressed in July 2004 at Penrose Library, and three progressively designed solutions to address both the immediate and long-term needs of the stacks, and ultimately, our users.

LITERATURE REVIEW

We found little mentioned about stacks maintenance policies and even less about "best-practice" procedures, particularly in recent publications of library literature. This lack of publishing on best-practices in stacks maintenance is reviewed in great detail by Roberta Stuemke in her 1997 article found in the *Associates: The Electronic Library Support Staff Journal*. Stuemke's observations highlight the surprising lack of evidentiary studies on the often discussed issues of the stacks as a physical place and as a processing unit. At the time of her writing of the article in 1997, and in 1985 when she first began working as a stacks manager, there was virtually nothing published about proper stacks management and this trend has continued. While many libraries have parts of their procedures and policies posted, there seems to be an acceptable rate of error and service that would be considered outside of acceptability if they were occurring in another area of the library.

In discussions with our staff, our librarians, and colleagues we have found that many consider the techniques so basic that they are merely intuitive. While it is not the intention to hypothesize why the low level of accuracy, proactive service, and out and out expectations are so low in the stacks, we know from experience that they can not only be corrected, but these challenges can also offer new opportunities for successful service throughout the library.

The first change must be made at the training and operational level. Our staff, in July 2004 and for many years prior, had come to expect high levels of failure in terms of searching for books. The Stacks unit was only responsible for shelving materials and the low quality of maintenance had the expected negative impact on morale. In terms of literature on the topic of morale and the role of the stacks in the library, we found our situation exactly matched that of Smith and Laning's observation that,

> Unfortunately, most library employees consider shelving one of the least appealing tasks in academic libraries and the task is usually relegated to student assistants, who do not have a strong appreciation for its importance. As a result, this critical aspect of library service moves to the bottom of everyone's priority list and receives inadequate attention until enough complaints are registered (p. 16).

Again, the literature on how to approach and resolve issues in this "critical aspect of library service" was scarce.

The task of unburdening the stacks from the stigma it so typically seems to be laden with starts by acknowledging it as a "critical aspect" of library operations and building successes into its operations. Unlike some of our service provision that is reactive, management of the stacks gives us the opportunity to be proactive in our service. This, however, does require leadership, some true implementation of policy and procedure, and accountability. As leaders, librarians define what is important, and service is generally at the top of that list. In addition, leaders define the values, responsibilities, and expectations of their departments and if the basics aren't right we can not expect to get the higher levels of service right.

Despite the lack of glamour in shelving, much has been written and published about the important role well-maintained stacks play in user satisfaction and the overall running of the library. We have often heard from all viewpoints in the library including reference, circulation, and technical services, that a book that is out of place is essentially "lost" or at least "unusable." Abraham Bookstein mathematically analyzed the problem of missing books in "Models for Shelf Reading," which first appeared in the April of 1973 issue of *Library Quarterly*. In this article, Bookstein calculates that "the amount of frustration generated in a brief period of time is proportional to the product of the number of uses" (p. 128). Bookstein's finding begged the question for us that no one wanted to ask: if there were an average of six missing book requests a day, how many were not being reported? The problem was so pervasive that for many years it defined the library's service standards, the role of the staff procedural, and through accretion became a problem that resulted in over 40,000 errors.

THE PROBLEM

Bookstein's mathematical calculations which describe patron frustration clearly exemplify the need for materials to be easily locatable. Penrose Library's mission echoes the access standards of most libraries, our error rate in the stacks told a different story. Access, in the strictest and most basic sense, was neither quantified nor enforced in any standing policies or procedural efforts. As a result, the missing book issue was pervasive. With so many errors, and a lack of policy and procedure, a point was made to approach each issue with a short-term tactic to empower staff with the responsibility to solve the missing book issue as quickly and directly as possible. We also had to adopt a realistic long-term view to strategically shift our processes. One long-term goal was to shelf read the entire library, but to make our patrons wait that amount time for their requested items to turn up was an unacceptable option as Penrose is comprised of roughly 50,000 shelves of monographs and serials alone.

This long-term process took a year and was worth every penny and minute. Ultimately, this concerted effort created a sense of pride throughout the stacks staff but it was by no means enthralling but was absolutely necessary. Our short-term approach was direct: we developed a standardized form for staff at the Circulation desk to use whenever a book was declared missing. This "Book Trace," is filled in by the staff member and records the call number or title of the missing item, the date, the patron's name, and an email address. The patron is told that their requested item(s) will be searched for by the end of the day and they will be contacted directly with the results. When we began this effort, we were receiving six reports of missing items per day and felt that this was a less efficient means of service when compared to the prior system of only requesting materials via ILL or from a consortial lender but that our patrons deserved more. This costly solution, in terms of fees and labor, and in terms of credibility in our community, helped to drive our reinvention. Procedures needed to be developed that would help identify what books were missing and resolve the patrons' requests immediately and systemically for the future. Methods needed to be built into stacks maintenance that would assure the shelves remained in good order and that patron reports of missing books would become the exception, not the rule. Finally, we knew what this was costing our library and we wanted to come out of transformation more efficient, more streamlined, and ultimately more cost effective. In the following pages, we will discuss elements of our transformation and how standardizing the missing books procedure actually served to overhaul not just the Stacks Maintenance unit but also redefined materials access service levels throughout the library.

THE SOLUTION PART 1:
IDENTIFYING THE MATERIALS AS MISSING

It is not always known how materials go missing. In our example, we found distinct patterns at work in our shelving errors:

1. One staff member had been purposefully mis-shelving since April of 2004.
2. Distinct patterns of common mistakes were made unintentionally by shelvers.
3. The majority of errors were on the top and bottom shelves (12% and 16%, respectively).

In the reactive library, materials are generally identified as missing in three ways. The first way that an item is discovered missing is by library staff going about their library work. For example, items are systematically searched for on system-generated lists such as inventories or for special projects such as weeding and pulling materials for off-site storage. The second, and less desirable way that an item is identified as missing, is by patrons being billed for a non-returned item even though they claim the item was returned. Third, is by patrons who are looking in the stacks for known items that they cannot find. We have all often heard a patron complain, "Your catalog says this book is available, but I could not find it on the shelf" or "I returned this book weeks ago, but it still shows it charged on my record." N. Andrew Spackman's recent article in the *Journal of Access Services*, "Reducing Check-In Errors at Brigham Young University through Statistical Process Control," discusses the issues of claims returned and a system for reducing check-in errors in more detail.

We wanted to build as proactive an approach to identification and solution as possible. Over the course of the last three years we have seen the Stacks unit become solely responsible for all pulling and shelving in the monograph and serial stacks. In the library, unlike a bookstore, the shelver puts the books away with little reward for a job well done. Currently, any book found to be missing while working through a list for weeding, ILL requests, catalog updates, and any myriad of other projects we spend our time on is, immediately researched by the staff in an effort to quickly and, through training, expertly track it down. Our stacks are now a point of pride and the expectation is success not failure. We consider it vital that our catalog match our holdings, and when it doesn't, we have direct techniques for offering immediate service and solutions. This short-term approach helped build morale, expectations among our internal and external users, and within the library team. Even when we fail we show intent to satisfy and always offer alternatives. Since implementing these new procedures we receive fewer than three Book Traces a week and 89% of those are generally either in the appropriate location, very recently returned, are currently checked out, or have special locations such as New, Reserve, Oversized. After addressing the immediate service issue, we set about to shelf read the entire library and sought to add transparency and accountability to the department in its day-to-day operations. For those items that remain unfound, we needed a passive method of tracking that would alert the shelver and the patron that the status of the item in question was missing. The solution is the tracer card.

THE SOLUTION PART 2: TRACERS–LOCATING THE MATERIAL EMPLOYING AN EFFECTIVE USE OF STAFF TIME

This brings us to the collaboration between Stacks maintenance and Circulation and the use of tracer card. It is a simple re-usable shelf marker made from heavyweight 8" x 3" card stock with clear pockets attached to be inserted into the precise location in the stacks where the missing item should be. A 3/4" extended tab holds the tracer in place makes it easy to spot and prevents it from getting pushed back and lost between books. The call number, a short title, the pagination, height of the missing book, and the date that the book was declared missing are printed on a card which is then neatly placed in the clear pocket. This is a clear marker for library staff and patrons that there is an ongoing search for a particular item. If the item is a claims return, the patron who claims to have it brought back can clearly see that it is not on the shelf, and instead, there is a marker where the item should be.

For our shelvers, every time a missing item is found, regardless of process, there is a record that the book about to be shelved is listed as missing and needs to be brought to the circulation desk and its missing status resolved. The missing book is then processed so that it can go on the hold shelf for a patron if a Book Trace was submitted, or so that the status of Claims Return can be taken off a patron's record and the fines waived. The tracers help us identify a problematic book in a semi-permanent, perpetual, low-tech method.

Anytime shelvers work in the stacks, they have the opportunity to provide excellent service to our patrons by finding the requested books. The following scenario illustrates this point: A book has been mis-shelved and was declared missing a year ago. During a shelf-reading project, a shelver finds the book and takes it to the shelf where it belongs. Seeing the tracer card, the shelver is alerted to the fact that this is a missing item. This helps us provide good service to our patrons without managing a list of books that need to be searched for every year. It also relieves any anxieties by staff and patrons that the search for the book has been forgotten. We have decided to keep tracer cards in place for a three-year period because missing and lost books will reappear as a result of processes outside those discussed. For example, missing books are returned to us from patrons themselves after many years and they may have been "Claims Returned" or suppressed because of check-out mistakes. Patrons do appreciate this service, as noted in William Warner Bishop's classic, *The Backs of Books*, "It is delightful, even somewhat uncanny, to receive back your slip, as I once did, marked in blue pencil, 'manca del 1682.'–'missing since 1682." (Bishop, 20).

The process for a patron-initiated missing item search begins at the Circulation Desk. If a patron is unable to locate an item on the shelf and wants us to search for it, a hold is placed on the material for the patron and the item status is changed to "Missing." This allows the catalog to alert patrons that the book has been identified as missing and allows the patron to request the item through Prospector[1] or Interlibrary Loan. A tracer form is filled out and the Stacks Maintenance unit is alerted to begin searching for the book. The basket where the forms collect is kept in a high traffic area and checked several times a day ensuring a quick turn around time. By changing the status to "Missing," a system message is generated which alerts the evening staff to search for the item one more time. Every evening, the night supervisor prints lists of all items marked Claims Returned or Missing (either identified as such by staff or by patrons throughout the day) and a final search is performed. After one day of intensive, concentrated searching, all unfound items change to a second form of Missing or Claims Returned–visible only to the staff to prevent the same list from being printed the next day. Finally, a tracer card is prepared for each missing item and the night supervisor places the cards in their designated places throughout the stacks. The next morning, the missing items become the sole responsibility of the Stacks Maintenance unit. At the end of the month, all missing book records are changed to "Lost." A physical review of tracers in the stacks is conducted semi-annually in conjunction with a review of system-generated lists of lost books. The list of any lost books that remain at this point, are then given to the cataloging unit to be suppressed. Finally, the subject selectors review the list of lost books and determine whether or not to replace the items. Patrons with claims returned items that are not found within the year are then billed.

THE SOLUTION PART 3:
MAINTAINING THE STACKS

The stacks maintenance unit at the University of Denver's Penrose Library is much like the one described by Smith and Laning at the University of Louisville in that it is a separate unit focused only on stacks related duties. Although Stacks Maintenance operates as a separate unit directed by the head of collection development, a highly developed system has been cultivated by creating close collaborative relationships not only between the Stacks Maintenance unit and the Technical Services units, but also the Access Services units of circulation, reserves, and interlibrary loan and has led to projects that are generally considered well outside of the stacks scope such as managing the microforms, current periodicals and newspapers, facilities maintenance, managing the flow of six skids of materials to an offsite storage facility per month, and a host of one-time projects such as moving furniture.

The Stacks Maintenance unit is managed by one full-time manager and an average of 250 weekly hours of hourly and student staff. Included in these hours are several fully trained "On Call" staff who are called upon during peak return periods and for special projects. The functions of this unit within the stacks specifically include the following:

1. Shelving all returned materials with a same-day-turnaround time for all returns.
2. Collecting, counting and reshelving materials used internally.
3. Maintaining current periodicals and new books, including the new book rotation to the regular shelving.
4. Retrieving materials for interlibrary loan, reserves, e-reserves, and Prospector.
5. Pulling materials destined for storage; pulling materials for special technical services projects.
6. Shifting materials in the stacks to make room for new materials.
7. Maintaining the stacks by keeping them neat and orderly, shelf-read, shifted, and inventoried.
8. Searching for books not found on the shelf and reported by patrons as lost, claimed returned, and in any other way missing.

This is a very demanding mission considering the statistics from last year: 97,541 items were checked out and returned, 25,691 items were retrieved for processing through interlibrary loan activities, and 6,644 items were retrieved for reserves. In addition, over 130 skids of materials were pulled, packed, and shipped to remote storage in support of a space-planning initiative. To keep up with this intense workflow, the staff hours are strategically scheduled for peak operating hours and at least one staff member is busy in the stacks nearly every open library hour.

From August 2004 to February 2005 the entire library was shelf read and over 41,000 errors were corrected in the collection. To prevent this volume of errors in the future, and to avoid ever having to do this much shelf reading again, many initiatives were begun to improve the collections and enhance collaboration with other departments without compromising quality or shelving time. Not surprisingly, we found that good order increased our shelving rates by nearly 18 minutes per 100 books. With our pace quickening, we found that we were able keep our turnaround times on returns to about 10 hours which we then established as our baseline.

Next, we moved the sorting areas for returned materials from behind the Circulation Desk, where it had occupied over 1,300 feet of linear shelving, to a well-signed, high traffic area on the floor they where housed called the Fine Sorting Area. This move developed transparency. We wanted to limit not only the amount of time a book waited to be reshelved but also to simplify access to the areas where it waited to be reshelved. To do this, we have converted to two three-tiered carts (one for each floor) that receive all of the returns from circulation, roughly sorted by alpha only. The expectation is that each shelver empties both carts at the start and finish of their shift. This eliminates a myriad of questions about where a book might be waiting for its return to the shelf–it is either in the Fine Sorting Area or it is missing and as we have discussed thus far, we have a solution for that–the Book Trace.

With the stacks shelf read and missing material searched for on a daily basis, the stacks maintenance manager trained the staff on best practices of stacks maintenance. This training was crucial to success. The amount of work to overcome our issues was staggering but we had momentum. As we shelf read, beyond putting things into perfect call number order, we initiated the "Theory of Flush," which is often practiced in bookstores. All materials are shelved with their spine flush with the edge of the shelf with enough slack that when a book is pulled out, it leaves the empty space open, which is referred to as shelf memory. While there is no hard evidence, experience tells us that visually messy shelves have a tendency to degrade into even messier shelves. Beyond the appearance aspect, the meticulously shelved books on the shelves visually queue the shelvers to areas that need attention and shelf-reading by the simple absence of a shelf being flush.

The vast majority of our materials, in accordance with the 80/20 rule, go years at a time without any activity. The assumption can then be made that a flush shelf is still in good condition and that shelvers can then prioritize shelf-reading and straightening areas less organized while shelf-reading very closely to identify potentially missing items. We have portioned out the entire stacks (based on a combination of circulation statistics and hours worked per staff member) into assigned ranges of contiguous call numbers and have found that within 30 minutes as many as 1,200 shelves can be reviewed using a brisk walk looking for the anomalous disrupted shelves. Thus, all section maintenance time is dedicated to areas that have seen activity. With 3 million volumes in the library collection, time is essential and the scale can certainly seem overwhelming.

As we are approaching our second year of using this method and we have turned every skeptical employee, new hire, and most importantly, patron into believers. From a management stand point, the expectation is order, and measuring how long a disrupted shelf takes to return to a flushed state makes accountability considerably easier. From a staff standpoint, the process is more active and yields a lot of error-correction in a short amount of time. This type of success in shelf reading is vital maintenance.

We know that our approach to maintaining order works well because we can check. Order is checked frequently through direct inspection and as a secondary result of our many pulling projects. Being that perfectly flushed shelves are not the natural state of publicly accessible book stacks, a flushed shelf took effort and that effort should be a signature of accuracy. An unexpected outcome is that the monotony of shelf-reading is now gone, quality is up, and staff turnover has hovered at zero for almost three years except for internal promotion, graduation, or completion of work-study award funding. We found that with the combination of removing the drudgery from maintaining the stacks, in tandem with removing the seemingly never ending backup of materials to be shelved, less than 1 hour of every 4-hour shift is spent shelving. This benefits shelving staff by enabling them to take on responsibilities that add variety to their day. The resulting efficiency has allowed this department to develop into a role of feeding materials into almost every unit around the library for specialized processing.

As we have just seen, not only is the identification of problem areas in the stacks is a helpful tool to the Stacks Maintenance unit but the passive tracer card allows us to actively pursue problems and quickly, visually, gauge areas of high density of errors in our stacks. Since the Stacks Maintenance unit is independently run, the shelvers work only in the stacks and thus know the stacks inside and out, especially in their assigned areas of shelf maintenance. This, along with a very low turnover rate, has allowed training to go deeper into the ILS modules and has allowed the department to spend more time on lingering issues such as long-term missing books, finding mislabeled books, developing a 100 item/hour inventory system, and mature staff development.

Much like Bookstein's systematic approach for setting shelf reading schedules determined by use patterns (Bookstein, 138), we have also found that each subject area has its own unique personality, including use patterns and complexity of call number ranges. The guide below is a copy of the actual training tool used for a semi-annual deep search for outstanding missing and lost books that have eluded initial searching efforts. The tracer system, as we discussed in section 2, plays an integral role in not just identifying missing items but also in driving the search well after the fact. We have found that our semi-annual search yields a 26% return on our efforts.

1. Pull the tracer card and make sure that the book isn't in fairly close proximity; generally, 3 shelves below and 3 shelves above. Really look closely.

2. Within the aisle you are standing, look for alpha changes or large numerical changes in the second line. For instance, the PSs are particularly difficult to maintain. When looking for PS 3555 A31 2000, look at all of the other PSs in that aisle first, at A31(PS3551 A31, PS3552 A31, etc.). In the QAs, look at the big numerical breaks–QA75, QA 75.1, QA75.12, through to QA 75.9. This step is the most productive. Ask yourself if you have any large numerical turns and check there for sure. In the PNs 1995-1999 this is exceptionally common.
3. If the above example isn't found in the aisle, next try PQ3555 A31, PR3555 A31, and PT3555 A31. We find them often this way as well. It works really well here and in areas like the BFs, Es, Fs, PNs, Qs and anywhere where alpha breaks change within the aisle. Take a look at the Ss for example where this occurs nearly 14 times. Check the alphanumeric portion within the aisle first.
4. Next, try Oversize. Even if the book is not oversized. This is common in the Es, Gs, Ns, and TRs.
5. If you use the above criteria, I think that you will have some success. If you want to spend a little extra time, looking at all of the P's from the first example, have at it. We really prefer to have the title with us when we search. We also like to have the size. Both help us find items that are labeled incorrectly which searching by call number alone will not equip you to do.

A final initiative that Stacks Maintenance began to aid in locating missing books is the use of a portable cart that carries a wireless laptop for routine in-stacks functions such as pickups/count-use capturing and item record updates and inventories. We partnered with the IT department of Penrose Library to receive two decommissioned faculty laptops along with a barcode scanner, and a mouse so that work could be taken to the stacks and done in real-time within the catalog. The goal of this initiative was to decrease the time that an item is unavailable to patrons because of internal processing. For instance, we are committed to quick turnaround and complete statistical gathering in terms of 'in house use' measurements; however, the process at our busy library was such that our staff gathered books on carts from the upper and lower levels of the library, parked the carts behind the service desk to await "Count Use" scanning, only to have the books be resorted by the circulation staff. Next, they were resorted by the shelving staff, and eventually made their way back to the shelf. We conducted a 5-week study and found that the average count use item was handled four times, by four people, before it was available again and what's more, over 95% of the items were used on the floor in which they were housed. By equipping the shelving staff with the equivalent of a wireless ILS, we are able to scan count use on the move, keep the materials available by sorting on the floor in front of our patrons, and we have real-time access to the availability status of each item. This final piece is surprisingly important because of the common reading lists used in core courses and in terms of popular items in our stacks. From a catalog maintenance standpoint, items that have an item record but no barcode are given one on the spot which also improves the future efficiency of use for both staff and patrons.

CONCLUSION

The authors feel that our innovations have stood up to rigorous testing within the laboratory that is Penrose Library. The tools, policies, and procedures for managing missing items isn't just the result of keeping a well-maintained stacks but actually served as the catalyst for moving the service of the library forward. We still have books that go missing and we still don't have all of the answers, however, we have discovered that there are best-practices that can have a profound impact well beyond the Stacks Maintenance unit. We sought to build all changes from a standpoint of improved service, both in the long-term and short-term. Through the implementation of new procedures and policies, we believe we have solved some inventory flow issues through simplifying process, increasing transparency, and finally, by building clear lines of accountability. In looking at the past five years of statistics, we annually use an average of 1,500 (120 per month) tracers and we average a 60% closure rate, helping keep the scheduled searching from lists low and turn-around time high. This also helps us maintain the one-to-one relationship between the status of material as noted in the catalog and the actual status of the material on the shelves. An added bonus is that books marked missing in the catalog and subsequently found are immediately reconciled in the catalog and appropriately marked as available instead of missing—and more importantly, put into the hands of the patron.

From conversations inside the library and with colleagues around the library community, we know there are issues with managing the stacks everywhere, and we know all too well the impact these issues have on our patrons and our staff. We were fortunate to have a team of librarians and library assistants willing to experiment and challenge the standards.

This was not always easy and as with all experiments, there were disappointments and resistance. But, the resulting missing books procedure exemplifies what we proudly believe to be a model of efficiency, productivity, and service. We invite questions and gladly offer copies of our documents, cards, and worksheets.

NOTE

1. Prospector is a unified catalog of twenty-three academic, public and special libraries in Colorado and Wyoming. Prospector provides access to over 20 million books, journals, DVDs, CDs, videos and other materials held in these libraries. With a single search you can identify and borrow materials from the collections and have them delivered to your local library.

REFERENCES

Bishop, William Warner. *The Backs of Books.* Baltimore, 1920.

Bookstein, Abraham. "Models for Shelf Reading." *Library Quarterly, 43*, no. 2, Apr. 1973, 138-141.

Bookstein, Abraham and Don R. Swanson. "A Stochastic Shelf-Reading Model." *Library Quarterly, 43*, no. 2, Apr. 1973, 126-137.

Brodart catalog *http://www.shopbrodart.com/shop/cb/product.aspx?pgid=1317.*

Smith, Margo and Melissa Laning. "Zen and the Art of Stacks Maintenance: Rethinking an Ancient Practice." *The Southeastern Librarian, 49*, no. 3&4, Fall/Winter, 2001, 14-17. *http://sela.jsu.edu/SoutheasternLibrarian/FallWinter2001.pdf.*

Spackman, N. Andrew. "Reducing Check-In Errors at Brigham Young University through Statistical Process Control." *Journal of Access Services, 3*, no. 3, 2005.

Stuemke, Roberta. "From the Bottom Shelf Up: A Personal View of Stacks Management in an Academic Library." *Associates: The Electronic Library Support Staff Journal 3*, no.3, March 1997 http://associates.ucr.edu/397stuemke.htm.

Circulation on the Go–
Implementing Wireless Laptop Circulation
in a State University Academic Library

June L. Power

PILOT PROJECT

In 2003, Sampson-Livermore Library began investigating the possibility of circulating wireless laptops to students to use in the library, especially for group work. The University of North Carolina at Pembroke is a rural school with one of the highest diversity rates in the nation, and supports 5,827 full time students and 255 full time faculty. As enrollment at the University increased, the funds became available to launch a pilot project. Four HP laptops were purchased and in spring 2004, the library began to circulate laptops.

The initial loan period for the laptops was two hours and the fines set at $10.00 per hour with a 15 minute grace period. The laptops were cataloged as reserve items and included pop-up messages in the item record to prompt staff to verify parts at check out and check in. The replacement cost for the laptops was $1,500.00, and prices for each part were available as well. To check out a laptop, a university-affiliated patron had to have a picture identification that was, and still is, held for the duration of the period in which the person had the laptop. These were clipped to a slip in which the staff person noted the number of the laptop and the time of check out and check in, so that if any problems were to arise, we would know which patron was responsible. Each laptop was circulated with a carrying bag and headphones were available for check out separately. The patron also had to read and sign the library's two page laptop agreement (Appendix A) at each checkout. We found this to be very time consuming, especially during peak check out periods between classes. We also found that students were the main source of patrons for this new service, with few to none of the University's faculty and staff taking advantage of the opportunity.

During the first semester of the pilot project, we had 108 laptop circulations, which we considered to be very successful. The decision was made to expand the project. For the following year, fifteen new HP laptops would be purchased to add to the four already in circulation. Additionally, in conjunction with the University's Digital Academy, five Mac iBooks would be added for use by faculty, staff, and students approved by the Academy to use the equipment. Preparations began for a full scale implementation of this popular service.

FULL SPEED AHEAD

While waiting for the new equipment to arrive, a task force met to discuss the pilot project, and what changes would be necessary based on things that had been learned in the pilot project, and with the idea that we would be circulating almost five times as many computers as in the pilot project. We wanted to be sure to be well-organized before just handing over the new equipment to the circulation staff and letting the patrons have access. I have learned over the last several years of working in libraries that a little planning ahead saves a lot of work in the end, and I wanted to make sure that my staff and I were prepared for the expected onslaught. In our planning several issues were tackled and resolved as the way was paved for full scale implementation.

Our first item on the agenda was the collaborative effort with the Digital Academy. Not only would we be circulating the five iBooks, but one of the larger study rooms upstairs was converted into a Mac Lab. Both the lab and the iBooks were to be limited to those individuals that had participated in one of the Academy's training sessions and were approved to use this specialized equipment. In order for circulation staff to limit access to the lab and the equipment, we needed a way to identify authorized individuals that was able to be frequently updated by the Digital Academy and that was readily accessible from the circulation desk. It was decided that the Digital Academy would maintain a web page with an alphabetic list of authorized individuals which would be bookmarked at each circulation workstation. When patrons request access to the Macs, circulation staff verify their name on the list, but otherwise these circulate just as the other laptops do, albeit with different parts to verify. At a busy circulation desk, keeping things as simple and consistent as possible for staff and patrons is the key to smooth operations.

After realizing how time consuming having to complete the laptop agreement was at a busy circulation desk (that had also just had all the DVDs moved from the stacks to behind the desk), it was decided to move to a once-a-semester laptop agreement. These were kept on file in the circulation office, and pop-up message placed in each patron record when the form is completed. At the end of each semester the pop-up messages are erased, the forms shredded, and we start the next semester fresh. After the first time they have filled out the full agreement, they need only initial the check out slip clipped to their ID card. Patrons have really have appreciated the saved step.

They also appreciated some of the new features of the new laptops. The new laptops were also HP, but were now $2,500.00 and had CD re-write drives, DVD drives, and a number of USB ports. As so many people had switched over to USB drives, the new laptops eliminated floppy drives in favor of the advanced technology. Wireless printing capabilities were added, and the wireless connections were much improved. Each laptop circulated with its own power cord and headphones. A second power cord was purchased for each laptop and kept in the powered storage cart for overnight charging. Each laptop was numbered and labeled for in-house use and programmed with Deep Freeze to keep staff from having to do more maintenance than necessary.

Another step taken to save staff time for circulation staff was to extend the loan period for the laptops from two to three hours. We found that we were doing a lot of renewals for people that just needed the computers for another half hour or forty five minutes. While we still have a number of laptop renewals, this extension has definitely reduced the potential number.

With our plans laid out, implementation proceeded full speed ahead. Laptop checkouts quickly predominated circulation desk functions and statistics skyrocketed.

While the per cent increase in laptop transactions is slowing down as the equipment has become more integrated into circulation functions, the absolute number of transactions continues to grow with the ever increasing popularity of the service.

Though we remain constantly amazed at the number of people that

Fiscal Year	Laptop Circulations	Percent Increase
Spring 2004	108	N/A
2004-2005	805	645%
2005-2006	3921	387%
2006-2007	5682	191%

will take the time to have us check out a laptop only to keep it fifteen minutes and return it saying they just had to check their email, apparently unaware that had they just stepped over to the wall terminal they could have been finished in half the time. But–we're happy to count their circulation, and chalk it up to one of those things we'll just never understand.

LESSONS LEARNED

However, some patron and staff behaviors can be understood, and allow for a learning experience on the part of the library. Despite the best planning, it is often impossible to predict how something will work until it has been tried, and often quite quickly needed adjustments are recognized.

Macros make life easier. In order to make our switch to a once-a-semester laptop agreement, we added messages to the patron records indicating that they had a form on file. We found that if the patron database is large, this is best completed using a global update as updating individual patron records would be counter-intuitive. To globally delete the message we have to search for the exact text of the message, which is supposed to be "Laptop Agreement on File." However, we found that occasionally, the message was not entered with the exact phrase. In order to make sure that this field was consistently populated and not leave a lot of clean up after the global update, we created a macro at each workstation. Now just pressing F12 enters the appropriate text, and end of the semester field deletion is a breeze.

Patrons don't read the form. If staff make occasional errors, patrons are even worse for their inattention to detail. Even though they only have to fill it out once a semester, patrons still do not read the laptop agreement form even though some will stand there and look at it. Occasionally, someone will read it, but that is a rarity. Patrons never seem to notice the prominent listing of the rental fee for laptops returned overdue, and we have had quite a few get very upset about their fines. They also have missed that they can't take the laptops from the building, and we've even had to chase a few people. They have let their children use them, a clear violation of the agreement that only University affiliates may use them, and they get quite upset if they are denied a renewal, even with other patrons waiting for them. But as with many other things patrons don't read, we can only provide them the material and hold them to the consequences. Not all patrons can be satisfied.

As soon as you get rid of something, patrons want it. There's a Murphy in every library, and ours is no exception. While not all patrons can be satisfied, the staff tried to fulfill all patron requests as much as possible. When we eliminated floppy drives believing that most of our constituents were using USB drives, we found quite quickly that there were still a lot of floppies out there. So we purchased two external floppy drives that plugged into the USB ports of the laptops, and soon expanded this to five. While they are rarely used anymore, they were used quite extensively in the 2004-2005 year and even a good bit the following year. This definitely taught us to stage transitions a bit more slowly.

Keep the laptops close to the circulation desk. This is a lesson we have learned, but are unfortunately limited in our capability to solve. The floor plan of our circulation department is not conducive to the high volume of circulations this service receives. Because it is the only locking room in our suite that all staff have access to, the powered storage cart for the laptops is kept in our storage room with the staff photocopier and Ariel workstation. This room is around the corner from the circulation desk, out of sight of the desk itself. This makes it difficult for staff assigned to the desk to retrieve the laptops. Our solution has been to put four or five laptops in bags on a book truck and park it in the large supply closet right behind the desk. Of course, there are times when all the laptops are checked out within the first half an hour the library is open, and all staff can do then is work as quickly as possible. We do have great plans for how we would change this arrangement should we get a new building one day.

"I knew something would get broken." The dire prediction did come true, and things did indeed get broken. Some of the problems were surprising–such as when we realized the closure clips had been ripped out of several laptops by patrons just yanking them open instead of pressing the open button. Others were expected– such as the usual non-connections, slow loading, and other general computer errors. We realized we needed a way to communicate laptop problems to systems staff. A web form was created to use in reporting laptop problems. The form allows circulation staff to

specify the laptop number, the problem, and also their name so that systems staff would know who to contact for further questions. Magnets were created for the storage cabinet. Circulation staff would place a magnet labeled "problem" next to the malfunctioning unit, and systems staff would place a magnet labeled "systems" next to the empty slot when they took the laptop to troubleshoot. This has proved to be very successful, but proved insufficient as several problems went unreported due to staff not realizing a problem existed, or were insufficiently reported. This led to the development of our daily laptop check form (Appendix B). Each night, all laptops are checked for parts, power, and connectivity, and all peripheral parts verified as well. This is time consuming and not the most enjoyable task. However, as we stop circulating laptops two hours before the library closes, staff have sufficient time to check all laptops and store them to charge for the following day.

Microsoft updates take forever! Not only did troubleshooting raise issues, but the regular updates and machine maintenance itself was a problem we had to tackle. Performing Microsoft updates alone takes days, as only a few machines can be done each day, as it's hard to get them between patrons checking them out. Luckily for us, these updates and other regular maintenance are performed by systems staff, but it is definitely one of the factors in our recent decision not to expand the number of laptops further, despite heavy demand.

Don't forget to renew and check in the peripherals. When we added headphones to the bags we thought we'd rid ourselves of having to circulate peripherals separately. Those thoughts ended with the purchase of the floppy drives, and later of USB external mice at the request of several patrons. So again, we were checking out peripherals, and found that it was quite easy to renew or check in the laptop and completely forget to do the same for the externals equipment, or not see them tucked into an internal pocket of the laptop bag. We had several instances of patrons ending up with overdue fines or bills for items that had not been properly renewed or checked in. This emphasized the need for attention to detail in these transactions, time consuming though it may be for both staff and patron.

BUT, WAIT! THERE'S MORE

As if all of the action surrounding the expansion of laptop circulation weren't enough, we also began to circulate other types of multimedia equipment. As we observed usage trends and with the desire to keep up with emerging technology trends to keep the library in step with the academic community, we looked for additional ways in which we could meet the media needs of our patrons.

Beginning in fall 2006, the library added five portable DVD players to its collection, also limited to three hour use inside the building. We purchased these players as a response to the observation that a great number of students were borrowing laptops in order to sit and watch movies on them. As sometimes there were students with academic needs waiting on laptops, which were quite often being used recreationally, we decided to provide some recreational equipment to help to alleviate use of the laptops for movie watching purposes, and making them available for individuals and groups needing to use the laptops other functions. Also, at one fifth of the price of the robust laptops, and requiring less maintenance we hoped to save wear and tear and staff time. We had a separately colored check out slip for the DVD players, and as with the laptops held the University affiliated patron's ID, but no agreement form was required. However, use of the DVD players was substantially less than we estimated, with only 58 circulations this fiscal year despite substantial marketing. We have realized patrons just prefer the laptops, and while we can inform patrons we have the DVD players, we aren't going to begin asking patrons what they want the laptops for in order to prevent them from using them to watch movies. Besides, watching a movie could be educational.

Also books are educational, of course, and with the addition of downloadable audio books to our Net Library collection, we wanted to make sure that all patrons had a way to access this material. To meet this need, MP3 players were added to the circulating collection. This was interesting, because unlike the DVD players, which had the same loan rule as the laptops, the MP3 players required us to create additional loan rules. I worked closely with our systems librarian to develop these loan rules, as we wanted the MP3 players to circulate outside of the library for as long as books do, and incur the same type of fines the other equipment does. When staff review circulation loan rules they often learn more about their ILS than they ever wanted to know. The MP3 players were then cataloged as reserves, like the rest of our equipment and peripherals, and they went into circulation in fall 2006. As with anything circulating outside of the library, we did have problems with damage, lost parts, and non-returns, including one student taking a MP3 player to his home for Christmas. Overall, it has been successful, and we expanded from our original ten to twenty in spring 2007, though with a change in model from the Zen Nano Plus to the Zen V Plus, which has an internal battery with charging cord rather than requiring AAA batteries. The new model also is sturdier, with less small, flimsy parts and seems to hold up better and cause fewer problems. Patrons must supply their own ear buds, and for the older model, their own batteries. Though circulations were moderate due to the longer loan period, 73 for the fiscal year, immediately they had long hold lists, as students, staff, and faculty awaited their use.

Next on our horizon to support the educational and recreational needs of our patrons with technology is the possible introduction of digital video and still cameras in spring 2008. While nothing is certain yet, we already have begun to consider the implications and practicalities, as we realize that this is not a change to be made overnight. The first problem to solve is developing storage in a library with severe space problems.

CONCLUSION

With so many changes in such a short amount of time, planning was the key component in leading us to successful implementation of equipment circulation for our patrons' various media needs. We have refined our procedures through an ongoing evolution as we learned from the practicalities of the circulation desk and the constraints of time and resources, both material and personal, added even more complexity to a department already short on both. Another key is to keep good statistics. When laptop circulation surged, we went beyond monthly circulation counts to circulation statistics by hour of day and day of the week in order to identify peak periods of use. Documentation, communication, and routine maintenance of equipment and database records all played an important role in our success. It is delightful to see all the work that goes into those tasks come to fruition in the students' direct expressions of appreciation for the service we are providing, but especially in those subtle comments heard around campus when they don't realize someone from the library is around. To know that what we are doing makes an impact in our community gives a meaningfulness to this endeavor that sheer numbers alone can't supply or measure. Change is ever on our horizon, but with our past successes to support us, we look forward to continuing to mold our services to the needs of those we are there to serve.

REFERENCES

Atlas, M. C.; Farza, F.; & Hinshaw, R. *Use of Laptop Computers in an Academic Medical Library.* Medical Reference Services Quarterly v. 26 no. 2 (Summer 2007) p. 27-36.

Duncan, Lucy E. *The World in Their Laps.* Community and Junior College Libraries v. 11 no. 3 (2003), p. 11-16.

Ellison-Nixon, K. *Policies and Procedures for Laptop Computers.* Book Report v. 19 no. 5 (March/April 2001) p. 33.

Ginzburg, B. *Goin' Mobile: Using a Wireless Network in the Library.* Computers in Libraries v. 21 no. 3 (March 2001) p. 40-4.

Lyle, Heather. *Circulating Laptop Computers at West Virginia University.* Information Outlook v. 3 no. 11 (November 1999) p. 30-32.

McAdoo, M. L & Tease, J. *The Mansfield Protocol for Laptop Computer Circulation: How a Library Can Provide Its Own Technical Support.* College and Research Libraries News v. 59 no. 7 (July/August 1998) p. 507-8 + .

Rogerson, H.D. *Lending Laptops at the Vineland Public Library.* Public Libraries v. 41 no. 6 (November/December 2002) p. 332-6.

Vaughan, J. B. & Burnes, B. *Bringing Them In and Checking Them Out: Laptop Use in the Modern Academic Library.* Information Technology and Libraries v. 21 no. 2 (June 2002) p. 52-62.

APPENDIX A. Laptop Agreement Form

Sampson-Livermore Library
The University of North Carolina at Pembroke
Laptop Computer Loan Agreement

By signing below, I, the undersigned borrower, agree to and acknowledge all of the following:

> - Prior to borrowing the laptop computer, I witnessed its physical inspection including its accessories. All checked parts are present and appear to be functioning.
> - I agree to allow the library staff to hold my second form of identification until I return the laptop to the Circulation Desk, and it has been physically inspected again after my use.
> - I accept full responsibility for the laptop computer and accessories I am borrowing. *I understand that the computer and accessories must not leave the Library.* I understand that if they do, the matter will be turned over to UNCP Campus Police and other appropriate UNCP authorities.
> - I will reimburse the Sampson-Livermore Library for repair or replacement costs of this laptop and/or accessories if they are damaged, lost, or stolen while checked out in my name. I understand that the replacement cost for this laptop computer will be no less than $2,500 and a $25 processing fee.
> - I will pay a rental charge of $10 per hour if I fail to return this laptop and all accessories to the Circulation Desk by the time it is due today.
> - I do hereby verify that I have read and understand this Laptop Computer Loan Agreement as it pertains to the circulation of a Sampson-Livermore Library laptop computer, and I agree to abide by these policies and all policies of UNCP relating to computer use. UNCP and its agents have the right to review any and all information in or on the laptop for any reason, at any time, without notice to me. I agree that the Library may terminate the loan of the laptop, without notice to me, if it appears that the laptop has been abandoned by the borrower, used in violation of UNCP policy, or used in a manner that is likely to damage the machine beyond reasonable wear and tear. I agree that my obligation, if any, to pay rental charges, replacement or repair costs, and any other fees relating to the laptop shall survive termination of the loan.

Full Name: _____
                    (Last)   (First)   (MI)

University ID: _____

E-mail Address: _____

Telephone Number: _____

UNCP Affiliation:
__ Student
__ Faculty
__ Staff

_____
        Signature of Borrower   **Date**

Checkout: *Employee's Initials* _____   *Date/Time* _____

Check-in: *Employee's Initials* _____   *Date/Time* _____

Used with permission.

APPENDIX A. Laptop Agreement Form (continued)

Sampson-Livermore Library Laptop Computer Circulation Policies

Eligibility
Only current UNCP students, faculty, and staff are eligible to check out laptop computers. Laptops must be used directly by eligible patrons. A valid UNCP ID and a second form of photo identification must be presented upon checkout. The second form of identification will be held at the Circulation Desk until the laptop is returned and checked by library staff. UNCP reserves the right to refuse to loan a laptop to any person who has damaged a UNCP laptop in the past (beyond reasonable wear and tear) or used any UNCP computer in violation of UNCP policy.

Loan periods and availability
Laptops can be checked out from the Circulation Desk from library opening hours until two (2) hours before the Library closes. Laptops circulate for three (3) hour increments, and may be renewed, if availability allows. Laptops are available on a first come, first served basis, and may not be reserved. Laptops are for use in the Sampson-Livermore Library only, and *may not leave the building for any reason*. Proper maintenance and care of computing equipment will be assured through a checklist review by library staff and borrower.

Rental charges and liability
The rental charge for returning/renewing a laptop late is $10 per hour. The maximum rental charge is $150. Replacement cost of a lost, damaged, or stolen laptop computer will be the cost of the item replacement plus a $25 processing fee. The *Laptop Accessories Inspection Checklist & Replacement Costs* is provided below. Whoever borrows the laptop is responsible for its safe return to the Circulation Desk. A receipt will be printed and issued to the borrower upon check-in of a laptop.

Limitations on use
Laptops may be used in the Sampson-Livermore Library only. Laptops should never be left unattended in the Library or upon return at the Circulation Desk. Food and/or drink are not allowed in the Library and should not be in the immediate vicinity of a laptop. Users may save their documents to their University account or e-mail their information to their e-mail account. Any software, files, plug-ins, etc. saved to the laptop will be removed automatically upon restart.

No borrower shall have any expectation of privacy with regard to any information on or in any laptop, and UNCP reserves unto itself and its agents the right to review any and all information on or in the laptop for any reason, at any time, without notice to the borrower. UNCP reserves the right to terminate the loan of any laptop at any time, without notice to the borrower, if a UNCP employee reasonably believes that the laptop has been abandoned by the borrower, used in violation of UNCP policy, or used in a manner that is likely to damage the machine beyond reasonable wear and tear.

Laptop Accessories Inspection Checklist & Replacement Costs

√	PC Item/Accessory	Price
	Power cord	$ 20
	Battery	$ 130
	Headphones	$ 50
	Carrying case	$ 50
	USB floppy disk drive	$ 50
	CD/DVD drive	$ 100
	Laptop	$ 2500

√	Mac Item/Accessory	Price
	Power cord	$ 75
	Battery	$ 130
	Headphones	$ 50
	Carrying case	$ 50
	Digital mouse	$ 50
	CD/DVD drive	$ 100
	Laptop	$ 2500

Used with permission.

APPENDIX B. Laptop Daily Checklist

Laptop Daily Maintenance Checklist

Date:

Please check each of the following items for damage. If any item is damaged or missing, please mark an X in the box instead of a √ and make a detailed note at the bottom of the page.

Laptop#	AC Adaptor	Power Cord	Laptop Battery	CD Drive	DVD Drive	Powers On	Network On	Initials
1								
2								
3								
4								
5								
6								
7								
8								
9								
10								
11								
12								
13								
14								
15								

Bag#	AC Adaptor	Power Cord	Initials
1			
2			
3			
4			
5			
6			
7			
8			
9			
10			
11			
12			

Old Bags - No Accessories

	Bag Present?	Initials
1		
2		
3		
4		

Used with permission.

Laptop Circulation at Eastern Washington University

Doris Munson
Elizabeth Malia

INTRODUCTION

At the behest of students, in 2001 Eastern Washington University Libraries began a laptop circulation program with seventeen laptops. The program grew over the next few years to 150 laptops, seventeen digital cameras, eleven digital handycams, and thirteen digital projectors.

Because the original equipment inventory was so small, the library was not prepared for the growing pains it encountered as the equipment inventory grew. The first pains were literally physical. Library staff started to experience overuse injuries from the constant handling of the laptops. The next growing pain was physical in terms of space. The library had to redesign a room to hold the laptops. In the last two years, the library had to re-structure its checkout and fine policies to ensure that the equipment was available for use by all students.

As outlined in this article, a large inventory of expensive equipment requires well thought-out policies and inventory control measures.

HISTORY

In 1999, Eastern Washington University (EWU) instituted a $35 technology fee, which students pay in addition to their tuition. The technology fee was a student-led state initiative backed by EWU administration and was enabled as by law as Revised Code of Washington (RCW) 288.15.051. Students decide how the technology fee money is spent through a Student Technology Committee (STFC). The committee chair is elected during student elections every spring quarter. Student members of the Student Technology Fee Committee are appointed by the Associated Students of Eastern Washington University. Other STFC members represent the faculty, the administration, and Information Services.

Every year, campus groups can apply for project funding from the STFC through a proposal process. In 2000, the STFC approached John F. Kennedy Memorial (JFK) Library staff and expressed an interest in having laptops in the library available for students to checkout. At the STFC's urging, a proposal was submitted. Although the proposal was for fifteen laptops, the STFC approved the purchase of seventeen laptops in the first half of 2001. The JFK Library laptop checkout program officially began in fall quarter, 2001.

The program proved to be so popular with students that the laptops were in constant use, and there was often a waiting list. Over the next four years, more laptops were added to the program, along with digital cameras, digital projectors, and handycams.

EQUIPMENT AND ACCESSORIES

The JFK Library currently circulates 152 laptops, ranging in age from those purchased in 2006 to those purchased in 2002. (The original seventeen laptops purchased in 2001 were withdrawn in 2004 because they were no longer under warranty.) Laptops loan for periods of 4 hours, 24 hours, or 7 days. In 2006, three seven-day laptops [not already defined, so this reference to what we later learn is the loan period is confusing] with special software were added to meet the needs of students with disabilities. Students must be registered with the Disability Support Services (DSS) office in order to use these laptops.

Originally, all laptops circulated for two hours, in house only. In 2004, the two-hour checkout period was changed to four hours, a 24-hour checkout period was added, and equipment could be taken out of the library. In 2005, when the laptops purchased in 2002 went off warranty, it was decided that they were still useful for less resource-intensive applications such as word processing. The seven-day circulating laptop came into existence to utilize these items and to meet student demand. Currently there are 94 24-hour laptops, nineteen four-hour laptops, and 39 seven-day laptops. Six of the 24-hour laptops are called "multimedia" because they contain extra software, mice, and a larger screen. This number will fluctuate some over the next four years because different quantities were purchased in each of the last four years. As explained in the "Lessons Learned" section, the library is working with the STFC to stabilize the total number of laptops in the program.

In addition to the laptops, the library circulates seventeen digital cameras, eleven digital handycams, and thirteen digital projectors, all of which circulate for 24 hours. Students who check out 24-hour equipment on Fridays are allowed to keep it until 10:00 a.m. on Monday morning. Four-hour equipment is not allowed to circulate overnight. All equipment is unavailable for check out during intercessions.

Checking out equipment with several parts has caused us to try various package concepts to maintain inventory of small parts and streamline checkout as much as possible. A standard laptop package currently consists of a bag, a CD/DVD drive, and the laptop. They all check out under the laptop barcode. All cords, including power cords, and remotes are also checked out to the patron but do not accrue fines. Patrons are charged replacement costs if they are not returned with the equipment.

SOFTWARE

One of the first questions we faced was what software to load onto the laptops, and how to protect them. As on most campuses, large site licenses that allow the university to use software on many machines are purchased for laptop software. We chose to focus primarily on the needs of students who are conducting research and writing papers. Most of the machines are identical to each other for ease of maintenance. Software was recently added to assist the computer literacy coursework required of all students. All laptops have the complete Windows Office package, Internet Explorer, print software, and Deep Freeze security software. These are obviously subject to change as the program progresses. The multimedia laptops have extra software including Movie Maker, MS Visual Studio, Gear Software, and MS FrontPage. An "image" is created for each type of laptop to facilitate maintenance. The image contains all of a laptop's operating system, settings, and software. If a laptop's software becomes corrupted for some reason, it can be "re-imaged" to bring it back to its original state. Re-imaging is done whenever a laptop is sent to Systems for repair work and during intercessions whenever possible. This process allows the library to install operating system upgrades and to get rid of any little software problems that have crept in.

Laptop hard drives are partitioned into two parts. One partition contains the software and is protected by Deep Freeze, which automatically removes unwanted items saved to the software partition of the hard drive and returns the software to its original state every time the laptop is turned off and back on. The other partition allows students to save their work to the hard drive and not automatically lose it to Deep Freeze. The STFC has also funded network storage for all students, and that currently provides five gigabytes of space per student as an alternative to hard drives and floppy disks. A separate lab for large multimedia presentations is housed in the Instructional Technology department.

PROGRAM OPERATION

The JFK Library submits one or more proposals to the Student Technology Fee Committee annually. When the proposal process is opened, library staff members meet to decide what equipment needs to be replaced and whether to increase the inventory of any type of equipment. Library staff then meet with a STFC representative to talk about the needs of the equipment circulation program. The results of these discussions are used to write the proposals.

It is important to note that communication between the library and STFC is an ongoing process, not just when proposals are submitted. Students initiated the program and think of it as theirs. STFC members work closely with library staff year-round to ensure that the needs of the students will be met and to communicate student requests and concerns. Because the program is funded with technology fee dollars, only students who have paid the technology fee are allowed to use the equipment. The technology fee is mandatory in fall, winter, and spring quarters but is optional in summer quarter. Circulation staff check a STFC database to ensure that the student has paid the technology fee. Staff and faculty may only check out equipment when demand is low, are not allowed to reserve the equipment, and are subject to the same checkout periods and fines as students. Professors cannot checkout multiple laptops to use in the classroom. (The enabling legislation specifically restricts the ongoing use of this equipment in classrooms by professors.) The university has many technology-enhanced classrooms for this purpose, and all departments have other funding to purchase their own equipment, as there is no central service on campus that delivers equipment for use in the classroom.

Self-booking became available and was turned on in the Millennium WebOPAC in 2005. This service instantly became popular with students, who had been requesting it since 2003. To allow as many students as possible to access to the laptops and keep one person from continuously having a laptop, students can only book one piece of each type of equipment at a time.

Some of the 24-hour laptops have been made unbookable. The primary reason for this is to have a laptop available if a reserved laptop is not returned on time. Another reason is to have some available for walkup clients.

When a piece of equipment is returned with damage, its status is updated to "Equipment Unavailable" and it is sent to the Systems Unit. Systems Unit staff do any simple repairs that can be done in-house. If the repair cannot be done in-house and the item is under warranty, the item is shipped to the manufacturer for repair. If the item is not under warranty, it is withdrawn and a note is made to request a replacement in the next STFC proposal.

When the program began, laptops were purchased with a three-year warranty and were on a three-year replacement cycle. In 2003, the STFC began purchasing laptops with a four-year, no-questions-asked warranty and the program went to a four-year replacement cycle. At the end of the 2006-2007 school year, four-year old laptops will go to seven-day checkout. All laptops five years old or older will be withdrawn.

EVOLUTION OF FINE STRUCTURE

The hourly equipment fines were originally low enough that some students found it more convenient to keep the equipment than to return it on time. This problem became greater when self-booking was implemented in 2005. Students who were not returning laptops on time were depriving other students of the laptops they had reserved.

Several discussions were held with the STFC to come up with a fine structure that would encourage students to return equipment on time but that was not overly punitive. Fines are not seen as a way to generate funds for the library but as a way to encourage students to return the equipment on time so that other students also have a chance to use the equipment.

As a result of the discussions, equipment has a tiered fine structure. The fine is $4.00 for the first two hours a piece of equipment is overdue and $2.00 for every hour the library is open thereafter. Fines accumulate until they reach the maximum, $368.00 for laptops. This fine is non-refundable. This amount is roughly equivalent to two weeks of overdues. Three overdue notices are sent during this period. When the maximum fine is reached, the student is billed for the replacement cost of the equipment. (Patrons can appeal a fine. Circulation staff makes a decision based upon our policies.)

Because laptops are covered by an excellent warranty program, it was originally thought that it was not necessary to fine students who returned equipment with damage outside of normal wear and tear. Since the longer checkout periods were instituted in 2004, we have found that the longer an item is checked out, the more susceptible it is to damage. Some damage, such as a cracked screen, may be accidental but other damage, such as destruction of all USB ports on a laptop, is obviously not accidental. The Systems and Media Units are currently in the process of proposing that students be charged a flat fine for equipment returned with damage beyond normal wear and tear but still usable if sent in for warranty work. The fine is to encourage students to take better care of the equipment and to deter willful damage. If library administration approves the proposal, the next step will be to negotiate what the charge will be with the STFC.

LESSONS LEARNED

The laptop program broke new ground in the library when it was started. It was small enough that not much thought was given to the integrated library system (ILS) codes used in the item records. The program is now large enough that the codes were redone last year to make it easier to create reports and track the equipment.

We also found it wise to include the EWU equipment ID number and serial number in each item record. A laptop was stolen last year, and the library was unable to provide the police with the serial number because it was not in the item record. It is difficult to pull a serial number off an invoice when there were 39 identical items purchased at the same time.

Demand for equipment is slow the first few weeks of classes, gets heavy at midterm, and remains heavy the rest of the quarter through finals week. Demand for digital projectors is higher than for cameras or handycams because students use a laptop and projector to give class presentations. The library hopes to increase its inventory to fifteen projectors next year and, by student request, add a portable screen.

When circulating laptops, it is necessary to have extra batteries, power cords, and drives to help keep the equipment in use. Staff often do not have time to charge a battery between the time a laptop is returned and when it goes back out. Batteries also wear out over time but it is often difficult to purchase batteries for a laptop model after three years. A multi-bay battery charger is purchased every time a new battery model is acquired. Laptop cords are easily damaged or lost. A frequent cause of damage is pets chewing on the cords. Replacement parts are occasionally needed, such as drives and batteries, and the after market vendors generally meet this need. The fine monies collected are used for these purchases.

CD and DVD drives have proven fragile. A broken faceplate can often be glued back on but the drive is still out of commission for several days. If the drive has internal damage, it must be sent in for repair under warranty.

The library currently has to send all equipment to the manufacturer for warranty work. This process will take a piece of equipment out of use for ten to fourteen days. We have found that about five percent of laptops are in repair during heavy use periods. Not surprisingly, the longer the circulation period, the more likely the laptop will be returned with damage.

A large inventory of equipment made it necessary to start tracking repair records of equipment. Systems Unit staff are in the process of creating a web-based equipment repair history database that library staff and the STFC will be able to access to check on the status or repair history of a piece of equipment. The program is too large for staff to be able to remember if one particular laptop is prone to breakage.

Physical space is an issue. A secure room was remodeled three years ago to accommodate the laptops and battery chargers. Extra electrical power had to be added to the room to handle the heavy electrical requirements of the battery chargers. The room has now reached capacity. Also, the Media Circulation Desk area was not designed for a large staff or circulating equipment.

Library staff found a physical cost to the program as it grew. Staff developed backaches, tendonitis and other physical complaints from frequently lifting the equipment as it was checked out and then back in. Full-time staff have reached the limit of how much equipment they can physically handle.

The number of staff is also an issue. The library currently employs two full-time staff and about fifteen student workers who operate this program on site. We have found that adding more student staff sometimes results in increased errors in processing and that our physical space cannot handle more bodies. A third full-time staffer has been proposed to cover the later hours of service provided.

Security became an issue in 2005 when the library had a circulating laptop stolen for the first time. The theft occurred when the Media Circulation Desk was very busy and staff were distracted. In the same year, the library found it was missing a digital camera from where it was stored in a room behind the desk. To help combat theft, a daily inventory was instituted. Also, the university will be installing a security camera system to cover the media circulation area. The videos will only be viewed by campus security when there is a security problem.

For these reasons, the library has capped the number of laptops it can manage at 160. This amount includes 157 regular circulating laptops and three disability laptops. The library wants to keep 150 in circulation but has allowed for 157 because there are usually five to seven laptops in repair during busy periods. Although students would like to see more laptops and other equipment in the library, they understand that the staff and space issues must be solved first.

With number of laptops capped at 160 for now, the library and STFC have agreed upon a more planned approach to the purchase of laptops. Instead of requesting the same number of laptops to replace the ones going off warranty, the library will be requesting 32 laptops a year. This cycle will stabilize the total number of laptops to a predictable number in a few years, although there will be some fluctuation in numbers until then. When the library is in a position to raise the cap, the increase will be over four or five years to allow for the replacement cycle.

CONCLUSION

The equipment checkout program at Eastern University Washington was started by a student grassroots effort. The program was a success and grew from 2001 to 2005. However, it has become necessary to cap the number of laptops until space and staffing issues can be resolved.

Although the program in the library is successful, it cannot meet the demand. To alleviate the additional demand, STFC members have encouraged the computer lab in the Pence Union Building to start another laptop checkout program on campus. The lab has submitted a proposal to create a program in January 2007, which is pending at the time this article was written. The computer lab considers the library's program to be successful and plans on implementing the same policies and fine structure the library uses.

The library suffered growing pains as the equipment inventory grew. A large inventory of expensive equipment requires well-thought out policies, fines, and inventory-control measures. It also requires a secure storage space with adequate electricity to recharge batteries.

Demand on staffing is another issue that needs to be considered. Constant handling of large numbers of equipment can result in physical injuries. In addition, during busy periods there can be lines of ten or more patrons waiting for a laptop or other equipment, which produces stress and distractions. The distractions can make it easy for equipment left unattended for "just a moment" to be stolen.

Eastern Washington University Libraries have learned many lessons since the first laptop was checked out in 2001. We are developing our policies towards future growth and the introduction of new technologies that students will need to access for their class assignments.

Beyond "Classroom" Technology: The Equipment Circulation Program at Rasmuson Library, University of Alaska Fairbanks

Karen Jensen

INTRODUCTION

The library at the University of Alaska Fairbanks (UAF) has all the usual contemporary services offered at other academic libraries–virtual reference, electronic reserves, online journals, document delivery–but one service distinguishes itself from the programs offered by other academic institutions, the UAF Rasmuson Library's "Media Desk," a major media equipment lending program.

Fairbanks, Alaska, has an area population of 82,000 and is located in the Interior region of Alaska, connected by road to Anchorage, the largest Alaskan city. The University of Alaska Fairbanks is the flagship campus in the Alaska University system, with an enrollment of more than 5,630 students and 311 faculty members at the main location in Fairbanks; there are many more faculty and students at the other 6 branches of the UAF system. Rasmuson Library is the main library for the UAF campus, and is also the largest library in the state of Alaska, with 1.1 million volumes; it serves distance students, faculty, and students as well as the general public.

Libraries of all types have been providing media or audiovisual, "AV," equipment to patrons for many years, despite the public's conventional image of libraries as being storehouses for books. In a 1979 article on the integration of AV and library services in *American Libraries*, Maxine Jones summarizes a survey of public libraries offering media equipment; half of those surveyed allowed only in-house use of equipment, the other half had a variety of checkout periods or rental policies and fees, but all experienced significant demand for equipment, usually 16mm film projectors, slide projectors, and cassette players (Jones, 1979).

Public elementary and secondary schools often house the AV equipment in a combined library/media center; school librarians often assist teachers with equipment use. Equipment use is considered so crucial for school libraries that the American Association for School Librarians mentions "technology" extensively in their new "learning standards" (American Association for School Librarians, 2007). Articles in the library literature about school library media centers and school library media specialists abound, evidence of the importance of using media technology in the learning process at the K-12 levels for many years.

Academic libraries have offered limited audiovisual equipment checkout for many years, mainly to allow access to audio-visual media owned by the library, such as 16mm films, audio cassettes, or LP records. Published information on contemporary academic library media equipment lending programs however is scarce. Many of the programs described in the literature feature in-house use of equipment only, or have such serious restrictions on the use of equipment that it is not possible to fairly compare those programs with ours. Some institutions have a separate technology department that handles academic equipment support.

In recent years, with the advent of personal-use digital media, some academic libraries, including the University of Alaska Fairbanks Rasmuson Library, have expanded equipment lending to include many more options. A recent article in the *Journal of Academic Librarianship* (JAL) describes the development of the equipment lending program at the State University of New York at Cortland in 2004, a program with a heavy emphasis on digital cameras and image editing (Wood et al., 2004). That same article summarizes some of the issues we've had to resolve in our equipment program, from methods of cataloging equipment, to finding ways to provide adequate technical support to users. An older article in *College and Research Libraries* describes the startup of a digital camera lending program at University of Oregon (Holman, 1999). Many of the other recently published program descriptions feature laptop-only loan programs in academic libraries, such as Temple University (Myers, 2001), Mansfield University (McAdoo, 1998), University of Nevada-Las Vegas (Vaughan and Burnes, 2002), and New York University (Young, 1997). Considerably more information is available on library web sites, describing laptop loan or rental policies, surveys, and even patron checkout agreement forms. But few comprehensive equipment lending programs are described in detail in the published library literature, perhaps because it is seen as less worthy of an academic library; this will likely change, as more academic libraries realize the potential for expanding circulation services, and the library's role in enhancing campus technology options. Wood sums it up with a faculty member's quote cited in the recent JAL article, "collections are not what we are about anymore" (2004). The academic library's relevance to non-book-oriented youth can be greatly augmented by offering equipment checkout services, services that we are already set up to provide with efficiency.

The Rasmuson Library equipment program is unique among academic libraries, offering a wider variety of equipment than most, patron access through the Circulation Desk, use not limited to classrooms or the library, 3-day or longer checkouts, and substantial user support available weekdays, evenings, and weekends. Equipment is mainly but not solely used in support of classroom teaching or assignments, but also to enhance student, staff, and faculty learning in all aspects of their academic and personal education. The library has recognized the importance of keeping current with technological change, and ensuring that students and faculty have awareness of and access to that technology. This program directly supports the University's latest strategic plan, which emphasizes the need for technology in learning, including "lifelong" and "experiential" learning (University of Alaska Fairbanks, 2007).

HISTORY AND STAFFING OF OUR "MEDIA DESK"

Rasmuson Library has reorganized its administrative departments numerous times, with the most recent restructuring in 1998 resulting in the library handling equipment checkout responsibilities. At the last reorganization, we integrated the media lending program with our Circulation Desk, making the checkout process convenient for patrons; getting a laptop is as easy as getting a book. Making our equipment lending policies generous and eliminating paperwork and use regulations has enabled many more students to utilize equipment. Our lack of restriction has especially helped UAF's many "non-traditional" students, many of whom have families and full-time jobs. Other students who might not be enrolled in a class that uses media equipment have the opportunity to try out new equipment on their own and expand their learning outside of the classroom.

The library has been fortunate to have Circulation area support staff interested and knowledgeable about evolving electronic technology. It is due primarily to these staff that the media equipment checkout program has expanded and succeeded beyond initial expectations; staff abilities are critical to the success of such a program. One staff person, the Media Technician, has the primary responsibility of assessing needs, researching and selecting equipment, cataloging items in our ILS, monitoring bookings and overdues, and the physical processing and labeling of equipment. Another Circulation Supervisor assists with patrons' technical questions and training during evening and weekend hours, and provides general backup support for equipment. Between the two media positions, the library is able to provide technical assistance almost all hours the library is open, about 86 hours per week. The Media Technician and Evening Supervisor provide in-depth assistance with equipment and one-on-one training for faculty and students. Patrons with special equipment needs must contact one of these two support personnel directly, as far in advance as possible. All Circulation personnel however, including regular library staff and student assistants, provide booking and circulation support for the equipment collection; patrons do not have to wait for specialized personnel for most checkouts, and manuals are always available for check out as needed. The checkout process involves only the patron's University identification card, and a confirmation of good standing, to borrow any equipment item.

SELECTION, INVENTORY, AND BUDGET

The equipment offered has been selected both on the basis of customer demand and on the interests and abilities of the two library staff that support the program. Available equipment is added to a database that displays on our library web page, and includes specifications and checkout status, as well as an email reservation feature (see http://uaflibrary.us/media/equipment/).

The inventory changes frequently, as equipment is purchased or withdrawn. The most popular items include laptops and digital cameras, followed closely by computer projectors and camcorders, but we have many more items in the database, and even some less used equipment not featured on the web page, but available upon request.

Equipment is purchased from a variety of sources, online and locally, and is selected using product reviews and staff knowledge of brands and models. We purchase extended warranties for most equipment, and they have frequently paid off, given the lack of local technical repair options, and the significant hours of heavy use. Most of the equipment is purchased with departmental supply funds, supplemented annually or biennially with grants supported by our University's student technology fees, a per-credit charge to all students.

CIRCULATION POLICIES AND PROCEDURES

Probably the most notable aspect of the Rasmuson Library's equipment program is our generous circulation policy. Program descriptions from other library websites and in the above-cited journal articles typically outline an in-library-use-only policy for laptops, with 2-4 hour loan periods, and other equipment is often subject to similar or added restrictions, such as signatures of course instructors verifying use, or lengthy forms for checking out items. Rasmuson Library currently maintains a 3-day loan period for all equipment except data projectors.

We have experimented with a variety of loan periods, adjusting for specific types of equipment to meet demand and extend our supply.

BOOKING EQUIPMENT

One of the most significant challenges we have encountered in our equipment lending program is finding an adequate reservation system. Due to the high demand and limited number of pieces of equipment, reserving items in advance for important projects or events is essential. In the beginning, we used 3-ring binders with tabs for each type of equipment, reserving individual items by scribbling in patron names and phone numbers and hoping that the writing would be legible, the date correct, and that those working the Circulation Counter would pay attention to the written bookings before checking something out. The system was prone to failures on many accounts, especially given that most of our Circulation staff are part-time students with minimal training! Needless to say, that primitive system had to be upgraded, first to an Excel spreadsheet, then to the Meeting Maker software program, and now to Sirsi's Unicorn booking system, which integrates with our circulation system. Despite the significant limitations of Sirsi's booking module, we have managed to make it work for us, by primarily using the checkout system and booking only when absolutely necessary. We evaluated a number of booking systems, with none being optimal, due to the complexities of reserving and circulating multi-part equipment. By using our ILS however, patrons do have a single library "account" they can check to see what items they have and when they are due, and availability information for specific pieces of equipment can be accessed on the web in real-time.

OVERDUES

The greatest frustration for staff and our patrons is the lack of patron compliance with our overdue policy. It has been challenging to find a way to ensure that equipment is returned in a timely manner so as not to inconvenience the next user, without creating excessive restrictions for all users. We have thus far avoided using fines for both practical and philosophical reasons but instead have a graduated system of penalties for late equipment return, the first infraction resulting in a warning, the second a 60-day block from equipment use, the third a one-year block from equipment use, and the most dire penalty, a permanent ban from use of equipment at the library, a level only a few egregiously naughty patrons have reached. Despite promoting patron awareness by posting the policy on our web page, on our fliers, at the desk, and having all patrons sign our policy agreement, most proclaim complete ignorance of it when they are caught with a penalty, hence the warning at the first violation. It has been difficult to try to gain some patrons' understanding of why we enforce these stringent policies. For most patrons though, our current system "works," and ensures their reserved item will be available when they need it. After the first warning, most patrons abide by the policy.

MAINTENANCE AND UPGRADES

Daily maintenance of electronic equipment is essential to an efficiently-functioning media program, and to ensure patron satisfaction. The Media Technicians provide day-to-day maintenance and repair for all equipment, with extensive use of service-center warranties, especially for laptops. While most laptop warranties pay for themselves due to the heavy use they receive–sometimes 200+ checkouts annually–other types of equipment, such as digital cameras, reach technological obsolescence, and get retired from service before extensive repair is necessary. All equipment items are looked over at check-in by Circulation staff, and problems referred to the Media Technicians. Batteries are removed and charged immediately; we have purchased sufficient spares so that we can put a fresh set into each piece of equipment at every checkout. Sometimes damage occurs that does not prevent use, such as a broken "door" on a laptop drive; in those cases we continue to circulate the piece after adding a note to the item record. Occasionally we charge patrons for damage, when it is evident that the item was damaged during the last checkout period.

We purchase new laptops on an annual basis, with a continual cycle of replacement, so that we are within 3 years of current technology for most machines. Cameras and camcorders tend to be replaced entirely, so that we maintain a set of the same models, retiring all the old models when new ones are added to the collection. LCD projectors are also purchased in groups, so that we don't end up with a few of each type, making patron assistance and item reservation unnecessarily complicated. Other items are purchased on an as-needed basis.

USES

UAF students, staff, and faculty use equipment for a wide variety of course-related and personal projects. Camcorders and editing equipment have been used by film-making classes, sign language programs, and for field research. Many students have experimented with film-making on their own, contributing to a student film festival offered every year; one recent graduate has gone on to graduate-level education in film. Cameras have been used for web page design, in-class presentations, documenting events or lab procedures, and photo enhancements to oral histories. Computers are used for term papers, power point presentations, thesis defenses, and conferences. Audio recorders and sound systems help with visiting speakers, and musical and theatre programs. We try to provide as much variety in our equipment offerings as possible, and patrons have helped drive the program through their requests for new items.

USER SURVEY

In February 2006, we conducted an online user survey, with the following five objectives:

- To obtain a description of current equipment users.
- To measure satisfaction with current media equipment and media services.
- To determine which campus information sources were most appropriate for disseminating information about equipment and services.
- To make non-users more aware of equipment services.
- To determine user priorities for future equipment purchases and training opportunities.

SURVEY DESIGN

The survey was made available online to all library users, through a web page, using phpESP, Easy Survey Package, an open source software program. We compiled 23 questions which fit into four general survey categories:

- User affiliation and description of use.
- Type and condition of equipment used.
- Publicity and information - awareness.
- Training and assistance.

We also included several options for respondents to contribute information of their choosing, including free-form fields of considerable length, a choice that resulted in valuable feedback for our program.

SURVEY PROCEDURE

We advertised the survey in the campus student newspaper, on our library web page, in the faculty/staff newsletter, at the Circulation Desk, and by distributing tabletop "tent" ads to the main student center. To encourage participation we offered a raffle incentive to respondents, featuring a drawing for an iPod Nano; we believe this attracted many of the participants to the survey, as it elicited much verbal feedback and questions at the Circulation Counter.

SURVEY RESULTS

Of 426 online respondents, 83% were students, 9% faculty, and the rest a variety of categories, numbers that along with annual use statistics lend weight to our biennial grant applications for the student technology fees, which greatly support our equipment budget. The most popular equipment items borrowed were laptops, with 21% reporting having checked one out, followed by digital cameras (14%), media players (VHS or DVD or CD players) (13%), computer projectors (13%), and camcorders (11%). We have such a wide variety of equipment that the rest of the responses break down into many types of equipment. We were not surprised that laptops were our number one item however, as our circulation statistics and anecdotal evidence at Circulation also verify this information.

We were very pleased to find that most users (72%) were "always" or "usually" satisfied with the condition of equipment, something we work hard to maintain, through staff training and constant vigilance. When asked how patrons found out about the equipment program, 53% indicated they discovered it when in the library, 26% learned of it from friends. Our web page informed only 18%, and our other outreach efforts definitely need work as well, with less than 25% having been made aware of the service elsewhere.

While 49% of users expressed no need for staff assistance with equipment, another 45% indicated they would attend equipment training workshops of 30 minutes or less, a service we have considered but not yet offered. A whopping 87% indicated they would "possibly" or "definitely" use online tutorials, another service under consideration. Despite our many varied attempts to inform users of our late return policy, 50% claimed no knowledge of it at all, and many of the rest only found out when being informed by staff, and 60% preferred being informed by staff rather than a web page or flier.

Users expressed an interest in longer checkouts; at the time of the survey our standard loan period was 24 hours; the overwhelming response was that checkouts should be 3 days, even if that meant less equipment available overall.

CONCLUSIONS

We made quite a few changes in response to the survey suggestions. We concluded that a longer loan period was popular, and that it was warranted, with students doing more extensive projects like video editing that require more time to complete; the standard loan is now 3 days for most equipment. So that we could minimize the waiting time even with the longer loan period, we committed to purchasing additional laptops annually, with a 3-year cycle of replacement. We have expanded our outreach efforts as well, finding ways to publicize the service in order to reach students who do not normally use the library, including ads in the student newspaper, public service announcements on the student radio station, and fliers on campus bulletin boards.

The survey also generated a number of free-form responses offering many suggestions for improvements, but also expressing overwhelming appreciation for the media equipment lending program. This documented enthusiasm for the program allows us to continue to be successful at getting financial support for more equipment, and encourages us to maintain our standard of service excellence and the library's high profile on campus. The Media Equipment desk will continue to be one of the most popular services offered at the University of Alaska Fairbanks Rasmuson Library.

REFERENCES

American Association of School Librarians. (2007). AASL Learning Standards. Retrieved January 16, 2007, from *http://www.ala.org/ala/aasl/aaslproftools/learningstandards/ standards.htm.*

Holman, J. (1999). Checking out digital cameras: Providing tools for Web publishing and interactive multimedia at the University of Oregon. *College and Research Libraries News*, 60, 83-5.

Jones, M. (1979). AV services: Frills no longer. *American Libraries*, 10, 555.

McAdoo, M. L. (1998). The Mansfield protocol for laptop computer circulation: How a library can provide its own technical support. *College and Research Libraries News*, 59, 507-8.

Myers, P. (2001). Laptop rental program, Temple University Libraries. *Journal of Interlibrary Loan, Document Delivery and Information Supply*, 12, 35-40.

University of Alaska Fairbanks (2006). Strategic plan: UAF 2010. Retrieved June 14, 2006, from *http://www.uaf.edu/strategic/plans/2010.*

Vaughan, J. and B. Burnes. (2002). Bringing them in and checking them out: Laptop use in the modern academic library. *Information Technology and Libraries*, 21, 52-62.

Wood, G. M. Melita, L. & Wildman, M. (2004). Lights! Cameras! Action!: Digital media equipment and the academic library. *Journal of Academic Librarianship*, 30, 410-415.

Young, J. R. (1997). New York University allows students to borrow laptops in the library. *Chronicle of Higher Education*, 44, A26.

Computer Reservation System

Sandra L. Cannon

Ten years ago no one would have conceived that customers would visit a library and never read or look at a single item in it. Today we have customers that have never read a book, listened to a CD, watched a DVD, or availed themselves of any of the library's programs. Some don't even have a library card. Who are these customers? They are working adults who don't have computers at home and are rushing in after work to fill out forms online. They are teens that come in after school to grab the first available computer to play games or email friends. They are people looking for jobs online. They are street people trying to connect with family or just pass the time of day. The computers are used from the minute the library doors open until they close.

Ten years ago Austin Free-Net, a non-profit organization, partnered with the Austin Public Library System to make possible public access to computers and the Internet at the Central Library, 22 of its branches, and the Austin History Center. Austin Free-Net assured staff that it would not have to do anything except turn the computers on and off. The public would just come in to use the computers and maybe they'd get a library card. A win-win situation; however, this was not the case. There were issues: many users didn't know how to use the computer software, customers didn't have disks, pornography was being accessed, there were all-day users, and the list continued to grow. Also, library staff spent too much time collecting money for print jobs and the library was losing money because print jobs were never wanted or picked up. Management of the computers became an issue.

BEFORE PHAROS

Before the implementation of Pharos, improper use of the computers was a daily occurrence. For example, a man one day came into the library with a rolling file box. He signed up with a staff member, sat down at a computer and set up his office. He did this on a daily basis. When staff bumped him off he'd close down, go to another location, and set up his office again. We discovered that this was not an isolated case. Austin had a lot of entrepreneurs setting up offices within the Austin Public Library!

We, also, had adults arguing with children. Adults wanted the children to get off of the computers because playing games was not as important as an adult's activity. There were street people who wanted to have something to occupy their time so would stay on the computers until we closed! There were people who would print out documents then decide they really didn't want them but wouldn't pay for them. They'd just walk out of the building! Reams of paper and toner cartridges were being depleted, yet we could not reconcile the receipt of money with the needed order of paper and toner.

Parents complained about minors being able to view pornographic sites–through their own web searching curiosity; or passing by and viewing another customer's monitor. We couldn't change settings on the individual computers; therefore, everything was filtered. Censorship then became an issue.

The process of registering users was also unmanageable. The staff manually recorded the individual's name and the time they got on to the computer. Although there was suppose to be a time limit it required staff to monitor the usage of time for each computer. This was a problem! Staff would get involved with their "library" duties and forget about the users on the Free-Net computers. Sometimes staff would discover that an individual had never signed up for a computer! Either way when individuals were asked to get off of the computers they would become quite angry. Fistfights, shoving matches, and angry disputes occurred quite often. At times staff was accused of playing favorites. At some locations staff was not as busy with library tasks; therefore, they did a better job of monitoring the computers. If customers signed up during Children's Storytime days those individuals might stay on the computers for 3 hours or more without being bumped off. The busier locations soon had a reputation for allowing customers to stay on computers indefinitely! The result was more customers began to visit the busier locations to access the computers. Customers were lined up outside the doors prior to opening. The minute the doors opened people rushed in to grab computers. Library staff felt as if they were policing computers and dealing with frustrated customers more than performing their traditional library tasks. The whole situation was soon unmanageable. Something had to be done!

SOLUTION EXPLORED

Various computer reservation systems were reviewed. At the time there were computer reservation systems that allowed registration of users, but it didn't monitor the time. Another system could monitor the time but did not allow the registration of users. What was needed was a user-friendly system that encompassed both needs. It was decided that the Pharos System was the solution.

The Pharos Systems, www.pharos.com, definition of its product is, "... an automated computer reservation system that combines immediate and scheduled reservations to ensure orderly, equitable access to the machines during times of peak demand and removes the random, lottery aspect of an unmanaged environment. In addition, the ability to reserve a machine for future use removes the stress of uncertainty for patrons."

AUSTIN PUBLIC LIBRARY DECISIONS

Before implementing the Pharos System we decided that there would be a daily limitation of 120 minutes for each customer. Each location could decide the user's limitation of time per session on the computer without having to signup again. Most have increments of 30 minutes to an hour and the Express computers are limited to 15 minutes. The system will not permit more time even if the computers are not being used. Staff can modify the time, but for consistency of policies this is rarely performed. The user will receive two warnings before the eminent ending of his/her time. The system will reboot at the end of the time and any unsaved data is lost. "Acceptable Use Policy for Public-Use Workstations" and "Public Computer User Agreement" forms were developed. Each is given to a customer at registration.

Only one account is allowed for each customer. Using more than one Logon ID or using someone else's Logon ID, with or without approval, is not permissible and doing so will result in the loss of computer privileges system-wide for a period of a designated time. The account is disabled from the Nerve Center on the Register User computer behind the Circulation Desk. Staff writes a brief reason why the account is being disabled, adds their initials, date and the location acronym. Staff never deletes an account. At registration of the user, the customer's birth date is entered in the comments field. This determines whether or not a customer over 18 is placed in the Unfiltered Group, or if under 18 is placed in the Youth Group. Customers requiring screen reading or magnification software are placed in the Adaptive group. An alias is automatically created by the system upon registration. The aliases are displayed on the Queue Station Computer that displays the user's start time and specific computer.

HOW DOES IT WORK FOR THE CUSTOMER?

A customer comes to the Circulation Desk and shows his/her identification to staff. We prefer our library card barcode number; however, any photo ID may be used if the customer does not have a library card. This enables anyone to access the computers regardless of their status–library card user, out-of-towner, or street person. Staff registers the user, as previously mentioned, and the identification number is the customer's Login number. The customer may log on to a vacant, unreserved workstation for the time limit stated on the screen or for the remaining time on the customer's account whichever is less. If all workstations are in use, the customer may reserve a workstation using the Signup and Print Release Computer by logging on and clicking "Reservation." The customer accepts the next available time on a workstation and notes the reservation length, the workstation number, and the start time assigned then "Logs Off." A customer may also *select* their reservation. After logging on the customer clicks "Reservation" then the "Change Details" button. Details that may be changed are time of day and type of computer (Express, General, or Unfiltered). The reservation options are updated as selections are made. Once the reservation is made the customer notes the computer number, the start time, and reservation length assigned, then "Logs Off." The customer has seven minutes to log on to the reserved computer before the reservation is automatically cancelled. If the customer decides to cancel the reservation, s/he logs on at the Signup and Print Release Computer. Details of the reservation are displayed. The "Cancel Reservation" button is selected and either the customer may select a "New Reservation" or exit the Pharos Station by clicking the "Log Off" button. A new reservation cannot be made until the previous one has been cancelled.

Once the customer is logged on to the computer and wants to print a job there is a process in Pharos to release the print job. We have posted signs reminding customers to preview the print job and decide which pages to print. After the customer clicks the "Print" button a Pharos Pop-Up Box will appear and the customer names the print job. The customer clicks "OK" and the print job is in the queue to the print server. All print jobs waiting to be printed are saved in the print queue for 24 hours. If a customer wants to retrieve the print job during the computer session, the customer may lock the workstation by holding down the CTRL and ALT keys while pressing the Del key, then press the K key to lock the computer. The Austin Public Library has Copy Card Vending Machines where the customer purchases a copy card for obtaining print jobs. At the Signup and Print Release Computer the customer logs on, inserts the copy card into the card reader and clicks the "Printing" button. The Print Job Name that the customer has used for the print job is clicked. If there are multiple print jobs the CTRL key is held down and each print job name is selected and clicked. The customer clicks on the "Print" button and "Log Off" button. The customer retrieves the copy card from the card reader and picks up the printed pages from the printer. Pharos is easy to use!

CONCLUSION

Computer Users		
2002	*2003*	*2006*
24,629	818,319	898,204

Internet Printing Revenue		
2002	*2003*	*2006*
$6,957	$10,144	$14,342

Within the first year of implementing Pharos there was a 322% increase in users and 9.76% within the next 2-year period. The Internet printing revenue increased 45% the first year and 41% within the next 2-year period.

However, the greatest outcome of having a computer reservation system has been the reaction of our external and internal customers. Our customers now feel as if they are in control. There seldom is a need for them to interact with staff. The customer enters the library, logs on to a vacant computer, decides what to print, uses their print card, and picks up their copies. It has eliminated most conflicts! Our problem now is not having enough computers!

The mediation of customer problems, scheduling computer time, and unwanted print jobs is almost non-existent. Now staff time is commonly limited to registering a customer into the database, disabling accounts, and hand-delivering print jobs. The management of computers is now minimal due to the computer reservation system.

APPENDIX A. Acceptable Use Policy for Public-Use Workstations

 ACCEPTABLE USE POLICY FOR PUBLIC-USE WORKSTATIONS

I understand and agree to comply with all of the following conditions:

- I will comply with all state and federal laws and the Austin Public Library policies and procedures.

- I understand that the City of Austin reserves the right to change its public use workstation access policies and procedures.

- I understand that individual Library staff members are not authorized to modify these policies

Daily Time Limit

- I understand that I may use the Library's public-use workstations up to 120 minutes per day.

- I will not violate the time limit policy by having or using more than one login ID.

- I will not share my logon ID with family, friends, or other users.

- I will not use the logon ID of family, friends, or other users.

Fees

- I will pay for all of the pages I print.

Use the Public Computers Responsibly

- I will not harm or harass any City employee or member of the public.

- I will not violate any state or federal statute including those regarding obscenity, pornography, or delivery to minors material deemed harmful to them.

- I may not access sexually explicit sites on any filtered Austin Public Library workstation and may be asked to leave the Library if I do so.

Used with permission.

APPENDIX A. (continued)

- I must be 17 years of age or older and be able to provide my photo identification that includes my date of birth to the Library staff in order to use an unfiltered Austin Public Library public-use workstation.

- I will not permit others to use or view an unfiltered public-use workstation during my session unless they have also provided Library staff with photo identification proving that they are 17 years of age or older.

- I understand that I can be held responsible for any damage I may cause to the Library's computers including repair/replacement costs resulting from the use of damaged or virus-infected diskettes

Use the Public Computers at Your Own Risk

- I understand and acknowledge that the Internet contains information, both written and pictorial, which may be offensive or harmful to me or to others.

- I release the City of Austin and the Library from all liabilities associated with my viewing of, use of, or exposure to any information, machine-readable file, picture, graphical representation, or illustration I may encounter while using any public-use workstation, whether or not such information appears or is delivered through the station I operate.

- I understand that I create, store, and use personal files at my own risk and that the Library is not responsible for the loss of personal electronic documents, diskettes, and/or files.

Loss of User Privileges

- I understand and accept that my failure to comply with Library policies and procedures will result in Library penalties that range from suspension of Internet privileges for a week through permanent eviction from the Library.

Used with permission.

APPENDIX B. Austin Public Library Staff Responses to Public Computer Use Policy Violations

AUSTIN PUBLIC LIBRARY STAFF RESPONSES

TO PUBLIC COMPUTER USE POLICY VIOLATIONS

| Using more than one account or any other method* to gain access to Austin Public Library Internet computers for more than the maximum of 2 hours per person per day throughout the system. | 1st Offense | Account disabled & computer privileges suspended for **1 week** |
| | 2nd Offense | Account disabled & computer privileges suspended **Permanent** |

*Includes: Using a friend or family member's ID with or without permission; using another customer's ID with or without permission or using multiple or fake IDs to deliberately create duplicate accounts.

Person In Charge at each location will make decision to disable or enable Pharos accounts.

• Before a disabled account is reinstated, customer must sign an agreement acknowledging that computer usage is limited to 2 hours per person per day and agreeing not to violate APL public computer use policy again. Use "APL Computer User Agreement" form located on Common Drive.

Person in charge at each location should add notes to the comments field in Pharos Screen for each disabled account:

For example see Pharos account for SUSIE Q. PATRON with Logon ID sqp100

This is what is entered in the comments field for that account:

Violated time limit policy by using 2 IDs - sqp100 & 12121212- both disabled 12/2/02 suspended until 12/09/02 ATO/dfp/ Public Computer User Agreement signed - Acct sqp100 reactivated 12/09/02 ACB/etc/ 2nd violation- Permanent suspension 12/20/02 APH/rfk

(Since this field is limited, shorten as needed to include all facts.)

Staff entering messages should leave all previous notes in field and add new ones after them. Be sure to enter location where violation, reactivation, or suspension occurred and initials of staff member in charge.

Used with permission.

APPENDIX C. Austin Public Library Public Computer User Agreement

AUSTIN PUBLIC LIBRARY PUBLIC COMPUTER USER AGREEMENT

Before a deactivated Austin Public Library Internet/Public Computer Account can be reactivated, the account holder must read and sign the following statement:

- I understand that my ability to use public computers at the Austin Public Library is a privilege and that I must share this resource with others. While using the computers I will comply with all state and federal laws and Austin Public Library policies and procedures.

- I understand that I am limited to using Austin Public Library computers up to 120 minutes per day. This daily total includes all computers in the Austin Public Library System and is a not a separate total for each location.

- I understand that I may have only one active logon ID registered in the user database and that I must not share my logon ID or use the logon ID of family, friends or other users.

- I understand that I must pay for all the pages that I print.

- **I understand and accept that one more infraction of Library polices and procedures concerning public computer use will result in permanent suspension of my Internet and public computer use privileges throughout the Austin Public Library System.**

_____   _____

Signature   Logon ID

_____   _____

Printed Name   Location/Staff Witness

Used with permission.

The Impossible Takes a Little Longer: Implementing a Copyright Policy for Electronic Reserves

Susan Clayton

INTRODUCTION

"From digitization projects to interlibrary loan and from electronic reserves to electronic books, copyright law is having an impact on librarianship." (Dames, 1). While many librarians would like to ignore this impact, it is here and we must somehow deal with the realities of the impact of copyright law in many areas of the library. This article will attempt to shed some light on just one aspect: that of copyright and electronic reserves. A review of the recent literature shows that library practices regarding electronic reserves vary from one extreme to the other. Some libraries consider all electronic reserves to fall under fair use while others are more restrictive about the items that can be placed on e-reserve. This article takes the middle ground and by examining one electronic reserve policy will assist other librarians in formulating their own copyright policy for their electronic reserve systems.

REVIEW OF RECENT LITERATURE

Rebecca Butler in the article "Copyright Law and Organizing the Internet" provides an excellent overview of current copyright law including the concepts of fair use, the Digital Millennium Copyright Act (DMCA), copyright term extension, public domain, and the Technology, Education, and Copyright Harmonization (TEACH) Act. This article also provides a helpful checklist for items to consider when placing materials on electronic reserve. Anna Pilston and Richard Hart present a discussion of the advantages and disadvantages of developing an electronic reserve system in their article "Student Response to a New Electronic Reserves System." As is true at the University of Redlands, the authors found through a survey of students at the Pennsylvania State University–Erie campus that "The results were overwhelmingly in favor of electronic reserves" (Pilston 149). A lengthy and informative article by Elizabeth Buchanan, entitled "Copyright Policies and the Deciphering of Fair Use in the Creation of Reserves at University Libraries," includes a thorough study of research library policy regarding the copyright law and electronic reserves. There have been several articles on the controversy over the University of California–San Diego's (UCSD) electronic reserve system. One article is by George Pike titled "Academics Test Copyright Law" and another is "Battle Brews over E-Reserves" by Andrew Albanese in *Library Journal.*

To add to the complexity of this issue, there is a chapter in *Off-Campus Library Services* edited by Anne Marie Casey that discusses electronic reserves and copyright in regard to distance learners. As you can see, the issues surrounding electronic reserves and copyright are numerous. This paper will give one example of a small private university library's electronic reserve policy and how we are "Treading Carefully through the Murky Legalities of Electronic Reserves" as Judy Anderson and Lynne DeMont have so aptly titled their article.

DEVELOPING THE POLICY

The University of Redlands Armacost Library began using the Innovative Interfaces Millennium electronic reserve module in 2002. Once the staff was familiar with the module and the new equipment including a scanner, they began placing materials on electronic reserve. The procedures for placing materials on electronic reserve were in place, but the issue of copyright had not been addressed nor included in the procedures. Faculty embraced the electronic reserve service and quickly grew. The dilemma was that there was still no copyright policy in place and the service continued to grow at a rapid rate. Both faculty and students were enthusiastic about the availability of electronic reserves.

In August 2003, a new off-campus services librarian was hired who had previous experience with copyright issues, policies, and permissions. During the fall semester 2003, the librarian drafted a copyright policy for electronic reserves and the policy was put into practice during the spring semester 2004. There are a number of factors to keep in mind regarding this policy. First, the University of Redlands is a small, private liberal arts university with a student body of approximately 4,400 students (2,400 undergraduates and 2,000 graduate students) and a faculty of approximately 200. Second, the electronic reserve system is a fairly new service and to date primarily articles and book chapters are placed on e-reserve which is reflected in the policy. So far there have not been requests for streaming audio or video to be placed on e-reserve. As this begins to occur, the e-reserve copyright policy will be revised to accommodate these formats. Currently, CDs and DVDs are placed on traditional reserve, but not on electronic reserve. Third, while a number of students are distance or off-campus students, there have been few requests by the School of Business and the School of Education faculty to place materials on e-reserve. Our system and our copyright policy can easily accommodate these requests, and the library staff expects this to be the next area for growth in the electronic reserves system.

Since the fall semester 2003, the electronic reserves copyright guidelines have been through several revisions. The policy consists of two pages of copyright guidelines with an additional summary page to be used as a faculty hand-out. Also, the policy is in draft form as it is waiting for university administration approval. Several resources were used to develop the University of Redlands Library policy including the ALA Model Policy for Library Reserve Use, the CONFU guidelines (Driscoll 46-47), and guidelines from the University of Texas "Crash Course on Copyright." The guidelines address several topics regarding electronic reserves: materials which do not need copyright permission, materials for which copyright permission should be requested, storage and reuse of electronic reserves, access to electronic reserves, and the copyright notice on electronic reserve items. Since the University of Redlands policy is in draft form, other examples of electronic reserve policies and guidelines are included in the list of additional resources at the end of this article.

IMPLEMENTING THE POLICY–
SEMESTER BY SEMESTER

The current procedure for placing materials on electronic reserve includes several steps to cover copyright issues. When the e-reserve request is received, it is reviewed by the reserve staff for any copyright questions. If there is a question regarding the request, it is given to the off-campus services librarian for review. If there is no problem, the material is returned to the reserve staff for scanning into the system and labeling. One print copy is added to the traditional reserve collection.

If there is a copyright question, for example, multiple articles from one journal issue, the librarian requests permission first through the Copyright Clearance Center. If it is not available from the Copyright Clearance Center, then she sends a request for copyright permission directly to the copyright holder. There are several steps in receiving copyright clearance and while this is being done, the item is scanned and added to the e-reserve system. This is a controversial point and is handled in different ways in various libraries. Because the University of Redlands Armacost Library has a relatively small electronic reserves collection and the copyright permissions are closely monitored, it was decided that for practical reasons the material would be posted while permission was being sought. So far only once has permission been denied and then the item was immediately removed from electronic reserve and the faculty member was contacted. The item was kept in the print reserve collection.

To give an idea of the number of items added to electronic reserves and the number of permissions requested, spring semester 2006 and fall semester 2006 will be used as examples. There were 143 electronic reserves; 2,202 traditional reserves; and 45 copyright permissions requested for the spring semester. For fall semester 2006, there were 160 electronic reserves; 2,252 traditional reserves; and 58 copyright permissions requested and received. It is clear, and not surprising, that the numbers are increasing each semester. In addition, during the summer 2006, the part-time reserves staff member retired and a new full-time reserves/circulation staff member was hired. With the additional staff hours devoted to reserves, this has increased both the number of electronic reserves which can be scanned into the system and has also increased the number of copyright permission requests.

The cost of copyright permissions is an additional consideration. Currently at the University of Redlands, the library is paying for copyright permissions. As the e-reserve numbers increase, the budgetary amount will become a greater issue. During the sample spring 2006 semester, the cost for copyright permissions was approximately $1,500. In the fall 2006 semester the cost was closer to $2,000. The library administrative assistant, who processes many of the library invoices, also processes the invoices for copyright permissions. As an additional note, only one request for copyright permission for electronic reserves was denied during the spring 2006 semester and none were denied in the fall 2006 semester.

THINGS TO CONSIDER
REGARDING COPYRIGHT AND E-RESERVES

First, consider the faculty and their needs for electronic reserves. At the University of Redlands, currently it is the on-campus faculty who are using this service. Potential users of electronic reserves are the School of Business and the School of Education faculty. The two professional schools offer classes in the evenings, on weekends, and primarily off campus. The availability of electronic reserves would be a great benefit to these students. In fact, the Blackboard Course Management System is heavily used by both schools. It is through this online delivery system that faculty members in the professional schools are making their reserve materials available, but in doing so they are bypassing the library reserve system. The library staff is working proactively to encourage the School of Business and School of Education faculties to begin using the library electronic reserve system more for their students if they wish to do so.

A second consideration is that there should be a staff member whose task it is to track copyright information for electronic reserves. Ideally this task would reside with the reserve staff. At the University of Redlands, there are future plans to move the copyright responsibility to reserves with the off-campus services librarian acting more as an advisor than the person actually tracking copyright permissions and payments. Until then, copyright permissions are the librarian's responsibility.

Third is the question of who pays for copyright permissions. As mentioned earlier, even with the relatively few copyright requests during the spring 2006 semester, the cost was significant. There should be a place in the budget for copyright permissions and registration for the Copyright Clearance Center. Some institutions have the individual departments pay the copyright costs while others have a budget line in the library budget. This issue must be decided within the institution itself.

The fourth and final consideration is the software and equipment. If a library does not already have a course reserve module in its online circulation system, the module or the software must be purchased. Also, a reliable and easy-to-use scanner is a necessity. Training for the reserve staff and student assistants in the use of the course reserve software and the scanning equipment is another necessity.

CONCLUSION

Through the use of the example of two semesters of electronic course reserves at the University of Redlands Armacost Library and the policy and procedures developed for reviewing copyright compliance for each request, this example will hopefully encourage other libraries to approach copyright issues with less anxiety. With the information presented and the resources cited, it is hoped that other libraries will feel prepared to develop their own electronic reserve copyright policy.

REFERENCES

Albanese, A. (2005). Battle brews over e-reserves. *Library Journal, 130*(9), 16-17.

Anderson, J. and L. DeMont. (2001). Treading carefully through the murky legalities of electronic reserves. *Computers in Libraries, 21*(6), 40-44.

Austin, B. (2004). *Reserves, electronic reserves, and copyright: The past and the future.* Binghamton, NY: Haworth Information Press.

Buchanan, E. A. (2005). Copyright policies and the deciphering of fair use in the creation of reserves at university libraries. *Journal of Academic Librarianship, 31*(3), 182-197.

Butler, R. P. (2003). Copyright law and organizing the Internet. *Library Trends, 52*(2), 307-317.

Casey, A. M. (Ed.). (2001). *Off-Campus library services.* Binghamton, NY: Haworth Information Press.

Dames, K. M. (2006). Library schools and the copyright knowledge gap. *Information Today, 23*(2), 1-3.

Driscoll, L. (2003). *Electronic reserve: A manual and guide for library staff members.* Binghamton, NY: Haworth Information Press.

Pike, G. H. (2005). Academics test copyright law. *Information Today, 22*(6), 19-20.

Pilston, A. K. and Hart, R. L. (2002). Student response to a new electronic reserves system. *Journal of Academic Librarianship, 28*(3), 147-151.

ADDITIONAL RESOURCES

Copyright Clearance Center. Copyright.com. Retrieved January 30, 2007 from http://www.copyright.com

Crews, K. D. (2006). *Copyright law for librarians and educators: Creative strategies and practical solutions.* Chicago: American Library Association.

Electronic reserves and fair use. (2004). *ARL, 232,* 7-8.

Harper, G. Crash Course in Copyright. Retrieved January 30, 2007 from *http://www.utsystem.edu/ogc/Intellectualproperty/cprtindx.htm*

Hoffman, G. M. (2001). *Copyright in cyberspace: Questions and answers for librarians.* New York: Neal-Schuman Publishers.

Hudock, S. L. and Abrahamson G. L. (2004). Embracing fair use: One university's epic journey into copyright policy. *Journal of Interlibrary Loan, Document Delivery & Information Supply, 15*(1), 65-73.

Lowe, S. and Rumery, J. (2001). Services to distance learners: Planning for e-reserves and copyright. In A. M. Casey (Ed.), *Off-Campus library services* (pp. 319-330). New York: Haworth Information Press.

Rosedale, J. (Ed.). (2002). *Managing Electronic Reserves*. Chicago: American Library Association.

Russell, C. (Ed.). (2004) *Complete Copyright: An Everyday Guide for Librarians.* Chicago: American Library Association.

Electronic Reserves, Copyright, and CMS Integration– Six Years Later

Jodi Poe
Sonja McAbee

BACKGROUND

Jacksonville State University (JSU) is a medium-sized, public comprehensive university offering both undergraduate and graduate programs. It was founded in 1883 as Jacksonville State Normal School. Its purpose in 1883 was to provide a preparatory education for citizens of a rural Alabama county and the surrounding areas. The mission and the student population of the university have changed over time. The current enrollment is approximately 9,000 students. The University hosts students from all over the United States and from almost every corner of the globe. The institutional borders have expanded beyond its actual physical space. The library's collection has also expanded in this way. It has grown from microforms and print resources such as books, journals, and newspapers to include electronic resources such as CD-ROMs, databases, web sites, e-journals, and e-books. In this same vein, reserve readings have also extended beyond the physical structure with the implementation of electronic reserves.

INTRODUCTION

In 2001, with the proliferation of web access and the implementation of the Voyager library management system, HCL began to look for ways to electronically disseminate reserve readings. Doing so would accommodate the needs of the ever growing population of distance education students, make documents accessible to multiple users at the same time, address staffing utilization issues, and meet possible accreditation requirements. These electronic reserves would consist of documents that are scanned or downloaded onto a server or direct links to articles in full-text databases.

Because of past experience with system changes and re-education of the users, the staff was reluctant to train the users to use yet another system. The goal was to use a recognizable interface which would provide a common portal to facilitate one-stop shopping. It was also advantageous to give the students added access points as an alternative to simply searching by instructor or course. Since many students do not remember the name of their professor or the course number, the decision was made to purchase a document management system and integrate the electronic reserve documents into the traditional reserves using the Voyager system.

The Docutek ERes system was selected because of its history as an easy to use product and its price. With this decision came some problems associated with integrating a foreign product and the existing Voyager/EZProxy infrastructure. Neither vendor, Endeavor or Docutek, offered much assistance with the integration process. With some fine-tuning, JSU implemented electronic reserves in spring 2002. McAbee and Walter (2002) reported on the HCL experience at the 2002 Southeast Voyager User's Group meeting. Their presentation on this implementation can be found at <http://www.jsu.edu/depart/library/personal/walter/sevugm/>.

Although the Docutek system allows for the inclusion of photographs, audio files, and video files, the library administration decided not to incorporate these file types into the reserve system. This decision was based on several concerns. First and foremost is the lack of funding for additional server space and limited bandwidth throughout the campus. It is just not a priority nor is it affordable to acquire the servers to accommodate the larger size files used for images, audio, and video. Further, the students at JSU monopolize most of the bandwidth visiting entrainment sites such as user-generated videos, MP3/iPod sites, streaming files, and social networks. At this institution, the high volume of users accessing such files could only be handled by an outside source, not through Docutek. There are vendors offering such hosted services, including copyright verification, but at this institution the current demand cannot justify the costs.

Additional concerns are relations to copyright laws. Verifying that a print document is copyrighted is much easier than identifying the status of an image. The library staff lacks the expertise to verify that an image is copyrighted or free.

Also, there are questions as to how far the library's mission evolves around offering such services. The Distance Education Department (DE) already has the ability to mass produce DVDs for distribution. It seems that the digitizing of multimedia for web access might be an area more appropriately handled by their experts.

MARKETING

The first announcement to the faculty regarding the move to electronic course reserves was at the "New Faculty Orientation" meeting held in August 2001. In December 2001, a lengthy flyer was distributed to every faculty member employed by the University. Concurrently, the DE Librarian used a listserv to notify instructors involved in distance education of the availability of the service. Information was also distributed to department heads and departmental liaisons through the library's liaison listserv. Each announcement addressed access, submission, copyright issues, viewing requirements, and contained contact information. These announcements were followed by a presentation at the university's monthly Academe meeting by Graham and Poe (2002). Students were educated about the system through library instruction sessions and an article, "Library Reserves enter the Digital Age," that was published in the student newspaper (Poe, 2006).

COPYRIGHT ISSUES

From fair use to the TEACH Act, libraries have always dealt with copyright issues. Ensuring libraries are in compliance with copyright is a goal that must be met head-on. E-reserves present librarians with a special challenge. HCL implemented several things to address copyright compliance: copyright statements for faulty, copyright notices for students, and authentication. HCL provides an online form faculty members can use to request reserve items. The "Course Reserve Request Form" (http://www.jsu.edu/depart/library/graphic/coures.htm) includes a statement regarding copyright that the instructor must accept prior to placing a request. This statement includes a link to the copyright code and a notation that the faculty member will be responsible for all copyright costs (see Image 1). Once the faculty member's request has been received and processed, the reserves are made accessible through the library's catalog or Blackboard courses. Upon retrieving a document, users must accept the copyright notice (see Image 2) prior to receiving access to the document, thus complying with copyright restrictions. Copyright restrictions require that e-reserves be limited to authorized users. To comply with this restriction, users off campus must be authenticated through HCL's EZProxy system by entering their last name and University identification number (see Image 3).

HCL does not solely rely on these measures for managing copyright. Docutek incorporates certain functionality, which HCL utilizes, to assist libraries with managing copyright issues from creation through delivery. The system provides other options that are detailed on their site.

IMAGE 1. Copyright Statement on Request Form

Do you have copyright permission to place this item on electronic reserve? ⌒ Yes ⌒ No
If you are not sure please see our copyright permission information page for details

COPYRIGHT ACKNOWLEDGEMENTS

Submitting this request indicates that you have read the warning concerning Copyright Restrictions
and agree that the materials submitted to the Reserve Department are in compliance with the
copyright law of the United States (Title 17, United States Code)

By submitting this request, you agree to assume all charges incurred for any
Copyright costs. In addition, I have read the warning concerning Copyright Restrictions.

Submit | Reset |

IMAGE 2. Copyright Notice

Please be advised that to use electronic material, you must agree to
the following by clicking the 'Accept' button below:

The copyright law of the United States (Title 17, United States Code) governs the
making of photocopies or other reproductions of copyrighted materials. Under
certain conditions specified in the law, libraries and archives are authorized to
furnish a photocopy or other reproduction. One of these specified conditions is
that the photocopy or reproduction is not to be used for any purpose other than
private study, scholarship, or research. If a user makes a request for, or later
uses, a photocopy or reproduction for purposes in excess of fair use that user
may be liable for copyright infringement.

Course Info: SPES86 - Practicum in severe disabilities (Spring 2007) - Gardner
Document Title: Children with disabilities who use assistive technology: ethical
considerations

Accept | Cancel |

"Docutek ERes provides complete copyright workflow management. All bibliographic information can be stored in the Docutek ERes
database, letters to publishers and rights holders can be generated automatically, and a powerful set of reports and tracking summaries can be
created with the click of the mouse. Through a partnership between
Docutek and Copyright Clearance Center (CCC), libraries can also
seamlessly connect with CCC's online system to obtain instant electronic permissions on many documents. To assist libraries in enforcing
copyright compliance, Docutek ERes requires users to accept a statement of the libraries copyright policy before viewing documents in
Docutek ERes. In addition, the access to any document or reserve page
can be limited via an encrypted password. Docutek ERes tracks the

IMAGE 3. EZProxy Login Screen

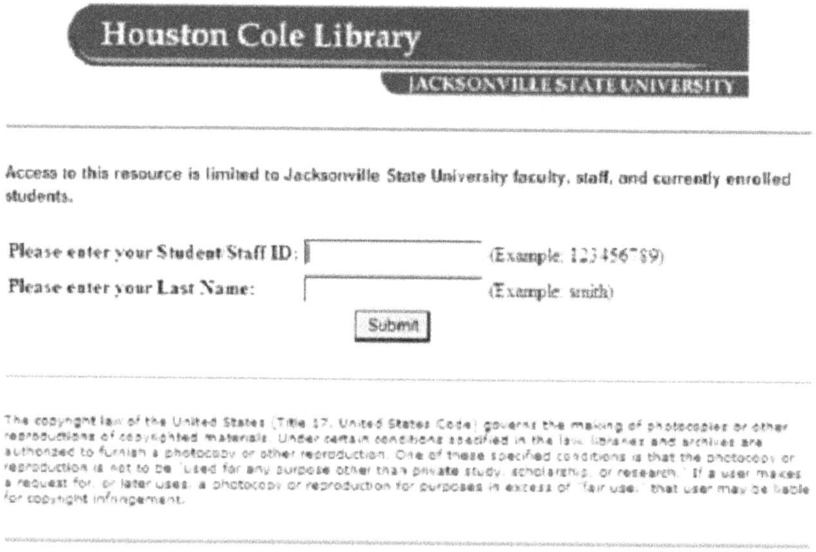

number of times copyright-protected documents have been accessed, and if royalties are to be paid, Docutek ERes will "track the charges" (Docutek, n.d., para. 2-3).

Direct linking to articles in full-text databases is preferred, because electronic articles from these sources are not subject to the same copyright scrutiny as those from print sources that are scanned into the system. However, there are license restrictions that must be adhered to when providing access using these persistent links. Because of this, and since most database vendors provide methods for creating persistent URLs (PURL), direct linking is very popular with the library staff. If the article is available in one of the databases, there is no need to scan a copy of the article. Such scanning often results in poor image quality, making the article nearly impossible to read. In addition, the subscription price for the databases makes up a substantial portion of the library's budget. Thus, the library has made it a priority to promote these resources as much as possible and encourage their use. Finally, the turn-around time it will take to make the article accessible to the students is greatly reduced (Warren, 2003).

However, each vendor creates PURLs differently and the Library must add a proxy pointer. To address this issue, HCL created a document, "How to Link to Electronic Content in Courses, Web Pages, and Other Electronic Documents" <http://www.jsu.edu/depart/library/graphic/ Persistentlinks.pdf>. This document provides detailed instructions for creating PURLs for some of the frequently used databases available through JSU. The document was also placed on the Library's "Faculty Services" web page <http://www.jsu.edu/depart/library/graphic/facserv. htm> and distributed to the faculty through the two listservs used at JSU. In addition, it is included in email messages to professors requesting links for Blackboard courses.

At JSU, the faculty are still responsible for securing copyright permissions. Library staff will assist them as much as possible using the CCC link available through Docutek. The library has an established CCC account and will pay the fee and bill the department. However, when confronted with the estimated cost for permissions, most faculty simply remove the item from their course reserves.

COURSE MANAGEMENT SYSTEMS (CMS)

Due to the growing demand for courses offered any time at any place, distance education programs are increasing. Online courses seem to be the preferred method of delivery. Many universities are using course management systems to facilitate the delivery of these courses. JSU offers a number of online courses using the Blackboard Online Course System.

The DE Librarian works closely with the Office of Distance Education (ODE). She is a member of the Distance Education Advisory Committee and attends ODE staff meetings and workshops. Her close association with the ODE has enabled her to ensure that the library has a presence in Blackboard. This presence is evident through the addition of a button or link to the library in the navigation pane in all of the Blackboard course shells. Unfortunately, the version of Blackboard used at JSU, Blackboard Academic Suite™, Release 7.1.391.3 - Enterprise License, only allows the ODE to add buttons and/or links to the course shells; it does not permit control of the tabs at the course level. Thus, faculty may remove links that they do not wish to appear on their course page, making the library link vulnerable to removal. The benefit of having tabs instead of buttons or links is that tabs cannot be deleted, so the library's presence would be static. Blackboard produces a version that allows institutions to manipulate the tabs, Blackboard Community System™, but JSU cannot migrate to this version at this time.

Working closely with the ODE has also provided the DE Librarian with an administrative login and the needed skills to assist faculty and students with common Blackboard problems. In addition, the DE librarian collaborates with the ODE and the faculty to incorporate electronic reserves into Blackboard courses. According to McManus, Brown, Hulbert, Maximiek, and Rushton (2006), this is important because "Collaborating with faculty to provide course support and instruction via Blackboard will help further the libraries' instructional mission and goals" (p.91). Having the DE librarian as part of the OED team has proved beneficial as more and more courses are either being transferred to or supplemented by electronic course delivery. JSU faculty members can request that a link be added to their Blackboard course for their reserve items. If the item was scanned and placed in Docutek ERes, a link, automatically assigned to the document, is used to add the e-reserve to Blackboard. If a PURL was created, this link is added to the Blackboard course page. The DE librarian will either add the link directly into the Blackboard course or email the link to the faculty member for them to add. All links provided by the DE librarian include some type of notation indicating that the item is available through the library. This "branding" notation is important because those students using Blackboard, as well as all distance education students, are surveyed every semester to determine how well the library is meeting their needs.

The popularity and increased use of electronic reserves has not gone unnoticed by CMS vendors, as is indicated by the recent introduction of an electronic reserves module in Blackboard: Blackboard Content System™. Blackboard partnered with CCC to ensure copyright management was an important element for the module and introduced this system as a way to integrate electronic reserves directly into the course. This system would eliminate the problem of inconsistent placement of reserve items, since it is an integrated feature and included in a tab that cannot be deleted. Since HCL already provided this service to JSU faculty and the addition of this system would involve a significant extra cost, the ODE declined to subscribe to the enhanced system.

Even without the additional module, using Blackboard provides the library with a variety of benefits. This method of delivery: (1) provides easier access to the reserves through a system the students are using to access their other course materials, (2) allows the library to become an integral part of the course and the university as a whole, and (3) encourages the students and faculty to see the other resources the library has to offer. This presence illustrates to the teaching faculty that the library is an essential part of the students' education and an effective collaborative partner. At the same time, it demonstrates to students that the library is the best place to start and finish their research–sometimes without ever leaving their computers. Additionally, as Bell and Krasulski (2004) illustrate, the use of Blackboard, ERes, and the library's databases complement each other and can be used together to provide quality materials to the university's CMS users while increasing their ease of utilization. By using all three of these systems in cooperation, the library creates "greater faculty member's awareness about library resources" (Bell & Krasulski, 2004, p.75-85).

There are some disadvantages in using Blackboard. First, there is not a standard placement for electronic reserves. Some JSU faculty members place reserve items under the "Assignments" area, others use the "Course Documents" area, and finally, some use the "Course Information" area. This inconsistency makes it difficult for the DE librarian to add links to each course where the professor wants them, so the DE librarian has initiated the practice of adding the content to the "Course Documents" area but not activating the content. Once the faculty member is notified about the additions, they are responsible for moving them to the appropriate location and making the content available to the students. Another disadvantage is that incorporating course reserves into CMS programs does not address items on traditional reserve. However, most faculty using the CMS to deliver course content tend not to use traditional reserves. And lastly, only the more costly versions of CMS products address tracking items for copyright compliance and customize report management.

Docutek ERes has reporting features to analyze all aspects of the system, including how it's being used by instructors, the library, and students. Access Reports show how frequently specific items are being accessed within Docutek ERes. Summary Reports offer a snapshot of the system tracking growth.

IMPLEMENTATION OBSERVATIONS

The administration deemed that using a dual system (photocopies and/or electronic formats) would be confusing for the staff and the users. Further, it would permit those faculty opposed to digitized formats with a method to circumvent using the electronic system. Therefore, it was decided that the reserve staff would no longer circulate print copies of documents for photocopying. Surprisingly, only one member of the faculty was disgruntled at this change and removed the course readings from the library.

After the initial scanning of the documents at the beginning of the semester, the reserve staff had more time to do other things. As a result, the reserve desk was relocated to the lobby and the personnel were merged with the circulation staff. This relocation/merger has allowed HCL to better utilize the staff. Until the relocation, reserve staff was only involved in reserve matters. With the merger, the circulation and reserve staff are cross trained and better able to assist our patrons. As far as training, integration to facilitate a single user sign-on is more difficult for the staff than using Docutek exclusively. However, it is easier for the users because they are using a familiar interface and the integration is transparent. It also requires more in depth training of the reserve staff in the use of the cataloging client. Since the temporary catalog records entered by Reserve staff usually do not comply with standards, the cataloging staff must be flexible and willing to accept these temporary entries.

Moving around in the Docutek system can be frustrating because it requires several mouse clicks to get to the location that is needed. This is one of the factors that led to HCL's decision to do all of the electronic reserves management in-house instead of training the faculty. Training would be constant and the staff would not have time to process the materials, whereas the reserve module of the catalog is very user-friendly with simple drop-down menus from which to select. The service itself is extremely popular, yet most faculty do not want to set up course materials themselves. Thus, the practice of in-house management is still employed and will be for the foreseeable future.

Despite all the disadvantages of e-reserves and its integration with Blackboard, the statistics in Table 1 indicate that e-reserve activity is on decline. However, these numbers are not all-encompassing. First, Docutek did not provide a way to track retrievals during 2001-2003. Those retrievals were counted using the Library's EZProxy statistics, which did not reflect the number of times a specific reserve was retrieved, but counted the number of pieces retrieved (e.g. pages of a pdf document). In 2003/2004, Docutek began to provide a method for obtaining several statistic reports. One report reflects the number of documents retrieved during a given date range. The statistics listed for 2003/2004-2005/ 2006 are taken from this report. Still, these numbers reflect a decline in

TABLE 1. Electronic Reserve Documents Added/Retrievals

Date	Documents Added	Retrievals
(January) 2001/2002	479	27,505 (statistics taken from EZProxy server which duplicates PDF pieces)
2002/2003	251	26,141 (statistics taken from EZProxy server which duplicates PDF pieces)
2003/2004	312	18,002
2004/2005	259	15,077
2005/2006	139	10,225

e-reserve activity. This can be attributed to the use by faculty of direct links in their Blackboard courses.

To gauge the actual activity rate, HCL would need to keep statistics for the number of reserves requested through Docutek and for those direct links added to Blackboard. Blackboard does provide a method for tracking the number of views a document receives, but the individual faculty member must activate this feature. Currently, the DE librarian has not requested faculty use this option, but as more and more e-reserve links are added directly to Blackboard courses it may be worth exploring. To address this problem, the DE librarian has begun maintaining limited statistical information about those requests that are directed to her; however, this approach fails to count those that faculty create independently.

THE FUTURE

HCL strives to bring the needed resources directly to the students and to provide these resources in a manner students can easily utilize. "Electronic resources management at HCL has often been a complicated process, and it is a process that continues to evolve as the Library discovers new and better ways to pursue its goal of one-stop shopping for e-resources" (Skaggs, Poe,& Stevens, 2006, p. 205). The staff has consistently met this goal by anticipating the users' needs when implementing new technologies. The idea of one-stop shopping is appealing to HCL staff for a number of reasons, most importantly in delivering resources to the users through a system that is user-friendly and easily navigated. The other benefit to using the catalog is that students have already been trained on using this system. Proactive thinking such as this should allow the HCL staff to improve the delivery method of e-reserves and to resolve some of the management and copyright compliance issues that are prevalent with e-reserves.

The HCL staff are constantly rethinking current practices and workflows to ensure that the delivery method used for e-reserves is the best possible. One new technology on JSU's horizon is in the migration of the financial and student systems to Banner <http://www.sungardhe. com/default.aspx?id = 80> and integrating it into the Luminis portal <http://www.sungardhe.com/default.aspx?id = 115>. Both of these systems are provided by SunGard. With this implementation, the university is moving to an environment where the users' needs are met online with real-time delivery of information and resources. The SunGard systems include the added benefit of easy access to the entire range of university resources with a single sign-on, or allowing users to login only once to access everything within the portal, including Blackboard. Because of the implementation of the Luminus portal and given that each course is assigned a Blackboard course shell for supplemental learning, it is expected that as Blackboard is developed to address the library's tracking concerns, the library will eventually migrate from Docutek and rely on Blackboard for electronic reserves.

REFERENCES

Bell, S. J. and M. J. Krasulski (2004). Electronic reserves, library databases, and courseware: A complementary relationship. *Journal of Interlibrary Loan, Document Delivery & Electronic Reserve, 15*(1), 75-85.
Docutek, a SirsiDynix company. (n.d.) *Docutek Eres features.* Retrieved March 5, 2007, from http://www.docutek.com/products/eres/features.html
Graham, J. B. and J. Poe (2002, March 18). *Course reserves made easy: An introduction to the library's electronic course reserve system.* Presentation at the monthly meeting of Jacksonville State University's Academe, Jacksonville, AL.
McAbee, S. and D. Walter (2002, July 22-23). *Integrating electronic reserves with Docutek, Voyager, and EZProxy.* Paper presented at the Southeast Voyager Users Group Meeting, Auburn, AL.

McManus, A., E. A. Brown, D. Hulbert, S. Maximiek & E. Rushton (2006). Implementing electronic reserves using the Blackboard Content System. *Journal of Interlibrary loan, Document Delivery & Electronic Reserve, 16*(4), 85-92.

Poe, J. (2006). Marketing electronic reserves at a University library: start spreading the news. *Journal of Interlibrary loan, Document Delivery & Electronic Reserve, 16*(4), 93-102.

Skaggs, B. L., J. W. Poe, & K. W. Stevens (2006). One-stop shopping: A perspective on the evolution of electronic resources management. *OCLC Systems & Services: International Digital Library Perspectives, 22* (3), 2006, 192-206.

Warren, S. (2003). Deeplinking and e-reserves: A new generation. *Journal of Interlibrary Loan, Document Delivery & Information Supply, 14*(2), 65-81.

Tackling Copyright in the Digital Age: An Initiative of the University of Connecticut Libraries

Barbara Oakley
Betsy Pittman
Tracey Rudnick

Has your university been visited by the RIAA recently? Are you re-considering your e-reserves because of what you hear in the news? Are patrons asking library staff for advice about copyright issues related to their teaching, research, and learning? The University of Connecticut Libraries faced exactly these concerns in the spring of 2005. Inspired by an influx of questions–many associated with new electronic services at the university–and the rapidly changing legal landscape, the library de-cided to tackle the issue of copyright head on.

BACKGROUND

The inevitable questions arose right away. Does the university not have a policy? Why should the library get involved?

Before 2005, the issue of copyright within the university community, including the libraries, was handled on an ad hoc basis, addressed by in-dividual areas and divisions as issues arose, independent of other areas and services. A few university policies did address some overarching is-sues: ownership of works created at the university; the illegal distribu-tion of software or other material via university computing and networking systems; and procedures for handling DMCA-infringement complaints. However, these documents were general in nature and vague in approach; readers would not find specifics to answer day-to-day questions, nor would they find policies related to the use of copy-righted information in the course of teaching, learning, research, and publishing. The university does have a Center for Science and Technol-ogy Commercialization to handle trademark and patent concerns for the university, but similarly it is not in their purview to deal with general in-tellectual property or copyright issues.

US copyright law, especially section 110(2) (the TEACH Act), now requires universities to establish institution-wide policies and identify contact persons in order to take advantage of privileges afforded to aca-demic uses, especially in the context of distance education. The univer-sity had identified a person assigned to handle reported abuses. University staff could also consult the Office of the Attorney General on copyright issues that arose within the context of their public employ-ment. Neither of these offices was equipped to handle the potential vol-ume of questions that might result if everyday issues were directed to them, and the university did not have any other clearly identified office or individual to handle routine copyright questions from the university community.

Members of the university community often turned to library staff for their copyright questions, and library staff frequently faced similar questions in their own day-to-day work. Due to the nature of their responsibilities, librarians were in a position to know and keep up with fundamental copyright principles, though no one on the library staff was qualified or claimed to offer legal advice. In addition, the number and variability of questions increased as electronic access to copyrighted material grew. This ultimately led to a wide range of understandings among staff and users about the law as expertise and context varied.

Thus, the minimal direction at the university level, the changing nature of copyright enforcement, and increasing questions and complexities faced by the library staff prompted the libraries to launch a copyright initiative as a strategic priority for two consecutive fiscal years, 2005-2007. This objective was just one component of the libraries' strategic plan, in which the library was called to "provide leadership and expertise for the university community as scholarly communication systems are transformed." Among other activities, the library set a goal for itself to "articulate evolving library copyright issues for the university community."[1]

In July 2005, the Copyright Project Team, made up of three librarians, was charged to develop policies and guidelines on copyright and related legal issues for the libraries to follow; to develop guidelines for staff, patrons and researchers, as appropriate; to recommend further actions to introduce these issues to the larger university community; and to maintain current and evolving knowledge of this area within the libraries. The project team was not responsible for enforcing copyright compliance at the university or providing legal advice to staff or users. Nevertheless, the activities of the project team have permitted the libraries to serve as a leader for the university and regional professional communities.

Over the two years of its existence, the Copyright Project Team engaged in a wide range of activities to fulfill its charge and to raise awareness of copyright issues in the library and across the university. This article highlights some of the primary activities and tools used by the team to involve stakeholders, to provide educational opportunities, and to stay current on copyright issues in higher education. Many more activities and events than can be detailed here were part of the process. For a timeline of major milestones, see Table 1.

GETTING STARTED

Where would the team begin? Was there not good information about copyright on the web already? Why reinvent the wheel?

With these and many other questions looming, the team's first project was to get a feel for the copyright landscape. Each team member had some knowledge of copyright issues because their respective job responsibilities required it, but none felt they had a truly comprehensive view. The team began by performing an environmental scan of copyright web sites and policy statements across higher education. After viewing dozens of sites, the team identified several that were useful or even outstanding in one or more aspects. Each had some particularly relevant content or effective approach to site organization. While no one site addressed all of the needs the team had identified, each helped formulate the team's early thinking and provided content and layout ideas for subsequent website design.

The team also performed an internal environmental scan. The team inquired library-wide about known policies or guidelines put out by the library, in addition to issues, questions and concerns, and staff knowledge and self-identified expertise. Armed with this information, the team developed a survey for staff. (See Table 2 for sample survey questions). Conducted in December 2005, the survey assessed the general level of library staff knowledge and awareness of copyright, fair use, and the relationship of both to library materials. The survey also asked library staff to prioritize library services and types of questions that would most benefit from copyright policies or guidelines. The survey not only helped the team assess the state of knowledge and staff concerns, it also served as a vehicle for inviting library staff participation. It was clearly understood that everyone had a stake in the development process. Later meetings with individuals and library teams focused on library services such as interlibrary loan and reserve, and related library activities such as scholarly communications, a new institutional repository, and digital collections. The substantial level of staff input from the beginning and throughout the project fostered a general spirit of "buy in" when the team rolled out a new copyright web site.

PEOPLE TO HAVE ONBOARD

It was not enough to have buy-in from just the library staff. Copyright is an important ongoing issue for the university, so it is valuable to have

TABLE 1. Timeline of Events and Important Milestones

	Administrative	Policy & Web-site Development	Staff/Public Events
Spring 2005	Team formed		Webcast on orphan works
Summer 2005	Scan of internal and external copyright environment		Webcast on applying fair use
Fall 2005	Staff survey to assess knowledge and identify expertise/needs	Assemble outline of web-site topics and potential policies	
Spring 2006	Identify and secure approval for use of outside legal counsel	Develop web-site framework and prototype	Copyright forum and web-site preview
Summer 2006	Consultation with administrators across university*	Web-site content development;* secure content permissions	
Fall 2006	Consultation with library units*	Draft library policies; reviewed by legal counsel*	
October 2006	Web-site and progress report for library leadership	Informal web-site release*	Web-site introductory sessions for library staff
November 2006			Article in library newsletter
December 2006	Presentation to library's faculty advisory committee		Boston Library Consortium copyright forum
January 2007	Submit charge for a university-wide copyright committee to the President's Office	Formal web-site release*	Article in university newspaper
February 2007	General library policy statement approved by library leadership		
March 2007	Link to copyright web site added to university's policies web page		Authors' rights brochure (with Scholarly Communications Team)
May 2007	Team's final report to library leadership		
Future	Library participation on university committee on copyright?	Continued web-site development	Additional outreach and resources for library staff and university community

*Activity or development continued beyond this time period.

TABLE 2. Sample Survey Questions

Each question was offered as true/false.
The library should seek permission to use any copyrighted materials for course reserve.
An author must register a work with the Copyright Office to receive copyright protection.
Copying at the university is fair use because it's for educational purposes.
To take advantage of the benefits of the TEACH Act, an academic institution must have an institution-wide copyright policy.
Fair use allows libraries to circumvent encryption technologies in digital formats for the purposes of research and scholarship.
Contractual arrangements and licensing agreements take precedence over fair use.
The survey was distributed to all library staff in December 2005. Forty-seven percent of the staff completed the survey.

the endorsement and support from offices and individuals who can help advance the agenda and knowledge of all members of the university community. The libraries' Copyright Project Team sought out individuals and groups within the university who had a stake in the presentation and dissemination of knowledge of copyright and intellectual property issues as part of their responsibilities. The team built relationships with these stakeholders to further its work and to raise the profile of copyright issues within the university community. In the process, the team sought the approval of the university for its efforts and sought the university administration's engagement as a central, authoritative voice in disseminating information and policies.

As counsel for the university, the state's attorney general on campus was a key representative from whom the team sought information and endorsement of its work. The attorney general's office provided the team with the perspective of the state with regard to the work of the university and all of its units, including the library. Members of the office worked with the team to provide overarching parameters for the team's work, to formulate general statements, and to approve specific language of key policies. The team consulted with members of the attorney general's office regularly throughout the process of developing the copyright web site to ensure that interested university offices were not working at cross purposes and that the library was not overstepping its bounds.

The university's compliance officer played a similar role in guiding the work of the team in accord with university policies. Members of that office were especially effective in disseminating information to the entire university community as a part of the ethical conduct training they provide. Moreover, it was at the suggestion of the compliance officer that the library's copyright web site was added to the University's ePolicies web site *<http://policy.uconn.edu/pages/main.cfm>*.

For detailed legal advice and oversight of the team's policy development, the libraries obtained outside legal counsel, with the approval and endorsement of the attorney general's office. This legal advisor was essential in helping the team create clear, understandable and legally supportable guidelines and policies that reflected the requirements of the local environment and respond to the needs of the local community.

The libraries have ongoing relationships with university curriculum support divisions that assist faculty in creating new courses and provide technical assistance with enterprise tools like course management software. In the course of their work, curriculum support specialists encounter questions from faculty about copyright and what materials can or cannot be used for instruction. The copyright team continues to capitalize on these relationships to share information and to help develop policies and guidelines for campus users that reflect their experience and needs while working within copyright law.

The university has a robust program for technology commercialization, turning university research into marketable products through patents and licensing. The primary concern of this office is necessarily related to new intellectual property developments and, as such, comes from a very different perspective than the team encounters when members of the community want to use the intellectual property of others; this had implications for the team's work on the web site. Work with these patent experts reinforced for the team the importance of balancing the rights of creators and those of users. Regular contact with this office keeps these issues close in the team's thoughts as the team continues to develop resources and teach users on campus about appropriate uses of copyrighted information.

FORUMS

Each spring, the university libraries sponsor an open forum on timely and forward-looking topics of interest to libraries and the academic community. Some examples of recent forum topics include the future of libraries, institutional repositories, universal web-site usability, and mass digitization projects.

In April 2006, the Libraries' forum was on the topic "Whose Rights & Who's Right: Copyright in the Digital Age" <*http://www.lib.uconn. edu/copyright/whoseRights_Oakley.html*>. Speaker Robert Oakley, Law Librarian and Professor of Law at Georgetown University and Washington Affairs Representative for the American Association of Law libraries, gave attendees a brief history of US copyright law, highlighting some of the landmark cases that have molded the copyright landscape of today. Using examples provided by the audience, Professor Oakley showed how current practice and issues are being addressed in public-policy arenas and how academics and librarians can play a part in changing the course of copyright legislation.

The forum was widely attended by members of the UConn community and beyond, from all aspects of academia. Because the forum was so successful, the university libraries arranged to have the talk repeated for the Boston Library Consortium at the Boston Public Library in December 2006. Key factors in the success of the forum include the timeliness of the topic, widespread and attention-getting advertising, the knowledge and reputation of the speaker and the relevance of the topic to the work of academia.

WEB-SITE DEVELOPMENT–LOGISTICS

Creating a web site with copyright policy information was central to the team's activities. What would be the focus of the web site: internal policies for library staff to follow; information for the library's users; or information for the broader university community? Would the library have sufficient resources to create content? Who would maintain the site? Would the university be interested in contributing content or in adopting the web site for use on a broader scale?

The team decided to create a web site for use by the entire university community <*http://www.lib.uconn.edu/copyright/*>, but recognized that some topics fell well beyond the library's purview. As such, the primary focus was on general copyright information and library services, with the understanding that the library could reach out to other service units and academic departments at the university at a later date. The team envisioned a modular web site that would be flexible enough to allow the addition of pages and cross-links that would accommodate new services, keep up with rapid changes in the copyright environment, and address a variety of user needs.

Using information from the environmental scan and the library staff survey, the team created a detailed outline of potential topics, noting places where outside input would eventually be needed. The outline was amended and approved by the university's counsel. Sketches for potential web-site organization began at the same time. These combined activities helped the team organize content, identify and prioritize issues, and map relationships between concepts.

Armed with the outline and sketches, the team worked with a library applications developer to create a template for the site's general appearance and navigation. Figure 1 shows a sample of the basic template. Over the next several weeks, one team member and the applications developer established site-wide templates, cascading style sheets, time-saving code-entry procedures, and documentation that would facilitate site-wide changes and ensure consistency. They also negotiated details related to the underlying organization and management of files, and fine tuned script-based navigation features such as the search box and drop-down menus.

As another timesaver, the team contacted several institutions and requested permission to adapt information, presentation, or structure of their copyright web sites for the University of Connecticut Libraries' site. In this way, the team could avoid starting from scratch. Over time, it was explained, editing to reflect local practices and policies, as well as legal counsel's input, would eliminate overt similarities or outright lifting. Several institutions kindly gave their permission to use elements of their sites.[2] Today's resulting content is a combination of original and researched content, pre-existing university library policies, and content originally created at other sites.

During its development, the site resided in a test directory. Library staff and interested parties had access to the URL and were welcome to comment at any time, but were asked not to distribute the URL or use it in public settings. In October 2006, the team moved the site into its public directory for a "soft" rollout. The team held a series of open meetings to introduce the web site to library staff. Staff members were then asked to use it in day-to-day transactions, share the URL as appropriate, and send further feedback about real-life experiences using the site. The formal release occurred in January

FIGURE 1. Image of a Sample Page Template

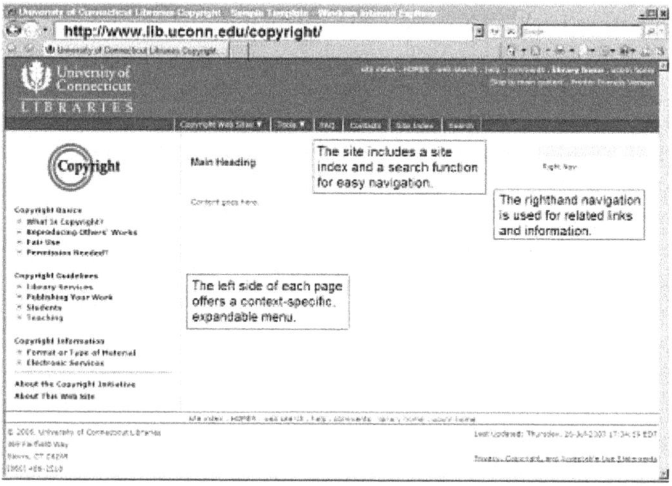

Used with permission.

2007, when the site was the focus of an article in the campus newspaper and the URL was distributed on brochures.

The web site serves a variety of important functions for the library and university. Most obviously, it is a central location where users from across the university (and beyond) can get useful and authoritative information about copyright that will answer many basic questions that arise in their day-to-day work. Beyond this, it provides a level of comfort and security to library staff to know that they can refer users to the site or rely on it themselves when assisting users with copyright questions in their work. Finally, involving staff and stakeholders in the development process allowed the team to address concerns and capitalize on expertise already available in the university. Because they were involved in the development, library staff members are also more likely to trust the information, to think of the resource in their day-to-day work, and to disseminate it further.

WEB-SITE DEVELOPMENT–
WORKING WITH LIBRARY STAFF

One of the first services the team addressed was course reserve. This involved staff from several service units at various UConn libraries.

The main library's reserve unit already had a copyright policy that other service units followed to some degree or another, but the policy had not been substantively renewed or updated in several years. Reserve handles copyright issues on a daily basis, gets frequent questions from faculty, and must regularly explain how US copyright law relates to reserve activities. Also, the proliferation of electronic resources used for reserve had raised new questions. The team undertook a complete overhaul of the policy statement, assembling relevant readings and sample policies from other institutions. Reserve staff brought their daily experience to the process and provided invaluable perspective and recommendations. The end product was a more comprehensive and up-to-date policy that better reflected the staff's work experience and answered many faculty questions–such as what could be placed on reserve, how to expedite service, and how the library defines ownership of material placed on reserve–thus freeing staff from this oft-repeated task. Figure 2 shows a screenshot of the Course Reserve Copyright Policy page.

Document Delivery/Interlibrary Loan (DD/ILL) statements were considerably easier to craft. The guidelines for ILL are more straightforward and less flexible, and therefore less ambiguous. Also, copyright management of DD/ILL requests is handled almost exclusively behind the scenes by DD/ILL staff. The copyright team found that while the guidelines themselves were clear, they were not widely known outside of the DD/ILL office. They needed to be articulated so that DD/ILL users and staff members outside the DD/ILL office would know how copyright requirements might affect their work. It was easy enough to relate the roles and responsibilities in a concise statement that is now available to all. Figure 3 shows a screenshot of the Document Delivery/ Interlibrary Loan Copyright Policy page.

In addition to crafting statements for different library services, the team spent considerable time developing information on "Copyright Basics"–What is copyright? When is something protected by copyright? What is fair use? When do I seek permission? With the basic tools in hand and copyright statements regarding library services, the team assembled topical "index" pages that pointed users to site pages of relevance to faculty and students. For example, the Teaching page pointed instructors to copyright information for course reserve, distance education, and course management software. The team also created cross-reference pages for specific formats–books, images, music, video, microforms, e-text, etc.–and electronic services–digital resources,

FIGURE 2. Image of the Course Reserve Copyright Policy

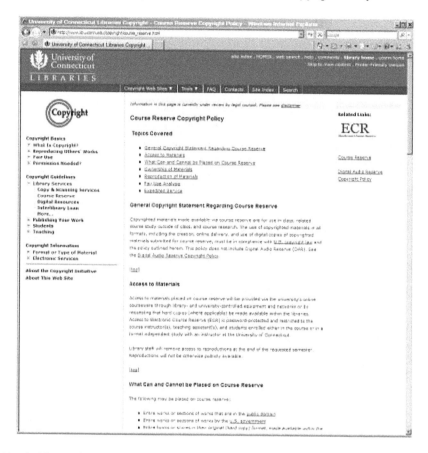

Used with permission.

ePortfolio, institutional repository, course management software, etc. Figure 4 shows a screenshot of the Teaching Index page.

As knowledge of the team's efforts grew among the larger university community, members found themselves fielding questions from far-flung members of that community. These may lead to a future page of exemplars or "scenarios" as object lessons. Examples of some of the more interesting or challenging questions include the following:

• A faculty member asked if she could show her class an episode of a popular talk show that she had taped herself.

FIGURE 3. Image of the Document Delivery/Interlibrary Loan Copyright Policy

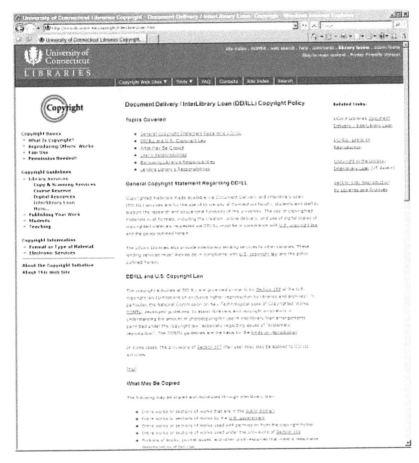

Used with permission.

- A graduate student wanted to know what his rights and obligations were to the university for software he had written for a class project, but that he thought had potential commercial value.
- A music major wondered if he could upload recordings of university music ensembles in which he had performed to ePortfolio, for use by his advisors, instructors, and potential employers.
- An instructor asked if he needed permission to translate a copyrighted work, or to publish that translation.

- A teaching assistant wanted to show her class the work of former students as examples of how to construct a well-written argument.
- A faculty member wanted to create a string of movie clips to put on electronic course reserve.

In addition to copyright, many of these questions spilled over into the areas of university policy, plagiarism, patents and contract law–topics all well beyond the purview of the copyright team's intended purpose. Still, these matters clearly were related, and users were in need of an-

FIGURE 4. Image of the Teaching Index Page

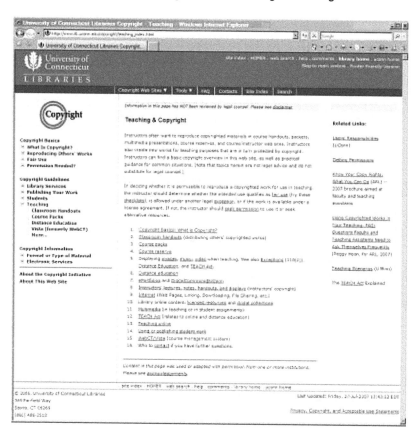

Used with permission.

swers and clarifications. The team found itself in the midst of a larger picture where questions could only be answered using a combination of tools and resources.

GESTALT–
THE WHOLE IS GREATER THAN THE SUM OF ITS PARTS

The Copyright Project Team is just one of several related and synergistic activities the University of Connecticut Libraries have pursued in recent years in response to internal and external demands and to the libraries' perceptions of the future of academic libraries. Others include a scholarly communications initiative, an author's addendum and informational brochure, an electronic resource management database (particularly regarding a staff/public interface for license information), and an institutional repository. All of these activities, resources, and tools support one another in an ongoing way and have a cumulative effect on the university environment that is greater than any of them could be as a standalone.

At the recent ACRL conference, members of the project team participated in a poster session *<http://www.lib.uconn.edu/copyright/presentations.html>* detailing their work over the two years of the team's existence. Presenters found themselves repeatedly asked if the University of Connecticut had these other tools or additional support from the university. Visitors to the session remarked that they had one or another of these resources, but not all, and that through work on the one they were becoming aware that they needed expertise in all of these areas to effectively respond to demands of their users.

Members of the Copyright Project Team have been involved in all of these projects as they have developed, both because of their roles on the copyright team and because they use the tools in their areas of primary responsibility. The copyright team worked with the institutional repository team and university counsel to develop copyright statements for authors placing materials in the repository. One member of the copyright team is also a member of the scholarly communications team, representing copyright interests to that team, and was instrumental in developing an informational brochure for authors about retaining their copyrights. Working in their capacities as selectors and service providers, members of the copyright team gave specifications and offered feedback to electronic-services librarians on an electronic resource management database that provides information to staff on licenses and acceptable uses. The simultaneous coordination and pursuit of all these activities highlighted the relationships between them and added momentum to the libraries' overarching agenda of transforming scholarly communications.

NEXT STEPS

In May 2007, the Copyright Project Team gave its final report to the library's leadership. As a result of the project team's recommendation, a new, permanent copyright team was charged to continue the work begun by the project team. One project team member will stay on permanently, another rotated off, and the third will stay on for one year to allow for transition. Three new members were added, including two from outside the university libraries. The new team will balance its activities to address a variety of constituents.

First and foremost, the team will continue to develop and refine library copyright policies to reflect changes in the law, university policy, and best practice, and to ensure that affected library staff and users of those library services are informed as to their rights and responsibilities. There will be ongoing consultations with affected parties to maintain stakeholder buy in and awareness of the issues.

Second, and related to policy development and dissemination, the web site remains central to the team's work. The new team will further assess, populate, refine, and promote the library copyright web resource in order to increase its utility, keep up with the fast pace of copyright law developments, and provide guidance for copyright issues at the university. The team especially plans reach out to other service and academic units at the university in order to facilitate discussion and bring more links or content under the umbrella of the library's copyright web site.

Third, outreach and training will be an ongoing focus for the new team, both in the library and to selected groups in the university. The team will develop or procure additional educational workshops and materials in order to increase the university community's awareness of rights, responsibilities, and strategies for approaching copyright. Such outreach will continue to foster relationships and partnerships at the university and beyond. It will also help to identify, create, and promote new copyright resources, lead to more pronounced and cohesive articulation of university expectations regarding copyright, and identify further actions to promote discussion in the larger university community.

Finally, the library has proposed the creation of a university-wide copyright committee with a library representative on the committee. The library's copyright team will work to coordinate its efforts with that committee and serve as a resource, with hopes of maximizing the library's investment to-date in its copyright initiative. If the university launches its own copyright web site, the library's site might be retired, or perhaps the university will consider adopting or taking over the library's site for a broader purpose. In either case, the library is positioned to be an integral part of any university-wide initiative.

CONCLUSION

The past two years have been busy, with the result that the members of the Copyright Project Team have built a valuable and authoritative resource for the university community. The importance of outreach to library staff and university stakeholders cannot be overstated. Public events, such as forums, open meetings, and advertised rollouts of a new web site or service are important milestones that raise awareness and keep stakeholders engaged. Throughout the process, the library has established itself as a leader on copyright issues for the university.

The new copyright team has an opportunity to build on the library's recent successes. Persistent news stories about copyright and intellectual-property battles and the frequency of visits to the University of Connecticut Libraries copyright web site illustrate that there is, and will continue to be, interest in and need for ongoing engagement.

NOTES

1. The University of Connecticut Libraries, "Strategic Plan 2005-2010," The University of Connecticut Libraries, http://www.lib.uconn.edu/about/administration/strategic/plan2010.doc.

2. The following institutions generously permitted the University of Connecticut Libraries to draw from content and design of their copyright sites: Brown University; Purdue University; Syracuse University; the University of California, Los Angeles; the University of Minnesota; and Washington State University.

BIBLIOGRAPHY

All web sites were accessed on 30 May 2007 unless otherwise specified.

Getting Started

Association of American Universities. *Campus Copyright Rights and Responsibilities: A Basic Guide to Policy Considerations*. n.p.: Association of American Universities, 2005. *http://aaupnet.org/aboutup/issues/Campus _Copyright.pdf.*

Association of Research Libraries. *Know Your Copy Rights: Using Copyrighted Works in Academic Settings*. Washington DC: Association of Research Libraries, [2007]. *http://www.knowyourcopyrights.org/.*

Crews, Kenneth D. et al. *Copyright Law for Librarians and Educators: Creative Strategies and Practical Solutions*. 2d ed. Chicago: American Library Association, 2006.

Lipinski, Tomas A. *The Complete Copyright Liability Handbook for Librarians and Educators*. New York: Neal-Schuman, 2006.

U.S. Copyright Office. *Copyright. http://www.copyright.gov/.*

Model Copyright Web Sites in Higher Education

Brown University. *Copyright and Fair Use. http://www.brown.edu/Administration/Copyright/index.html.*

Hoon, Peggy E. *Tutorial Series: Copyright Ownership, Copyright Use, Plagiarism, [and] Licensing Guidelines*. Raleigh, NC: Scholarly Communication Center of the NCSU Libraries, 2003. *http://www.lib.ncsu.edu/scc/tutorial/.*

North Carolina State University. *Scholarly Communication Center. http://www.lib.ncsu.edu/scc/main.html.* With Peggy E. Hoon, J.D., Scholarly Communication Librarian and Special Assistant to the Provost for Copyright Administration, and Annis Barbee, M.A., Scholarly Communication and Information Specialist.

Purdue University. *University Copyright Office. http://www.lib.purdue.edu/uco/index.html.*

Stanford University Libraries. *Copyright & Fair Use. http://fairuse.stanford.edu/.*

Syracuse University Library. *Copyright. http://library.syr.edu/copyright/.*

UCLA Library. *UCLA Copyright Policy. http://www2.library.ucla.edu/copyright/index.cfm.*

University of Connecticut Libraries. *Copyright. http://www.lib.uconn.edu/copyright/.*

University of Minnesota Libraries. *Copyright Information & Education. http://www.lib.umn.edu/copyright/.*

University of Texas at Austin. *The Copyright Crash Course.* http://www.utsystem.edu/ogc/Intellectualproperty/cprtindx.htm. With Georgia K. Harper, J.D., Scholarly Communications Advisor, University Libraries.

Washington State University, University Publishing. *Copyright. http://publishing.wsu.edu/copyright/.*

Useful Tools or Hot Topics

Association of Research Libraries. *Copyright & Intellectual Property Policies: Orphan Works. http://www.arl.org/pp/ppcopyright/orphan/index.shtml.*

Bailey, Charles W., Jr. *Open Access Bibliography.* Washington DC: Association of Research Libraries, 2005. *http://info.lib.uh.edu/cwb/oab.pdf.*

Copyright Clearance Center. *Copyright.com. http://www.copyright.com/.*

"Copyright Decision Map." In *Copyright Information & Education* at the University of Minnesota Libraries. *http://www.lib.umn.edu/copyright/map.phtml.*

Creative Commons. http://creativecommons.org/.

Hirtle, Peter B. "Copyright Term and the Public Domain in the United States." In *Copyright Information Center* at Cornell University. *http://www.copyright.cornell.edu/training/Hirtle_Public_Domain.htm.*

"Section 108 Study Group." In the *Library of Congress. http://www.loc.gov/section108/.*

SHERPA/RoMEO. "Publisher Copyright Policies & Self-archiving." In *SHERPA. http://www.sherpa.ac.uk/romeo.php.*

SPARC. "Author Rights: Using the SPARC Author Addendum to Secure Your Rights as the Author of a Journal Article." In *SPARC: Scholarly Publishing and Academic Resources Coalition. http://www.arl.org/sparc/author/addendum.html.*

"TEACH Act Toolkit: An Online Resource for Understanding Copyright and Distance Education." In *Scholarly Communication Center* at North Carolina State University (NCSU). *http://www.lib.ncsu.edu/scc/legislative/teachkit/.*

Textbooks 101:
Textbook Collection
at the University of Minnesota

Caroline Crouse

BACKGROUND

One of the major financial demands on undergraduate students is the need to buy standardized materials for their classes, particularly course packets and textbooks. The prices of textbooks increased by 186% from 1986-2005, with students paying an average of $898 for two semesters of books at four-year public universities (US Government Accountability Office, 2005). Two major reasons for these high prices are the publishers' use of "bundling" the textbook with supplemental instructional materials and the frequent revision cycles of texts.

Traditionally, academic libraries do not purchase textbooks for student use. In 2005, Hseih and Runner (2005) indicated that 61% of colleges surveyed have a specific policy against the collection of textbooks, while only 14% have a similar policy for leisure reading, another popular collection material for undergraduates. In order to provide better services to the undergraduate population, several university libraries, including the University of North Carolina–Chapel Hill (UNC) and Texas Tech University, purchase textbooks for large-enrollment classes and place them on reserve. Joe A. Hewitt, the University Librarian at UNC, describes the program there as "very popular" (Joe A Hewitt, personal communication, 24 March 2004). Other institutions, such as the University of Wisconsin–Madison, use special funds to purchase multiple copies of textbooks to place on reserve (Friends of the University of Wisconsin Libraries 2005).

In 2003, the Undergraduate Initiatives Council at the University of Minnesota libraries conducted a series of focus groups and interviews designed to help the libraries better understand undergraduate students and to identify and prioritize potential initiatives that would make an impact on student learning. One need identified through these assessments was a textbook collection; this need was again mentioned in undergraduate focus groups conducted in Spring 2005.

The University of Minnesota Libraries' collection policy currently excludes "[m]aterials that are of purely temporary and recreational interest, which are acquired only if they are needed to support identified instructional or research programs" (University of Minnesota Libraries 1996). Textbooks, which are often replaced with new editions, are generally classed as "temporary" materials in this exclusion. Although some selection areas in the U of M libraries do purchase textbooks if requested by faculty members, textbooks are generally not added to the collection.[1]

LITERATURE REVIEW

Surprisingly little has been written about collecting assigned textbooks. In a 1990 article, Robert Sommer and Marina Estabrook discuss the rising price of textbooks and the lack of faculty awareness of these prices. The conclusion of the article indicates that the library may need to play a role in educating faculty on these costs, but mostly to avoid purchasing unnecessary texts for the library (Sommer and Estabrook 1990). Jeremy Sayles addresses the benefits of collecting textbooks in a college library and recommends that textbooks be evaluated as regular monographs rather than adopting a specific "no textbooks" policy. The article, however, focuses on textbooks for general overviews of a subject or as recommended reading for specific courses, rather than required texts for courses (Sayles 1994).

In 2005, Cynthia Hseih and Rhonelle Runner created a web survey distributed to two library listservs, as well as reviewing thirty academic library collection development policies. Of the ninety-nine valid responses to the web survey, sixty-one percent reported that their library has a specific "no-textbooks" policy, with the leading justification being budgetary limitations (32%). Other leading reasons for these policies were "students should purchase own textbooks" and that the collection is "too difficult to maintain" (Hsieh and Runner 2005).

PROJECT DESCRIPTION

In order to meet student demands for textbooks, the Undergraduate Initiatives Council at the University of Minnesota organized a pilot project beginning in the Spring 2005 semester to collect textbooks in several subject areas. Student workers created a list of all texts used for classes in three departments: Ecology, Evolution and Behavior (EEB), Fisheries and Wildlife (FW), and Sociology. If the library already owned the texts used for a class, these copies were placed on library reserve. If the library did not own a copy of the text, the instructors were encouraged to place a personal copy or an unneeded copy designated for teaching assistants on reserve. Contacts to the department went either through the subject librarian to individual instructors (EEB and FW) or through the coordinator for textbooks within the department (Sociology). Since the donation of texts was voluntary, the library did not receive all of the assigned texts for the department; however, many faculty were willing to donate or lend copies of the texts to the library for this project. The ratio of books donated for each department is shown below.

The project was coordinated by one system-wide librarian who was in charge of compiling a list of texts used during the semester, advertising the project, working with reserves to arrange book access, and assessing the project. Subject liaisons were in charge of the contact with the departments about the program and coordinating donations with individual faculty members.

The pilot was expanded in the 2005-2006 academic year to include five departments in Fall 2005 and eight departments in Spring 2006. In addition, $2,000 was allocated to support purchase of texts that the departments could not supply. The selection criteria for purchased books were lower-division courses, high enrollment, and recommendation by the subject librarian. Approximately twenty titles were purchased using these funds.

RESULTS

Although the circulation rates were somewhat lower than expected from the textbook project, these books received much more use than most titles in the library collection. The average circulation of the textbooks on reserve was 4.35 times for Spring 2005, 3.27 times for Fall 2005, and 3.82 times in Spring 2006. In contrast, the Wilson General Collection Analysis (Crocker, Friesen, and Johnson 2005) indicates that items in the collection in the Humanities and Social Sciences Library have circulated an average of 2.5 times over the lifetime of the item. Based on an edition cycle of 3.5 years, the textbooks on reserve will circulate an average of 13.35 times in their lifetime, a substantially higher rate than the typical book in the collection (US Government Accountability Office 2005).

ADVERTISING

In addition to asking professors to announce the reserve texts in the syllabus and in class, the libraries placed advertising posters for the program in the departments and the libraries in early April 2006. These posters correlated with a substantial increase in the use of the texts, most notably from the Sociology texts, which increased circulation by 700% in the final month of the semester. Circulation rose by an average of 239%

Spring 2005

Department	Number of texts at the bookstore	Number of texts on reserve	Number of circulations	Average circulation
Fisheries and Wildlife	7	6	16	2.67
EEB	8	8	14	1.75
Sociology	71	12	83	6.92
Total	86	26	113	4.346154

Fall 2005

Department	Number of texts at the bookstore	Number of texts on reserve	Number of circulations	Average circulation
Fisheries and Wildlife	7	4	15	3.75
EEB	9	8	29	3.22
Sociology	49	33	26	.72
Applied Economics	16	7	31	4.43
Food Science	16	11	105	9.55
Total	97	63	206	3.27

across departments between April and May. The small advertisement seems to have substantially raised awareness of the project.

STUDENT FEEDBACK

The system-wide librarian prepared an on-line survey on the pilot project, which library liaisons distributed it to the represented departments, and asked them to send it out to students in all classes in both Fall

Spring 2006

Department	Number of texts at the bookstore	Number of texts on reserve	Number of circulations	Average circulation
Fisheries and Wildlife	4	4	5	1.25
EEB	6	5	15	3
Sociology	66	27	35	1.3
Applied Economics	31	20	132	6.6
Food Science	17	11	48	4.36
Anthropology	122	87	317	3.64
Finance	30	17	110	6.47
Economics	44	26	94	3.61
Total[2]	320	191	730	3.82

2005 and Spring 2006. The distribution and response rate was quite low in both semesters: enrollment in the classes for which the Libraries held books on reserve was 4,796 in Fall 2005 and 8,731 in Spring 2006. However, the surveys were visited only 86 times with 57 returns in Fall 2005, a response rate of .65%. In Spring 2006, the survey was visited 66 times, with 47 completes, a response rate of .71%. Although the response rates were relatively good, the low number of visits can most likely be attributed to lack of distribution to classes.

The student feedback from the survey was mixed. Although 64% of respondents indicated that the program is "valuable," 71% of the respondents never used the texts. Lack of awareness about the program seems to be one major reason that students did not use the texts. Forty percent (n = 17) of the students reported not knowing about the program, and 29% (n = 12) stated that they would have found the project valuable had they known about it. The vast majority of students who knew of the program heard through their professors, indicating that announcements on syllabi may be the most effective means of publicizing the availability of textbooks.

	January-April Circulations	Total Circulations (January-May)	% increase
Fisheries and Wildlife	4	5	125%
EEB	15	26	173%
Sociology	5	35	700%
Applied Economics	80	137	171%
Food Science	31	48	154%
Anthropology	201	355	177%
Finance	60	114	190%
Economics	57	124	218%

BENEFITS OF TEXTBOOK COLLECTIONS

Besides providing needed materials to students, this pilot project had several benefits, including positive public relations with students and an outreach opportunity for libraries. By reviewing the syllabus for individual classes, liaisons learned more about the classes offered in their departments and were able to connect with faculty members.

"I felt that it helped me learn more about the curriculum, who is teaching what, and what texts they were using . . . As often happens, my initial e-mail [to faculty members] led to other questions about library services, which is always good." –Julie Kelly

"As a liaison, it provided a connection point to my faculty, many of whom I had not had the opportunity to work with before. Those who responded to my emails were unanimous in their support for the program. . . . It helped me to get a better handle on what classes were being taught in my departments, which is always useful for collection development and reference assistance purposes."–Linda Eells

Additionally, the libraries were able to highlight this program in a campus-wide taskforce addressing the high costs of textbooks. One of the fi-

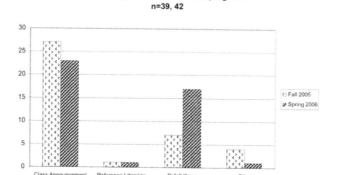

How did you find out about the program?
n=39, 42

nal recommendations of this group was that the pilot project should continue as a regular practice, with faculty members negotiating with publishers for an extra copy of the text for the library when agreeing to adopt a text.

CONCLUSIONS

Overall, the textbook collection pilot project at the University of Minnesota Libraries was a success; books circulated far more often than is normally the case for a typical monographs within the collection, even assuming the fact that the textbook will be in the collection for only 3-4 years. Additionally, student, faculty, and librarian feedback indicates that collecting the textbooks was extremely positive and represents a strong public relations component to the program. This analysis points to the fact that collecting textbooks through faculty donations and a small amount of monetary assistance from the library is beneficial to the patrons and library staff, without requiring sacrifices in other areas of the collection budget.

Greater advertising and awareness of the program will most likely increase usage of the texts. While the posters advertising the program increased the use of the collection, the majority of respondents to the student survey indicated that they found out about the project through their professors. In all likelihood, a combination of advertising from the library, along with an announcement of the program from professors, both orally and on the syllabus, would improve the usage.

One major challenge to this is the timing; often the collection of books for the library occurred just before or after the first day of classes, which is essentially too late for announcements on the syllabus. Better communication paths from the departments to the library may improve this planning problem, and faculty members will be asked to communicate their textbook choices to the library as well as to the bookstore. Additionally, a partnership with the bookstore could facilitate the communication about the number of books purchased.

NOTES

1. One exception to this is in the Mathematics library, in which the department and the library cooperate to make all current textbooks for the semester available through reserve circulation. This collection is popular with both faculty and students in the Mathematics department.

2. The departments of Applied Economics, Economics, and Finance had several overlapping texts in Spring 2006. Since there is no way to parse the class for which the book was checked out, some duplication is reflected in the individual subjects. There were a total of 191 unique titles and 730 total circulations during Spring Semester, averaging 3.82 circulations per title.

REFERENCES

Crocker, Francine, Betsy Friesen, and Michael Johnson. (2007). Wilson General Collection Analysis, October 15, 2006 2005 [cited April 24 2007]. Available from https://wiki.lib.umn.edu/Staff/WilsGenAnalysis.

Friends of the University of Wisconsin Libraries. (2005). Parents Enrichment Fund improves study space, provides textbooks. *Friends of the Library Magazine 45*(1).

Hsieh, Cynthia, and Rhonelle Runner. (2005). Textbooks, leisure reading, and the academic library. *Library Collections, Acquisitions, & Technical Services, 29*(2): 192-204.

Sayles, Jeremy. (1994). The Textbooks-in College-Libraries Mystery. *College & Undergraduate Libraries, 1*(1):81-93.

Sommer, Robert, and Marina Estabrook. (1990). Textbook prices and their implications for Social Sciences Librarians. *Behavioral & Social Sciences*, Librarian 9 (1):29-37.

U.S. Government Accountability Office. (2005). College textbooks: Enhanced offerings appear to drive recent price increases.

University of Minnesota Libraries. 2007. University of Minnesota Libraries Twin Cities Campus Selection Policy 1996 [cited April 12 2007]. Available from http://staff.lib.umn.edu//cdm/ppf/selection97.phtml?sectionList=%2Fcdm%2Fppf%2Fselection97.phtml&sectionAZ=http%3A%2F%2Fwww.aaup.org.

INTERLIBRARY LOAN
& DOCUMENT DELIVERY

IFLA Guidelines
for Best Practice for Interlibrary Loan
and Document Delivery

Joan E. Stein

INTRODUCTION

In March of 2006, the International Federation of Library Associations' Standing Committee on Resource Sharing and Document Delivery compiled, approved, and released a new document to assist resource sharing departments world-wide with working to their highest potential. This new document is the *IFLA Guidelines for Best Practices for Interlibrary Loan and Document Delivery*.[i] It is the hope of the IFLA Document Delivery and Resource Sharing Section that libraries around the world will find it a useful resource as they seek to continuously improve their resource sharing operations. These guidelines are based on solid research that has been replicated in various countries and they are relevant and applicable to any type of library conducting interlibrary loan and document delivery services.[ii] Before examining the guidelines at length, it is important to look at the process of the development of "best practices" in general.

Best practices come from the benchmarking process. Benchmarking can be defined as comparing and measuring your policies, practices, philosophies, and performance against those of high-performing organizations or services anywhere in the world. Everyone recognizes good service when they experience it. Many interlibrary loan practitioners have wondered if they were providing the best possible service to their service users and, if not, how things could be improved. Benchmarking provides service managers with the techniques to find out. Benchmarking investigations will provide the necessary insight into exactly what practices, processes, and procedures make a high-performing operation work so well. Librarians can then begin to introduce these practices into their own service. Benchmarking has several benefits:

- It supports a culture of change and of continuous improvement.
- It supports a learning organization.
- It helps to break established patterns of behavior and thought that may no longer be productive. "Because we've always done it this

way" is a poor reason to retain practices that may be contributing to poor service to customers. When service operations are customer-focused rather than process-focused, both the service and the customer benefit.
* It provides models for excellence.

It is important to understand why a library should consider implementing "best practices" in their own interlibrary loan and document delivery services. Many service managers feel that their practices, policies, and procedures have served them and their staff well for years or that they have trained their users to know what to expect from the service. Examining some data on customer service in general may help to address these attitudes.

Two decades ago, a customer experience research consultancy called TARP Worldwide was commissioned to conduct studies of customer services for several large and well-know corporations.[iii] Their results were sobering:

* The average business only hears from 4% of its unhappy customers. Of the 96% who don't bother to complain, 25% have "serious" problems. In other words, one complaint equals 24 others, six of which are serious.
* Complainers (4%) are more likely to stay with a company than are non-complainers. Complaints tell you what needs to be fixed in the system, and timely problem resolution has a positive impact.
* About 60% of the complainers will stay if their problems are resolved. Ninety-five percent of them will stay if they feel the problem was resolved quickly.
* Customers with a problem will tell between 10 and 20 other people about it.
* Customers who have had a problem resolved by a company will tell about five other people about their treatment.

It is important to consider these numbers when you think about your own service. No interlibrary loan and document delivery service can afford to ignore them because these findings apply equally to all services and affect how service users perceive and react to our manner of service provision. This is particularly important these days, now that our users can get many of their resources directly from the Internet.

- TARP also promulgated what they call the "85/15 Rule." This rule holds that 85% of service delivery problems are caused by poor systems or processes; only 15% are caused by individuals providing the service.

In other words, if good people are put in a poor system, the system will win 85% of the time. Looked at another way, by solving system problems, a service can solve 85% of its problems. Each person and each process has critical positive or negative potential. These findings provide libraries with powerful motivation to apply best practices in our own service. This finding is also useful in gaining staff acceptance of changes because it doesn't fix blame on any one person's performance.

Once we have the motivation to seek change, where should an interlibrary loan service look for benchmarking partners? Consider organizing a site visit to other libraries that have high-performing interlibrary loan and document delivery services. Another resource might be other libraries that have conducted their own benchmarking and best practices studies and published their results. It is important to also consider looking outside of the library world for benchmarking partners. Consider each process involved in the interlibrary loan and document delivery process. UPS or Fedex would make excellent benchmarking partners for shipping procedures. For quick supply of goods and services, consider an organization like Amazon.com, but perhaps closer to home.

The benefit of the *IFLA Guidelines for Best Practices for Interlibrary Loan and Document Delivery*[iv] is that they distill the research results from several studies in different countries and provide you with research-based recommendations. What the committee found in compiling these guidelines was that the various studies all had similar findings, which reinforces their validity and usefulness. The *IFLA Guidelines* are based on a combination of studies conducted in several countries and include:

- From the USA: the 1998 Association of Research Libraries' (ARL) interlibrary loan and document delivery study, conducted by Mary Jackson
- A national study from Australia
- A study conducted in the Nordic countries, and
- A study from New Zealand[v]

Because Jackson's ARL study was a major influence on the studies conducted by the other countries, we will examine the list of best practices that resulted from the ARL study.[vi] The following data has been provided courtesy of Mary Jackson. The ARL Interlibrary Loan Study looked at four major performance measures:

- Direct cost
- Turnaround time
- Fill rates, and
- User satisfaction

By analyzing the results of the multiple item data collection instrument, the ARL study was able to pinpoint high-performing borrowing and lending operations in comparison to their peers. Once these high-performers were identified, site visits were made to each institution to study what practices, processes, policies and procedures contributed definitively to their high performance as lenders or borrowers.

The ARL study identified the following practices that characterize high-performing borrowing operations:

- Maximize use of technology
- Use a single messaging system
- Maintain a paperless office
- Send articles directly to patrons
- Are willing to pay lenders/suppliers
- Use staff with interest in technology
- Have directors that support the activity

High-performing lending operations were found to have the following practices:

- Encourage borrowers to use their library first
- View lending as a business
- Maximize use of technology to speed the process wherever possible
- Ship materials via Ariel, fax, or expedited methods
- Oversee the entire process (mailroom to billing)
- Check the stacks for materials only one time
- Charge for sending books or articles
- Accept credit cards and IFLA vouchers as well as checks, and
- Have directors that support the activity

When the Standing Committee on Resource Sharing and Document Delivery was selecting and compiling the *IFLA Guidelines for Best Practices for Interlibrary Loan and Document Delivery*, the findings from the ARL study were combined with those from Australia, New Zealand, and the Nordic countries. Discussions were held at the IFLA Conference in Oslo, Norway, via email, and at the committee's 2006 Midwinter Business Meeting in Rome, Italy, where the final draft of the Guidelines was approved.

These Guidelines are divided into General Recommendations, Staff, Technology, Users, Recommendations for the Requesting Library, and Recommendations for the Supplying Library. The Guidelines advocate the following *General Recommendations*:

- Streamline the process within your own library.
- Define performance indicators for service levels and turnaround time and monitor performance against them.
- Evaluate routines and change them accordingly. Are they user-centered?
- Reduce the number of hands through which the requests are passing.
- All requests should be handled in one electronic system, preferably with the ability to interoperate with other ILL/DD systems.
- Keep statistics to suit national monitoring schemes and local needs.
- Make holdings available on Union Catalogues and keep them up-to-date, with an indication of availability for resource sharing.
- Explore reciprocal arrangements.

In terms of *Staff*, who are a crucial component of the service, the Guidelines recommend the services:

- Use the expertise of skilled staff members. Experienced staff can often tell how the system needs to be changed.
- Staff members should continuously be able to develop competencies and be trained in using new tools and resources.
- Encourage the exchange of experience at the local or international level.

The appropriate use of *Technology* is a very important component of best practices for resource sharing and document delivery, particularly in regards to speed of processing:

- Hardware and software must be up-to-date.
- Encourage or require users to submit requests electronically.
- Give the end users the ability to check the status of their requests online; this is particularly important to users and to service staff since having this capability cuts down on the number of times users need to contact the service for this information.
- Handle all communication about requests electronically.

As mentioned earlier, meeting *Users'* needs and expectations will make or break a service so it is important to include the user in these *Guidelines*:

- Focus on the needs and preferences of the end user.
- Perform user surveys on a regular basis.

Just because the users of library interlibrary loan and document delivery services often don't have anywhere else to turn to obtain needed materials doesn't mean that the way that service is provided isn't important. If users consider a library's ILL service to be poor, they can still tell others to avoid using our service or make complaints that affect a service's reputation. A library's reputation as a service provider is one of its best assets.

The Committee endorses the following *Recommendations for the Requesting Library*:

- ILL should be an integrated part of the library's service to users; it should be accessible easily from online databases and from the library catalog.
- Introduce new technology in all processes.
- Do not limit unreasonably the number of requests from users.
- Involve the end user as much as possible in requesting.
- Give end users access to union catalogues with requesting facilities.
- Process requests from end users quickly.
- Use experienced staff to select supplying libraries according to speed of service and cost.
- Adhere to the conditions set by suppliers and treat material with care.
- Offer IFLA vouchers as payment.
- Deliver the material as fast as possible to the end user.
    - Send copies electronically if at all possible.
    - Check speed of supply on a regular basis.

Recommendations for the Supplying Library include:

- Use experienced staff to collect requested material from the collections in order to minimize mistakes.
- Use the fastest delivery methods.
- Try to satisfy requests in the best possible way.
- Be sure that license agreements for e-resources will allow ILL/DD.
- Create online order forms and/or interoperate with other ILL/DD systems.
- Make library's lending policies available on web site and in policy directories.
- Accept IFLA vouchers.

The *Guidelines for Best Practice* are a solid foundation from which to work but they are not written in stone. Each library's or consortium's priorities may vary, depending on the needs and expectations of the institution, the consortium, or the users. Some examples of additional items would be:

- Design user-friendly procedures.
- Understand and meet users' needs–conduct user studies (surveys, focus groups, etc.).
- Use an ILL request management software package.
- Place regular borrowing requests with potential lenders the same day they are received in the office. (Problem requests may take longer.)
- Take complaints seriously and learn from them.

How should a library go about implementing the new *IFLA Guidelines for Best Practice for Interlibrary Loan and Document Delivery?* Don't be overwhelmed by the length of the list. Take incremental steps, focusing at first on some area that is problematic in operation. Making process improvements to streamline ILL workflow is another important step. One very productive method of doing this is to flowchart every single step in the interlibrary lending and borrowing processes. The creation of this flowchart will provide the opportunity to question procedures, to identify redundant or out-of-date processes, and give a good start on streamlining processes. Another approach to implementing these guidelines is to create a small group of libraries which agree to put them into practice together, or to introduce them into an existing group, such as a library consortium to which the library already belongs. Some of these guidelines may be cultural since the countries where they have been developed, and in which the research was conducted, have been similar in terms of infrastructure, economy, and other factors. Developing countries may find the need to adapt these guidelines or to conduct studies of their own to create relevant guidelines for their services. The next steps for the IFLA Standing Committee on Resource Sharing and Document Delivery are to disseminate and promote the use of these guidelines, advocating for and representing them to our colleagues worldwide, and educating our interlibrary loan colleagues on their use. Committee members plan to spread the word and lead by practice and invite other libraries to join in this effort.

NOTES

i. IFLA Document Delivery and Resource Sharing Section members. 2006. "Guidelines for Best Practice in Interlibrary Loan and Document Delivery". http://www.ifla.org/VI/2/p3/Guidelines_ILDD-en.htm

ii. See: Jackson, Mary. 1998. *Measuring the Performance of Interlibrary Loan Operations in North American Research & College Libraries: results of a study funded by the Andrew W. Mellon Foundation.* Washington D.C.: Association of Research Libraries.; Vattulainen, Pentti. 2001. "Nordic Study of Performance Measurement of Interlibrary Loan and Document Delivery Services", Nordic University and Research Libraries. http://www.nrl.fi/nvbf/versio1.5.pdf; Cullen, Rowena. 2004. " Interlibrary loan services in New Zealand: an environmental scan and national survey; subtitle: a report commissioned by the National Library of New Zealand and the Joint Standing Committee on Interloan". http://opac.lianza.org.nz/cgi-bin/koha/opac-detail.pl?bib = 60; Joint Standing Committee on Interloan. 2005. "Interloans Best Practice Handbook: March 2005 with Addenda May 2005 and August 2005". http://opac.lianza.org.nz/cgi-bin/koha/opac-detail.pl?bib = 17; Ruthven, Tom and Susan Magnay. 2002. "Top Performing Interlending Operations: Results of the Australian Benchmarking Study" in Interlending and Document Supply, v. 30, no. 2, pp 73-79. http://www.nla.gov.au/nla/staffpaper/2001/ruthven1.html; National Resource Sharing Working Group. 2001. "Interlibrary Loan and Document Delivery Benchmarking Study", National Library of Australia. http://www.nla.gov.au/initiatives/nrswg/illdd_rpt.pdf

iii. Unpublished material from Xerox' Total Quality Management training documents. No date.

iv. ibid

v. See endnote ii above.

vi. Jackson, Mary. 1998. *Measuring the Performance of Interlibrary Loan Operations in North American Research & College Libraries: results of a study funded by the Andrew W. Mellon Foundation.* Washington D.C.: Association of Research Libraries.

Books-on-Demand Pilot Program: An Innovative "Patron-centric" Approach to Enhance the Library Collection

Michelle Foss

SHRINKING COLLECTION BUDGETS
AND INCREASING ILL REQUESTS

The collection budget at the University of Florida Libraries has been flat the past few years despite the increase in new degree programs offered at the university. With the creation of new academic programs, the ILL borrowing and document delivery units have experienced an increase in ILL requests from both on and off campus. At the University of Florida Libraries, from January 1 to September 14, 2006, the Interlibrary Loan Office received a total of 17,814 borrowing requests, with 7,242 of these requests being for books that are not available in the UF libraries. With the high number of loan requests being submitted by UF patrons and the average cost of $27.83 per transaction, based on the ARL Interlibrary Loan study (Jackson, 1998), would the cost of purchasing a book be cheaper than processing an ILL request if the item was requested more than once? Despite what little literature is available, the trend of purchasing materials requested via ILL rather than submitting an ILL request has emerged. By purchasing ILL requests the patrons contribute in defining the collection. In addition to receiving a purchased book quicker than a traditional ILL request, it is often cheaper to buy than to borrow. Based on this analysis, a proposal was submitted to the University of Florida Libraries administration to create a six-month pilot program with a $15,000 budget allocation for purchasing books that were originally requested via ILL. This pilot project was touted as a "patron-centric" approach to supplement the current collection development program. The proposal also supports 2006-2007 the goals of the George A. Smathers Libraries to:

> build and manage library collections in support of academic programs; and provide timely access to requested material.

This pilot program will also foster a collaborative cross-departmental relationship to better serve the research and academic needs of the UF community.

PATRON-CENTRIC APPROACH
TO ENHANCING THE EXISTING COLLECTION

This approach is based on the Purdue University model (Ward, 2002) and other models in the literature, but tailored to meet the specific demands at the University of Florida libraries. To gain library-wide support for this patron-centric books-on-demand ILL program, an advisory committee comprising collection managers from Science, Special Collections, African Studies, and the Social Sciences was established with the goal to establish criteria for the purchasing of materials. The Advisory Committee identified and established the following criteria for purchasing books:

- Only faculty, graduate students and distance patrons' requests will be considered for purchase
- If requested books are marked as "lost" in the UF library catalog, they will be purchased regardless of the patron status (the ILL office receives 10 requests per week for "lost items" in the collection from UF patrons)
- $150 maximum cost per book. This cost was eventually raised for science books.
- No theses, dissertations, conference proceedings, technical reports
- No textbooks for courses
- Foreign titles are encouraged
- Out of print books and "core" monographs, if scholarly in nature

In addition to the advisory committee's criteria, the ILL unit had to satisfactorily meet the standards of the billing office. The original books-on-demand proposal included the purchasing of books from a variety of book vendors, including Alibris, Amazon, Barnes & Noble using a credit card and OCLC IFM. However, the idea of using a credit card was met with some resistance so the program proceeded with purchases only from Alibris using IFM through the ILLiad system. Using only Alibris for the purchasing of books via the OCLC IFM, monthly statistics allowed for the pilot program to obtain the following statistical information:

- ILL record number
- Title of the book, including the total monthly book count
- Patron: to identify department and status
- Request date of item

- Date shipped from Alibris
- Date received at the University of Florida Libraries ILL Office
- Cost of the book, including total fees for the month which could easily be reconciled by the billing office

Based on the IFM statistics from the last two weeks in December through the end of March, 80 titles were purchased. The majority of purchases were made from graduate student requests, followed by faculty and then undergraduate. The undergraduate requests comprised only titles listed as lost in the UF catalog. Only one title was purchased for a distance patron. Requests by department have also been analyzed. The majority of requests are purchased for the Humanities and Social Sciences. These top five departments for purchase requests include: English, Psychology, History, Sociology and Urban & Regional Planning (Appendix A). When the monthly IFM reports on Alibris purchases were sent to the libraries' collection managers, library administration, and the advisory committee, people commented on the lack of books being purchased for engineering and the sciences. After reviewing the monthly reports and ILL requests from the sciences and engineering patrons, three conclusions were drawn:

1. Science books that are requested are more expensive than the $150 maximum limit
2. Engineering and sciences requests are often for textbooks which are excluded under this pilot program
3. A majority of requests for science and engineering are for articles from core journals

With the goal of adding more engineering and science titles, the advisory committee recommended that the maximum dollar amount be increased for these books.

The turn-around time from the requested date to the date received by the University of Florida Libraries ILL Office averaged ~5 business days. Turn-around time for books sent from the UK or Europe obviously took longer. Unfortunately, Alibris does not always have the lowest cost of the book when compared to Amazon, but Alibris as of now is the only vendor in the WorldCat Resource Sharing (WCRS) using IFM for payment.

Survey results from faculty during and after the pilot projects at Purdue and the University of Wisconsin–Madison (Ward et al., 2003) show a high level of satisfaction regarding the fact that the library purchased items based on requests, and the quick turn-around time in which the book arrived. The University of Florida Libraries ILL Office also plans to conduct a follow-up examination of the items purchased through this program and how many times they circulated once catalogued.

Additional analyses on all relevant statistical data from the IFM reports, ILLiad reports and the returned questionnaire from patrons will be examined.

ADJUSTING THE ILL BORROWING WORKFLOW

The program is managed through the borrowing and document delivery units, and the workflow for this pilot has slightly changed for the staff, with additional steps implemented.

Step 1: The patron submits a book request via ILLiad. The request will first appear either in the borrowing queue, for on-campus patrons, or in the document delivery queue for off-campus patrons. The staff reviews the request to verify it meets the criteria for a purchase. If the item fulfills the requirements and is available via Alibris, then the Alibris symbol (ALBRS) is entered first in the borrowing string. ALBRS is listed first in the string because of the intention to purchase the item, not as a last resort if the request can not be filled by traditional ILL. If the book can not be purchased via ALBRS, additional libraries are added to the borrowing string so the request can route on to the next library as a part of the normal ILL process.

Step 2: If ALBRS is able to fill the request, they respond with a conditional that includes information on the delivery time frame (i.e. if the book is coming from the UK or Europe) and the cost of the book. The University of Florida Libraries has a set maximum cost limit of $50 per request so when a book exceeds this cost the ILL staff update the maximum cost and click "yes" to the conditional.

Step 3: Once the book is purchased, the ILL staff create a provisional record in the library catalog with the note "ILL-On Order." This additional step in the workflow will reduce the chance of the collection manager also making the same purchase, thus avoiding duplicate copies.

Step 4: When the book is received in the ILL office, it is checked in as an ILL book. The purchased book is banded with a different color band than the rest of the ILL books so both library staff and patrons know that it is a purchase. The book will have a two-week check out date with a one-time renewal. Similar to the Purdue model, a bookmark with questions is placed in the book. Four questions are posed to the patron:

1. Did the book arrive on time?
2. Did the patron find the book as a valuable addition to the collection?
3. Does the patron want to check out the book once it's catalogued?
4. Would the patron recommend the book to a colleague?

Question Three asks if patron wants the book to check out again. If this question is marked yes, the book is catalogued as a 24-hour RUSH. Out of 63 responses to this question, 47 patrons (74%) wanted to check out the book once it was catalogued (Appendix B). The ILL staff is responsible for dropping off and picking up the RUSH catalogued book. After retrieving the book from cataloging, the ILL staff informs the patron that the book is ready for checkout. The 24-hr RUSH cataloging, so the patron can check out the book for the normal loan period, is a very popular, value-added service.

While the additional steps are time consuming, the ILL staff manage the entire project and are able to follow the purchasing process from beginning to end.

BENEFITS FOR COLLECTION MANAGERS

Cross-departmental cooperation between collection managers and Interlibrary Loan benefit the library and the patrons. This project comprises materials based on patron requests, identifies existing gaps in the collection, and identifies trends of faculty research. Collection managers place orders for a specific duration of time. All orders must be submitted within this time frame and requests made after the timeframe are put on hold. The books-on-demand pilot, as seen by a few librarians, offer an alternative. One collection manager in the sciences wrote of this pilot program *"this ILL program is able to acquire books during a period when other options are put on hold. I think this is an important acquisition supplement at a time when it is needed most. This acquisition alternative is an option we have not had before and helps fill a gap in time when we traditionally have not been able to order materials."*

The collection managers are sent the IFM purchase report each month during this pilot project. As mentioned previously, this list is broken down by department, status, title of book, purchase cost, and turnaround time.

Another collection manager in the social sciences provided support for this aspect of the pilot with the following comment: *"The ILL purchased materialsare provided with quick turn around time, which is greatly appreciated bythe faculty I serve. After patron ILL use the items go through processing and become a permanent part of our collectionthat has a long term benefit to all of our users."*

EVALUATION OF THE PILOT PROGRAM

This program will evaluate three criteria. The first criterion is to monitor the faculty response to this program by having them fill out a mini-questionnaire at the time of picking up the item. This questionnaire gauges the satisfaction of having the library purchase the requested item, turn-around time frame for the item, usefulness as a permanent addition to the collection, recommending the book to a colleague, and comments. Based on the questionnaire feedback, the majority of the responses are favorable to this pilot program. The second criterion determines how often the item purchased through this service circulates over a two year period. Previous studies (Ward, 2002) have shown that items bought through this service have been circulated more times than traditional acquisitions in the same area of study during the same time frame. The third criterion evaluates who is using this service and why. Statistics can be broken down by department, status of user, department and status combined. Currently, the majority of requests purchased are from graduate students, with faculty requests a distant second, followed by staff and undergraduates. The titles purchased by the undergraduate population were for titles that are lost in the library catalog. There is no other way than via ILL to track the need for items that are lost in the catalog. These statistics may also lead to analyses of how a department is changing academic and research direction (e.g., psychology moving from behavioral to cognitive), growth of a department (e.g., more focus on biotechnology, optics, photonics), and identifying trends within research areas.

RECOMMENDATIONS
FOR IMPROVING THE PROGRAM

A few recommendations will be included in the final pilot project report. The most important recommendation would be if this pilot becomes a permanent library service it should expand beyond purchasing books from Alibris. The use of a credit card will offer a variety of vendor purchases, such as Amazon and Barnes & Noble. Requests for expanding the list of commercial vendors on the WCRS and being able to use IFM to purchase these books would provide a more competitive environment for book pricing. This issue was discussed during one of the "Hot Topics" sessions at the annual ALA conference last June, where OCLC representatives were in attendance.

CONCLUSION

The books-on-demand pilot project, while a work in progress, has been met with enthusiasm by the collection management librarians. They view this program as a supplement to their collection development activities. The Advisory Committee has unanimously recommended to library administration to move this pilot project in to a permanent library service as part of a final report on the pilot project which will be presented to the University of Florida Libraries administration. The ILL staff views this program as a patron-centric approach because it adds titles to the collection based on patron requests and they have adjusted to the new workflow with ease. The patrons appreciate this program because they feel that they are able to contribute to the library collections. A presentation was made to the University Library Committee (ULC), which is a faculty senate committee comprising nine faculty from various colleges who assist the Dean of Libraries in advocating the libraries to the UF community, and who review the role of the libraries and their affects on the academic and research programs. The ULC expressed their support for this program and recommended that this pilot program be announced to the full faculty senate. The announcement to the faculty senate may be a bit premature since this is only a pilot program but should be made once it becomes a permanent program offered by the libraries.

With budgets either flat or on the decline, innovative approaches not only save money, but to continue to build the collection that meets the needs of academic and research programs at the university. Purchasing materials via ILL requests demonstrates that this innovative program is popular with the university faculty, saves time, and is an excellent supplement to the traditional ILL service. Hopefully this pilot, which emphasizes the patron-centric approach to enhance the libraries' collection, will become a permanent library service.

REFERENCES

Allen, Megan, Suzanne M. Ward, and Tanner Wray (2003). "Patron-Focused Services in Three US Libraries: Collaborative Interlibrary Loan, Collection Development and Acquisitions. *Interlending & Document Supply, 31*(2): 138-141, http://vnweb. hwwilsonweb.com/hww/jumpstart.jhtml?recid=0bc05f7a67b1790e70e397f5ebc28d34f bec02af0eab02130f4f5cfe7404a15e208f3a1072f96732&fmt = C.

Anderson, Kristine J., Robert S. Freeman, and Jean-Pierre V. M. Herubel. (2002). Buy, Don't Borrow: Bibliographers' Analysis of Academic Library Collection Development through Interlibrary Loan Requests. *Collection Management, 27* (3/4): 1-11, http://vnweb.hwwilsonweb.com/hww/jumpstart.jhtml?recid=0bc05f7a67b1790e70e 397f5ebc28d346d066f3fa5d1465444c808c620f1f771916l1da5a9409bfa&fmt=C.

Atkins, Stephanie S., and Cherie L. Weible. (2003). Needles in a Haystack: Using Interlibrary Loan Data to Identify Materials Missing from a Library's Collection. *Library Collections, Acquisitions, and Technical Services, 27* (2), 187-202, http://vnweb.hwwilsonweb.com/hww/jumpstart.jhtml?recid=0bc05f7a67b1790e 70e397f5e bc28d34fbec02af0eab0213dc464bd674e2ccb45a2fa08ead058dcd&fmt=C.

Clendenning, Lynda Fuller. (2001). Purchase Express for any User Request: The University of Virginia Library Offers Delivery in Seven Days. *College & Research Libraries News, 62* (1), 2001, 16-17, Full Text; HTML: http://vnweb.hwwilsonweb.com/ hww/jumpstart.jhtml?recid=0bc05f7a67b1790e70e397f5ebc28d3475285a 693210cd57b531dadc9cb504e6f073773c10b1a101&fmt=H; PDF: http://vnweb. hwwilsonweb.com/hww/jumpstart.jhtml?recid=0bc05f7a67b1790e70e397f5ebc28 d3475285a693210cd57b531dadc9cb504e6f073773c10b1a101&fmt=P.

Jackson, Mary E. *Measuring the Performance of Interlibrary Loan Operations in North American Research and College Libraries.* Washington, D.C.: Association of Research Libraries, 1998: 21.

Perdue, Jennifer, and James A. Van Fleet. (1999) Borrow Or Buy? Cost-Effective Delivery of Monographs. *Journal of Interlibrary Loan, Document Delivery & Information Supply, 9* (4), 19-28, http://vnweb.hwwilsonweb.com/hww/jumpstart. jhtml?recid=0bc05f7a67b1790e70e397f5ebc28d343b9400de610fa4b5a65d74e2309d3 b0b379fcb7f852babbc&fmt=C.

Ward, Suzanne M. Books on Demand: Just-in-Time Acquisitions. In *Out-of-Print and Special Collection Materials*, 95-107 (2003). Haworth Press; Haworth Press, 2002.

Ward, Suzanne M., Tanner Wray, and Karl E. Debus-Lopez. Collection Development Based on Patron Requests: Collaboration between Interlibrary Loan and Acquisitions. *Library Collections, Acquisitions, and Technical Services, 27* (2): 203-213, http://vnweb.hwwilsonweb.com/hww/jumpstart.jhtml?recid=0bc05f7a67b1790e70e397f5 ebc28d34fbec02af0eab0213dc464bd674e2ccb47712 cdcdfea3b1fe&fmt=C.

Youngdahl, William E., and Deborah L. Kellogg. (1997). The Relationship between Service Customers' Quality Assurance Behaviors, Satisfaction, and Effort: A Cost of Quality Perspective. *Journal of Operations Management, 15* (1), 19-32.

APPENDIX A. Sample Titles Added Through the Books-on-Demand Pilot Program, January-March 2007

TITLE	PUBLISHED
Guy Debord : revolution in the service of poetry	2006
Cuenta hasta diez	2006
Thinking past terror : Islamism and critical theory on the left	2006
Objects : reluctant witnesses to the past	2006
Critical literacy/critical teaching : tools for preparing responsive teachers	2006
The body economic : life, death, and sensation in political economy and the Victorian novel	2006
Evolution and Christian faith : reflections of an evolutionary biologist	2006
Every other Thursday : stories and strategies from successful women scientists	2006
The price of whiteness : Jews, race, and American identity	2006
Genre, gender, race, and world cinema	2006
Learning from the left : children's literature, the Cold War, and radical politics in the United States	2006
Mainstreaming midwives : the politics of change	2006
The Womanist reader	2006
Europe undivided : democracy, leverage, and integration after communism	2005
Conscience, dissent and reform in Soviet Russia	2005
Applied social psychology : understanding and addressing social and practical problems	2005
Rethinking urban parks : public space & cultural diversity	2005
Designing small parks : a manual addressing social and ecological concerns	2005
Social work practice with children and families: a family health approach	2005
Electric bicycles : a guide to design and use	2005
The age of consent : a manifesto for a new world order	2004
Molecular host plant resistance to pests	2003

APPENDIX B

INTERLIBRARY LOAN PILOT PROJECT

Bookmark questions, January-April 2007

Did this book arrive on time?			
Yes	No	no response	
60	1	1	

How useful is this book as a permanent addition to the libraries collection?			
Very	Moderately	Marginally	no response
53	7	1	1

Do you want to check out this book once it is cataloged?			
Yes	No		
47	16		

Would you recommend this book to a colleague?			
Yes	No	no response	
60	1	1	

Comments:

- "3 days to arrive"

- "Book = Victorian Literature and the Victorian State by Lauren Goodlad." (She responded yes to the question that asked if she would check out the book.)

- "Very important book, in telecom field."

- "ILL rules!"

- "This is a rich source for graduate students and scholars to Chinese studies and Asian studies to understand and ponder upon fascinating issues in the biggest and ever changing socialist state. A work by leading anthropologists in this field, it is another 'must-add' in the reading list of courses on family, marriage, social change in developing world, and gender studies."

Having Java in the Library Doesn't Necessarily Require a Coffee Cart: Using an Object-Oriented Programming Language to Streamline Circulation Services for a Distance Education University

Sara Godbee
Mark deJong

Contemporary distance education (DE) comes in many forms, e.g., online via a course management system, at remote locations, video delivery/conferencing or a combination of two or more of these models. However, the underpinning for all of these delivery methods remains the same: technology. The same is true for library services in a DE environment. Because distance patrons are at the mercy of what is provided to them, i.e., they usually do not have the option of visiting the campus research library, academic librarians serving in a distance education setting should be proactive in applying available technologies to meet the needs of their patrons. However, the appropriate application of technology can potentially benefit all campuses and a wide variety of libraries.

Marshall Breeding noted in 2000 that, "while the dot-com world has embraced Java as its favorite programming language, the library world has been less aggressive in its adoption."[1] The authors believe this remains true today. Java is not as pervasive as it probably should be, or rather, object-oriented programming (OOP) languages are not as well-integrated into the world of libraries as they could or should be by now. There are several OOP languages with various strengths and weaknesses. Sun Microsystems' Java was chosen for this project primarily because the library associate was learning the language, but this circumstance was in part due to the language's popularity. Its relative ubiquity meant it was well-supported with many reference sources to consult and tools to utilize, making the design and coding far less burdensome. The project could also have been completed using Visual Basic, a Microsoft OOP language in which the document management librarian has had training. Irrespective of the specific language, OOP allows a fair amount of flexibility and ease for programmers, which is the great benefit of this iteration of programming languages. This paper discusses one such example, the development of a Java application to support the circulation processes for DE patrons.

The University of Maryland University College (UMUC), the second largest university in Maryland and the twelfth largest degree-granting university in the United States, began modestly in 1947 as a division within the University of Maryland College Park. The catalyst for creating UMUC was a hope to service the educational needs of a distributed military within the US and beginning in 1949, abroad. Classes began in

1948 with an entering body of 2,142 students. Nearly sixty years later, UMUC boasted 84,188 undergraduate and graduate scholars in Fiscal Year 2006,[2] 42,879 (51% of the total) of whom lived outside the United States. Many of the 2006 overseas students attended classes on military installations in face-to-face settings, but others took web-based classes or a combination of traditional and online courses. Even more noteworthy, 91% of all stateside courses were web-based. Accordingly, the distance education model of providing full academic services to a distributed student body is the primary purpose of UMUC.[3]

Regardless of whether UMUC students and faculty are taking or teaching classes at remote locations or in the virtual world, Information and Library Services (ILS) of the University of Maryland University College endeavors to provide the same level of support for all patrons. Of great advantage to ILS and UMUC in honoring its obligations to its staff and students is membership in a statewide consortium. As a constituent partner of the eleven campuses and sixteen libraries of the University System of Maryland and Affiliated Institutions (USMAI), ILS is able to provide a far broader range of materials than it could operating solely from its own collection. In fact, because UMUC has so few students who are able to visit campus, ILS's stacks hold only a few thousand books and a handful of periodicals. As most would imagine, the virtual collection is far more extensive. However, as ubiquitous as e-books are, they have not yet replaced the need for print resources. Therefore, ILS instituted a sophisticated circulation process to meet the need for print materials by its dispersed clientele.[4]

To dispatch books to DE students, ILS employs the integrated library system (Aleph 500) that is shared by the entire USMAI, UPS's WorldShip 8 (now upgraded to 9) application to manage shipments, an in-house developed Access database (DE Book Database) to facilitate and monitor shipping and circulation transactions and a University personnel database called Portico to verify address and patron information. ILS receives materials from its USMAI partners which have been requested by UMUC students via the University System OPAC, an element of Aleph. Once received, documents (primarily books) are charged to the appropriate requesting patron by means of the Aleph Circulation Module (see Figure 1). Then, a flurry of toggling between screens and data entry, some of it redundant, occurs while using the DE Book Database (Portico-held patron information is checked via a link through the DE Book Database) (see Figure 2) and WorldShip. The process begins anew when the patron decides to return the item(s) as ILS pays for and oversees the entire shipping process. The only real effort on the part of

FIGURE 1. Charging Items to Requesting Patrons

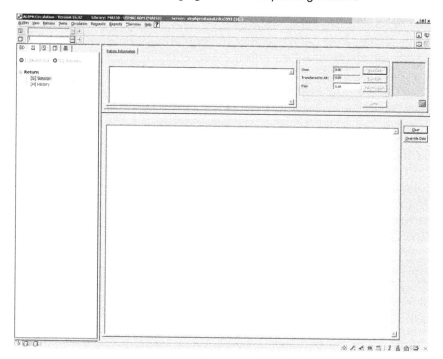

the patron is opening and sealing the packages. Initially, ILS did not give much thought to streamlining the process; student workers generally perform the work and when the program was instituted, volume was light. As years passed and the volume of shipments dramatically increased (515% increase from 2002 to 2006), the process was viewed as increasingly prone to error and too labor intensive, which slowed the delivery of materials to patrons.

In the fall of 2006, the ILS library associate began taking coursework regarding interface design and Java programming. Not long after, she conceived the idea to design a single graphical user interface (GUI) for simplifying the technical side of the DE circulation process. The concept, a database management system for distributed databases, allows for the importing and exporting of data between the various parts and the execution of perfunctory operations. The ILS document management librarian, supervisor for circulation and interlibrary loan, agreed with the associate as to the potential of the new model. He approached

FIGURE 2. Checking Patron Information–DE Book Database Link

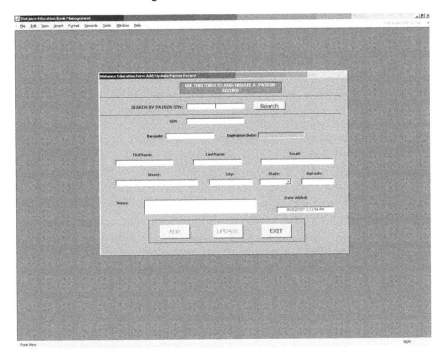

the library's management team for approval, which was granted immediately.

The library associate quickly recruited a team of three graduate students studying information management to participate in the design of the GUI and database management system. The document management librarian provided the necessary resources and guidance for the design and implementation process. The project team had three primary goals:

1. Create an intuitive and easy to use interface
2. Improve client service by reducing the probability of errors and processing time
3. Streamline the technical side of the distance circulation process by reducing the need for and redundancy of hand keying information in multiple databases

To realize the stated goals, the project was first divided into three phases. In phase one, learning about and mapping the current system, the team developed a comprehensive knowledge of the existing DE circulation system and its end-to-end workflow processes. This background treatment was essential for understanding the needs, limits, and practicalities of what was already in place, which was crucial for establishing the developmental direction.

Team members began by scrutinizing the different databases that are used to store data and would be federated through the new interface/ management tool. The team sought to examine the strengths and weaknesses of the individual databases and determine the potential interoperability each offered. In brief, the USMAI libraries use the Aleph OPAC which employs an Oracle database; the UMUC internal patron management database, Portico, uses MySQL; the UPS Worldship product uses Microsoft SQL Desktop Edition; and the DE Book Database was built with Microsoft Access atop the MS Jet 4.0 database engine.

After achieving a broad understanding of the databases, the team examined each part of the workflow and mapped the current system using the Unified Modeling Language (UML) method. UML is a standard language used by software developers to aid in creating models of specifications, visual layouts and more for complex software systems. More specific to this project, it has also been used extensively for modeling object-oriented software applications.[5] The design team used UML to help identify the classes, objects and activities in the existing DE circulation system. Then, using Microsoft Visio, they created activity, class, object and collaboration diagrams to map the current system and its associated workflows.

Using the diagrams developed for the existing system as a starting point, the team began phase two, Reviewing and Refining Workflows and Functionality for the new system. The designers initially worked on the interface prototype, visualizing the components of the new interface in terms of what functionality to include, how to organize the data flow and what information would be necessary on each screen (see Figure 5). Primary focus was on removing the redundancies and unwarranted steps from the existing workflow. Working from this premise, the team concluded that two operational modifications were required: first, the team would reorganize the shipping process to aggregate book processing based around patrons rather than books. This would eliminate repeated keying of the patron barcode each time an operator processed an item for a given patron. This decision resulted in a redesign of the Sending Book Input Screen (see Figure 5). In addition to an inclusive shipment for the patron, operators would have more flexibility to correct errors during the input of both patron and book information. Second, the designers determined that much of the information displayed in the various databases was extraneous to the circulation process; the screens were hard to read, which often led to confusion and errors. Therefore, only those data fields that would be needed for input or verification were included in the federated interface. This meant that while the existing databases and their inherent interfaces would remain unchanged, the federated interface would only display data relevant for the operator. For example, the differences between the screen for creating a book shipment (see Figure 6) and the screen for creating a patron shipping label (see Figure 7) shows that when books are the main entities being updated, patron information is pared down, but when the shipping label is created based on patron address information, book level information is absent, i.e., the book shipment list created in the Sending Books Menu is linked to the patron account, but it is not germane to generating a shipping label, therefore information about the books is not output for the Create Shipping Label screen.[6]

With solid design concepts and a work plan in place, the designers finally began Java programming and prototyping, the final phase of the project. The design team decided to utilize rapid prototyping and pair programming to maximize efficiency and productivity. Rapid prototyping is a model often used in the development of large, complex projects. It is an iterative process of design, development, testing and revision of a prototype until a final product is obtained. The great benefit is that it allows designers to uncover flaws or weaknesses quickly, and most importantly, before the implementation date.[7] In pair programming, two developers work side-by-side "continuously collaborating on the same design, algorithm, code, or test."[8] Basically, it is the application of the cliché, "two heads are better than one." Pair programming was especially helpful in reducing the number of mistakes during the actual Java coding. Using both techniques, the team was able to complete three prototype iterations during a six week span. After the three rounds of rapid prototyping, the team delivered a final prototype that included a primary interface (see Figure 3) and an interconnected database management system for DE circulation. While the interface was important to accomplishing the project goals, it was the linking of the various databases through the central interface that the real improvement in function was gained.

FIGURE 3. Primary Interface Screen
Collaboration Diagram

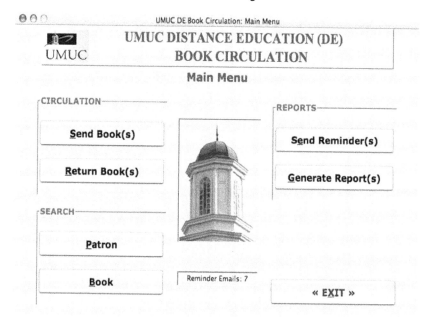

Used with permission.

However, the team suffered one impediment regarding interconnectivity. In researching how to interlock the unified interface to the various databases used in the DE circulation process, the designers found that connecting to the Aleph Oracle database could not be immediately realized due to outside administrative controls. The original concept for the interface/management system included interaction with this database to charge books out to patrons and retrieve bibliographic information for use in patron notifications distributed via the DE Book Database. To mitigate the impact of this set-back, the team reworked the workflows slightly: books would be charged out to the patron in Aleph before any other processing would begin. The team also recommended that ILS research a bibliographic database that could be linked to the interface and searched using the ISBN for importing relevant bibliographic information into the DE Book Database as a follow-up stage of development.

FIGURE 4

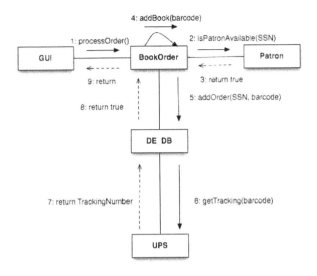

Now, within the new system, when a circulation operator processes a new or return shipment, they interact with only one interface. However, in the background, the interface/management system imports information from one database and integrates it with new information keyed by the operator or which is imported from yet another database. Then it outputs to a separate database for storage and later retrieval. The collaboration diagram (see Figure 4) represents how the databases interact through the interface and in what order interactions occur. From the GUI or main interface screen, the operator begins by creating a new or return shipment. When this action is started, the interface first checks the patron status and information by accessing the Portico database. If the patron is found, their information is verified and updated in the DE Book Database, books are then added to their account and a shipping order is created and sent to the UPS database. Shipment information is then passed from the UPS database to the DE Book Database, and the patron's account record is updated with the UPS shipment information.

This project represented a first stage of development for the new DE circulation tool. The team viewed the prototype as a proof of concept to gain internal approval and support in order to move forward with a broader de-

FIGURE 5. Distance Education Circulation Screen

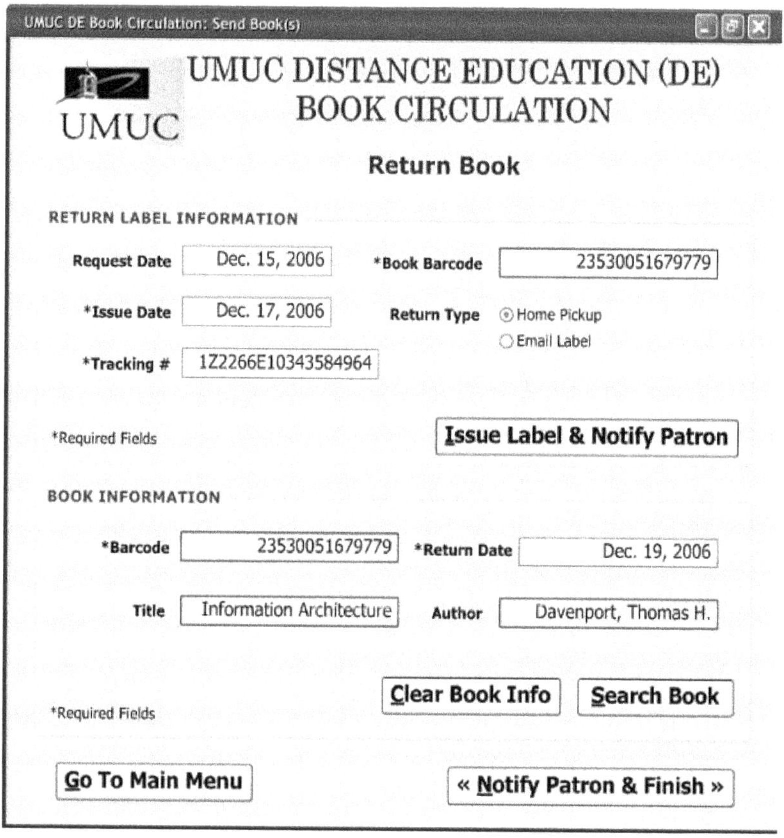

Used with permission.

velopment of functionality. Using the same model of research, design and rapid prototyping, the document management librarian and library associate plan to work with another group of graduate students to further enhance the system's search and report functionality in 2007/2008. For stage two, Java will remain the preferred programming language.

Some librarians consider technology to be anathema to libraries and librarianship. Various computer scientists consider libraries and librarianship to be anachronistic. Neither side is right, or wrong for that matter: the monograph–a relatively unchanged tool of learning for centuries–is

FIGURE 6. Sending Book Input Screen

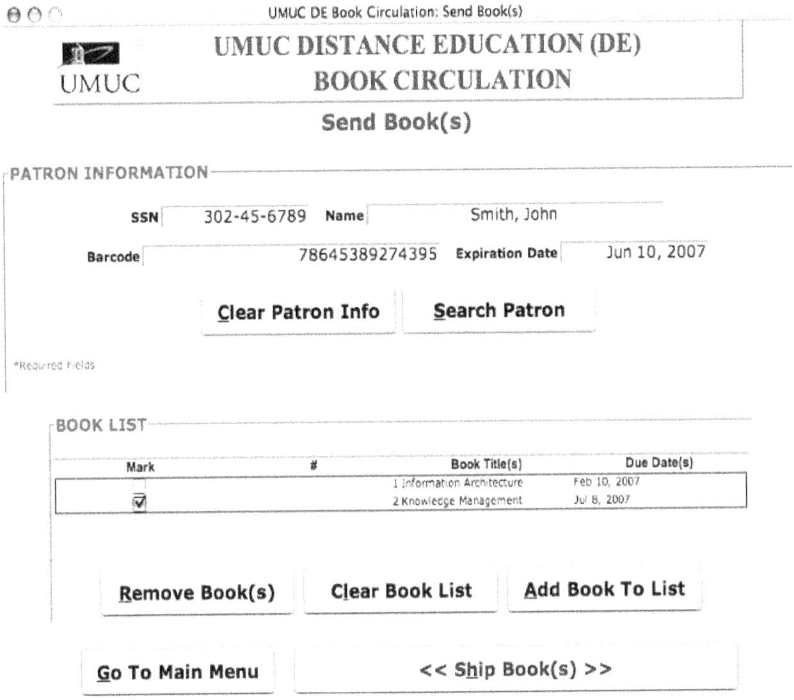

Used with permission.

a vital component of the academic library. However, this fact is not necessarily prohibitive of computers and programming languages; tradition and technology are not mutually exclusive, but they are often actively or passively treated as such by individuals and communities. The ILS DE circulation system project demonstrates that the two can be wed. However, preparation is of paramount importance. ILS also found that quickly constructing and deconstructing prototypes in conjunction with a team orientation was immensely beneficial. Though other libraries may not find this practical due to time/staffing constraints, rapid prototyping and pair programming reduce staff time costs in the long run. On occasion, a particular technology will be embraced by a library or the library community, but it is applied incorrectly or poorly due to haste. Possessing a broad understanding of current and desired work-

FIGURE 7. Creating Patron Shipping Label

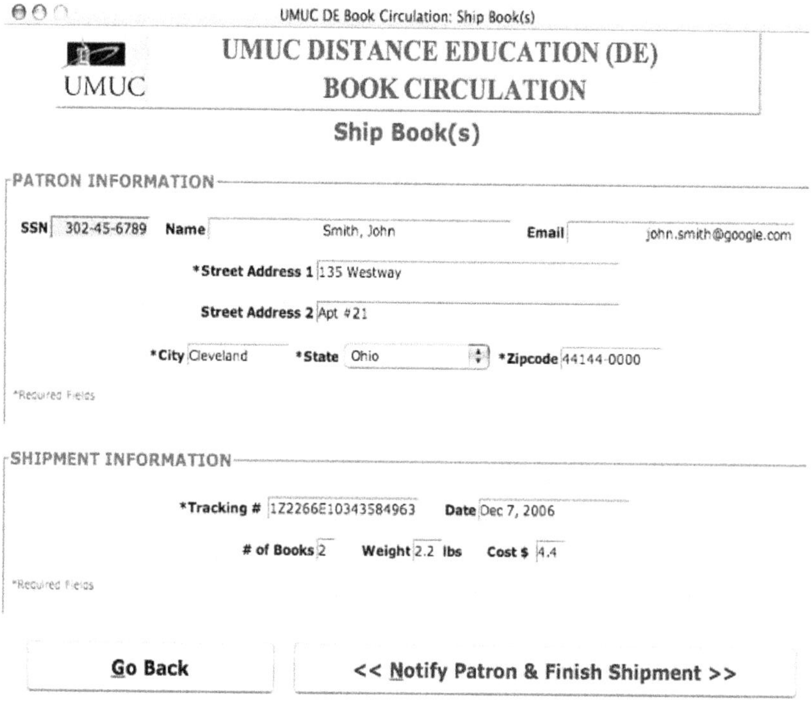

Used with permission.

flows, the technology available and its applicability (Java in this case), the potential impact on other systems, the necessary staff commitment, UML for modeling and similar concepts can greatly increase the probability of success–preparation, understanding and resource allocation are vital for any project's triumph.[8]

NOTES

1. Marshall Breeding. "Perking Up Library Applications: Java is Slowly Starting to Make a Presence in Library Automation" Information Today 17 no.11 (2000): 52.

2. July 1, 2005 to June 30, 2006.

3. Office of Institutional Research, Planning and Accountability, "Fiscal Year 2006 Factbook," (University of Maryland University College), http://www.umuc.edu/ip/

FIGURE 8. Workflow Review for Interface Design

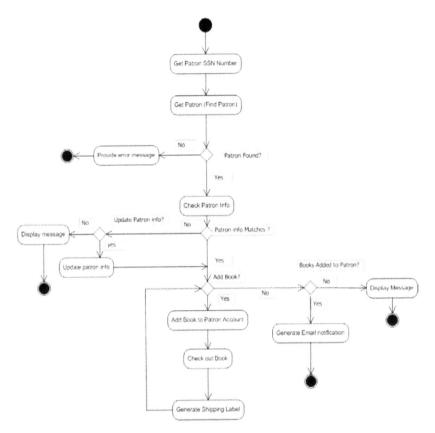

downloads/UMUCFY06FactBook.pdf, 3 (accessed April 30, 2007);University of Maryland University College, "UMUC–About Us," (University of Maryland University College), http://www.umuc.edu/gen/about.shtml (accessed April 30, 2007).

4. Board of Directors for the Association of College and Research Libraries, "Guidelines for Distance Learning Library Services" (American Library Association), http://www.ala.org/ala/acrl/acrlstandards/guidelinesdistancelearning.htm (accessed May 2, 2007); Clara Lantham. "Exploring the Guidelines for Library Services to Distance Education Programs" (Ph.D. diss., Texas Women's University, 2005).

5. Thomas A. Pender. UML Weekend Crash course (New York: Wiley Publishing, 2002), 6; Object Oriented Analysis and Design Team, Kennesaw State University, Unified Modeling Language (UML) Tutorial. http://atlas.kennesaw.edu/~dbraun/csis4650/A&D/UML_tutorial/index.htm (Last accessed May 12, 2007).

6. Michael J. Laszlo. Object-oriented Programming Featuring Graphical Applications in JAVA (New York: Addison Wesley, 2002); Richard Cooper, ed. Interfaces to

Database Systems: Proceedings of the First International Workshop on Interfaces to Database Systems, Glasgow, 1-3 July 1992 (London: Springer-Verlag, 1993).
7. Michael Thompson and Nina Wishbow. "Prototyping: Tools and Techniques: Improving Software and Documentation Quality Through Rapid Prototyping" Proceedings of the 10th Annual International Conference on Systems Documentation (New York: ACM Press, 1992), 191.
8. Laurie A. Williams and Robert R. Kessler. "All I Really Need to Know about Pair Programming I Learned in Kindergarten" Communications of the ACM 43 no.5 (2000): 109.

REFERENCES

Board of Directors for the Association of College and Research Libraries. "Guidelines forDistance Learning Library Services." American Library Association. *http://www.ala.org/ala/acrl/acrlstandards/guidelinesdistancelearning.htm* (accessed May 2, 2007).
Breeding, Marshall. (2000). "Perking Up Library Applications." *Information Today 17*, (11), 52-53.
Carey, Kelly, and Stanko Blatnik. Design Concepts with Code: An Approach for Developers. Berkeley, CA: Apress, 2003.
Cooper, Richard, ed. Interfaces to Database Systems: Proceedings of the First International Workshop on Interfaces to Database Systems, Glasgow, 1-3 July 1992. London: Springer-Verlag, 1993.
Gershon, Nahum, Stephen G. Eick, and Stuart Card (1998). "Information Visualization. *Interactions,* 9-15.
Lantham, Clara. "Exploring the Guidelines for Library Services to Distance Education Programs." Ph.D. diss., Texas Women's University, 2005.
Laszlo, Michael J. Object-oriented Programming Featuring Graphical Applications in JAVA. New York: Addison Wesley, 2002.
Niemeyer, Patrick, and Johathan Kundsen. Learning Java. Cambridge: O'Reilly & Associates, 2002.
Object Oriented Analysis and Design Team, Kennesaw State University, Unified Modeling Language (UML) Tutorial. *http://atlas.kennesaw.edu/~dbraun/csis4650/A&D/UML_tutorial/index.htm* (Last accessed May 12, 2007).
Office of Institutional Research, Planning and Accountability. "Fiscal Year 2006 Factbook." University of Maryland University Collge (2006). *http://www.umuc.edu/ip/downloads/UMUCFY06FactBook.pdf,* 3 (accessed April 30, 2007).
Pender, Thomas A. UML Weekend Crash Course. New York: Wiley Publishing, 2002.
Sun Developer Network. "Java Technology." Sun Microsystems, Inc. *http://java.sun.com/* (accessed April 30, 2007).
University of Maryland University College. "UMUC–About Us." University of Maryland University College. *http://www.umuc.edu/gen/about.shtml* (accessed April 30, 2007).

Bringing Delivery into the Fold: A Discussion of Cross-Departmental Document Delivery Service Implementation in Academic Libraries

Erik Mitchell
Cristina Yu

INTRODUCTION

Like many libraries, the Z. Smith Reynolds Library at Wake Forest University has been grappling with the need to integrate patron access to library held (both print and electronic) and remotely acquired (Interlibrary Loan and Document Delivery) resources. Wake Forest is a medium sized liberal arts university, supporting 6,500 students via three libraries (Undergraduate/Graduate, Business/Law, and Medical). The three libraries share an integrated library system (Voyager), and two of the three use ILLiad as their interlibrary loan (ILL) system. In 2003 the Z. Smith Reynolds (ZSR) Library transitioned to ILLiad from another system and began looking at ways in which ILLiad could be integrated with other library systems. During this time, the library also transitioned towards more electronic resources and worked towards integrating ILL request forms into our OpenURL resolver application.

Although the growth in remote availability of electronic resources has resulted in a shift in the nature of interlibrary loan requests, the ZSR library has seen a sustained demand for interlibrary loan and document delivery services due to three factors. First, the university support for remote patrons (students studying overseas, faculty working on sabbatical and from remote locations, and active duty students) means that resource delivery services still fills a valuable need, particularly for electronic delivery of resources. Second, an integrated resource request and delivery system means that our patrons are guaranteed a consistent level of service, regardless of their starting point. Finally, library commitment to providing exceptional service means that while electronic access enables a high level of self-service, added benefits from print resource delivery, digitization of print resources, and procurement of resources not held by the library through commercial vendors fills the immediate service demands of our patrons.

In order to address these demands, the ZSR Library began offering a number of different resource delivery services. These services include off-site storage retrieval, office based circulation services (delivery, pickup, renewal), and journal article photocopying. These services were all handled by the circulation department while the ILL department handled requests for items not held by the library. Both departments used separate request systems. In 2005, the ZSR Library decided to review these processes with a focus on streamlining fulfillment and delivery services. This project was motivated by feedback from University faculty requesting better access to local and remote resources and by the expectation that a consolidated approach would result in an expanded ability to offer delivery services.

This project quickly expanded to include system and process analyses and evolved into a discussion on the nature of 'document delivery service.' Much of the debate centered on deciding how our patrons would approach a document delivery request and how (and to whom) we could make expanded services available. While we considered a number of solutions, including preserving the split between obtaining resources from other libraries and delivery of items from Wake Forest University libraries, we ultimately decided to leverage the workforce of the two departments in conjunction with the ILLiad ILL/Document Delivery system in order to integrate these services.

This paper includes a discussion of the foundational issues that informed our decision, a presentation of common issues encountered during the implementation of delivery services, and a review of the specific technical hurdles related to implementing this approach in the ILLiad system.

REVIEW OF DOCUMENT DELIVERY SERVICES

ILL literature points to a split in definitions regarding the limits of service. In a recently published book on interlibrary loan, Lee Andrew Hilyar defines ILL in terms of the origination of the resource. "Interlibrary Loan provides access to materials not held in, or otherwise unavailable from, a library's collection" (2006, p. 8). In other cases, ILL departments fill requests both for items from other institutions and items held by the library itself. A recent case study of an implementation of this model is the article written by Zheng Ye Yang presenting the work done at Texas A&M in 2005. In this article, she discusses the success of the deliverEdocs service which electronically delivers up to 50 pages for free to most university patrons (2005, p. 49) including undergraduate, graduate and faculty patron groups.

While document delivery can be generically defined as a service that federates the provision of resources for library patrons, in reality, it can involve a number of specific services including resource provision, physical delivery services, and on-demand access to resources. While traditional definitions of ILL departments focus on obtaining resources outside of the institutional holdings, ILL departments are also positioned to adapt their infrastructure and processes to handle a wider set of delivery style services. At ZSR, the ILL office often receives requests for items already held by the library. The decision to begin filling these requests rather than canceling them represented a significant shift in the definition of ILL services in our institution.

A review of literature revealed five commonly used delivery services:

1. Real-time provision of electronic resources not held by the library through patron initiated requests.
2. Library mediated delivery (via print or electronic means) of materials held by the patron's home institution.
3. Federated handling of requests for materials held by sister libraries via expedited means.
4. Request and delivery of items held in off-site storage locations.
5. Door-to-door service for print circulation (checkout/delivery, renewal, and return/pickup) services. This may include library-to-patron or library-to-library services.

The ZSR Library employs all five of these forms of document delivery and was seeking to make the decision process for providing these services easier for both patrons and library staff. In recognizing the demand that interlibrary loan departments are placed under, Hilyar points to many current issues which informed our discussion of these services, including growing demand for quick, convenient service, and a perspective that looks at service levels in terms of user expectations in retail environments (p. 5).

This retail-informed model is a component of the Library 2.0 philosophy originally described by Chad and Miller (2005). In their article, they outline the impact that the web and services provided by companies like Amazon and Google are having on libraries. They mention two factors in particular: the "Internet-enabled way of life" and the "need for free" (2005, p. 4), which have raised the expectations for the level of service that patrons bring with them to the library. While Chad and Miller argue that "present Inter-Library-Loan (ILL) mechanisms are creaky to say the least" (2005, p. 4) they also argue that resource availability and delivery services represent a central component of the "pervasive library." Hilyar lists a number of 'best practices' in his chapter on ILL borrowing related to providing service in a '2.0' environment. Establishing service level definitions, meeting expected turnaround time, providing simplified request and delivery systems, and providing cost-conscious services are four major issues related to implementation that he lists (2006, p. 6).

Library 2.0 literature emphasizes user-centric services based on trust, rapid development of services and technologies, and integrated Web 2.0 style point-of-need service models (Casey & Savastinuk, 2006). Darlene Fichter's graphic on Library 2.0 (Library 2.0 = books 'n stuff + people + radical trust × participation) (2006) and Levine's comments on user centric business models in the Cluetrain Manifesto (Levine, 2000) are other examples of the service models that are influencing libraries. To realize this level of service in ILL/document delivery services can:

1. Include enhanced services as defaults rather than exceptions. Eliminate barriers to requesting exceptional service.
2. Eliminate 'don't-fill' reasons based on library ownership of materials.
3. Employ integrated authentication with campus resources; remove barriers to access.
4. Employ OpenURL based links wherever possible (Full Text Link resolver, Online Catalog, World Cat, GoogleScholar).
5. Provide document provision services outside of traditional library context/environments.
6. Eliminate mediation of requests where possible. Employ automated, real-time delivery of resources to patrons.

The concern over the ability of ILL departments to provide quality service in an open user-trust based environment is often represented in the literature. This idea is reflected in Zheng's comment regarding staff concern over their ability to support the request volume. In the end, their department decided that that rather than abusing the availability, "Users will use it when they need the service (2005, p. 51)." Zheng's report points to a successful implementation of a full open ILL/document delivery service based on the model of user trust.

PEER INSTITUTION PRACTICES

In preparing for this article the authors performed a small survey of peer institution ILL/delivery practices. In the survey of six institutions, we found both a shared vision for the need of ILL departments to be central to resource provision services and a wide variety of delivery policies and procedures. Jim Toplon at Vanderbilt University argued "It [Document Delivery] should be a core service for the faculty so they can make better use of their time" (Yu, 2007). Another librarian stated "Many [libraries] are doing [document delivery], more and more people coming here will be expecting it."

All of the libraries surveyed were using ILLiad as their ILL system. All six institutions offered some type of delivery service. While each of the libraries offered these delivery services free of charge, the specific services offered and the patron groups to which they were available differed. While all institutions offered these services to faculty, only one included delivery services to graduate and honors undergraduate students. No library surveyed currently includes staff in their policies although one is considering adding staff as an eligible patron group.

The formats supplied by the institutions also varied. Some institutions only offered book delivery services, while others only offered electronic article delivery. When physical delivery was included as a service the frequency was limited to one delivery per day and, in most cases, delivery meant that the item would be delivered to the departmental or branch library.

The institutions surveyed most increased staff and/or student hours while some also introduced more equipment to handle the increased workload. A third method mentioned by one library (and also employed at ZSR) is the collaboration with other departments for relevant services. In our case, ILL partnered with the Circulation Department, which is better positioned to handle the physical delivery and pickup of library resources.

DELIVERY SERVICES OBSERVATIONS

In deciding how best to implement or merge delivery services in the library, it is best to begin with an overview of current staffing levels, departmental processes, and expected service outcomes. While the ZSR Library chose to follow the cross-departmental implementation method, the success reported by other institutions that followed an expanded staffing model notes that there is more than one way to solve these problems. In addition, the ZSR Library chose not to obtain new equipment prior to implementing delivery services. The expanded workload has placed pressures on equipment time and staff availability.

PROJECT GOALS

The choices we made involved technical, political, and economic factors and represented a compromise of (sometimes) competing priorities. The goals were to simplify request mechanisms, provide users with context-sensitive links where possible, and to bring the services being offered by ILL and circulation together under one umbrella. In implementing these goals we found that services which had typically been handled by separate departments required integration and that cross departmental training and information sharing was involved. This section recounts some of the issues and motivations behind the implementation process and lays out a framework for ensuring adequate functionality.

To achieve these goals we decided to:

1. Combine resource request and delivery/pickup services into a single request/fulfillment system.
2. Employ staff from both circulation and ILL departments in workflows where necessary to eliminate duplication of effort.
3. Establish fair guidelines for providing resources regardless of location or holding library.

Through working with ILLiad support and by speaking with other ILLiad users, we identified a number of possible methods including: separate forms for document request vs. ILL, automated routing based on URL request values, and patron-specific access to request fields. Based on the idea that patrons should not have to make explicit decisions about where they want a document from but rather just that they want it, we decided to combine interlibrary loan and document delivery functions into a single interface that would be available to eligible patrons. While we kept the ILL and document delivery forms separate, by routing all requests into the ILLiad system, library staff is able to move requests between the Document Delivery and Borrowing modules seamlessly. In addition, by using ILLiad routing rules, we were able to route document delivery requests to specific queues automatically.

It became evident early in the implementation phase that the document delivery process needed clearly defined policies both to meet faculty expectations and moderate the demand on time of library staff. In discussing how best to present the service and balance demand and staff availability, we discussed:

1. Balancing student worker and staff responsibilities to ensure that delivery functions could be met in a timely manner.
2. How best to make essential services available to appropriate patron groups.
3. What additional hardware components might be required to enable efficient delivery processing.

MAKING IT WORK

This section contains specific discussion of ILLiad system setup and ZSR processes. To implement the document delivery system in ILLiad we needed:

1. A way to route delivery requests to the appropriate queue in the ILLiad module.
2. OpenURL connectivity from external systems (our online catalog and OpenURL resolver).
3. Cross-departmental workflows.
4. Consolidated billing systems.
5. A seamless web-based request system based on the ILLiad public interface.

REQUEST ROUTING

Initially, the ZSR library chose to route all document delivery-marked requests to the circulation desk for processing. In order to accomplish this, we used request routing rules and custom form fields in the public interface to mark records as 'document delivery.' Two excellent sources of information for setting up custom routing rules for ILLiad are the ILLiad user guides ("OCLC Illiad Document Delivery User's Guide," 2006) and a recent set of articles in the OCLC ILLiad Newsletter (Ford, 2006).

Custom document delivery pull slips were used to facilitate the request tracking process for student workers. As the process has matured, ILL has taken over initial document delivery processing and routes print items that need to be delivered to the circulation department.

OPENURL AND DEEP LINKING

In order to provide users with deep context-sensitive links into the ILLiad request database, OpenURL links were included in the Online

Catalog. These links create a request in the ILLiad system for eligible patron groups with the delivery request information pre-populated. In order to harvest data from the Voyager ILS and create a contextualized URL, JavaScript is used to create an ILLiad request URL and open it in a new window. In addition, OpenURL translation values were used to allow requests to be created that linked directly to document delivery functions. The JavaScript code harvests values from the Voyager Online Catalog screen (call number and resource type) and creates an OpenURL compliant link with this information for ILLiad (Gilbertson & Mitchell, 2007). The specific function is accessed via a link embedded in the Online Catalog interface for each record.

All other OpenURL based systems, including our OpenURL link resolver, use a default request format for ILLiad that forces eligible staff to select delivery as their preferred pickup choice. The default delivery status was set for the online catalog based on the expectation that if a user was requesting an item held by our library that it should fall under the delivery processing system. Additional information regarding using OpenURL and deep links in conjunction with ILLiad can be found in the OCLC ILLiad Administrative Guide ("OCLC Illiad Administrative Guide," 2006).

STAFFING & TRAINING

As the service has matured, processes have been shifted somewhat to incorporate document delivery into more regular ILL workflows. Circulation staff is now involved more in the delivery/pickup of physical resources than the provision of electronic copies or initial processing of articles. Initially, training and collaborative planning was held to make sure that the delivery processes that existed in circulation and the fulfillment processes that existed interlibrary loan worked well together. Two of the factors that influenced this shift were the balance of student/staff time and the familiarity of the ILL staff with ILLiad processing. Additionally, the physical location and availability of the equipment proved to be issues.

While the implementation group considered including item retrieval and scanning as part of the circulation process, the existing staffing level and technological infrastructure in the Interlibrary Loan Department meant that these processes could be handled with the least amount of disruption in ILL. Likewise, the connection to patron contact information and availability of student workers for on-demand pickup and delivery requests meant that the circulation department was much better equipped to handle print resource delivery requests. While the ZSR Library chose to implement this service without additional staffing, other institutions cite the addition of staff as a key component to implementing a delivery service. Some other staffing/workflow issues to consider are:

1. Availability of computers/scanners for delivery processing.
2. Availability of on-demand staff time to allow responsive processing of delivery requests. This may include both student and staff time to process, retrieve, and deliver materials.
3. Delivery schedules and turnaround times. The ZSR Library experimented with immediate to two hour periods and is now looking at a twice per day approach which attempts deliveries at 11 a.m. and 3 p.m.
4. Impact of document delivery functions on traditional ILL functions.

Each of these issues, depending on anticipated or realized use of the service, may require additional staff. In attempting to discover the extent to which a delivery service will impact staff, it can be difficult to get to a quantifiable number. Influential factors include level of staffing, amount of existing ILL volume, expected use of delivery services, and amount of time required to complete the delivery services. While using an integrated solution such as ILLiad and distributing responsibilities across library departments can help ease the burden, additional staff, student assistants, and technology components may be required to provide support for the added demand. Our recent survey found increased staffing was a component in most libraries although the types of staffing varied.

CONSOLIDATION OF BILLING

One of the major reasons that ILLiad was chosen to implement delivery was the ability to integrate charging mechanisms into the delivery process. While most requests remain free for faculty and administrative staff, if a charge does need to be applied, it can be done within the custom ILLiad billing system. In order to configure charging, stock billing rules needed to be created for photocopy items which exceeded 20 pages in length. Setting automatic billing levels in ILLiad has eliminated a significant amount of confusion regarding how/when to charge for document delivery items. More information on setting up default and item/patron/process specific billing levels can be found in the ILLiad Administrators User Guide ("OCLC Illiad Administrative Guide," 2006).

PUBLIC INTERFACE CUSTOMIZATION

We customized the public interface to include user-specific request forms and new request types based on the instructions in the ILLiad interface documentation for creating new request forms (Atlas Systems, 2007a) and handling patron groups (Atlas Systems, 2007b). These processes may or may not be relevant depending on the configuration of special services in other institutions. Because our document delivery service is only available to University faculty and administrative staff, special request pages were created which allow them to select the delivery option.

In addition to creating user-specific request pages, the ZSR Library also created a custom request type to handle pickup requests. The default values of the request form specify a document type (pickup) and title (pickup request). When used in conjunction with ILLiad routing rules, this creates a dummy request in the ILLiad processing queue which alerts circulation staff to the need to contact the faculty member regarding book pickup. This system works in addition to a phone pickup system which has been maintained. More information on creating custom document request pages can be found in the ILLiad Administrative Guide ("OCLC Illiad Administrative Guide," 2006).

CONCLUSION

By using an integrated system and bridging departmental functions where necessary, we succeeded in expanding an existing service without dramatically increasing workload on library staff. If delivery volume were to increase significantly, staffing and equipment availability would become larger issues. The ILLiad system allowed the library to avoid costly development and integration of public interface, authentication, and delivery mechanisms. Further, it enabled the creation of an integrated service request platform based on OpenURL interconnectivity and user-moderated request management. This enabled patrons familiar with existing functionality to happen across a service which had previously been buried in external systems, enabled them to capitalize on existing user accounts and skills, and allowed the library to use electronic delivery and billing mechanisms already in place.

REFERENCES

Atlas Systems. (2007a). Creating New Document Request Forms. In Illiad Administrative Guide.

Atlas Systems. (2007b). Setting Up Different Web Page Sets for Different Patron Types (Statuses). In *Illiad Administrative Guide*.

Casey, M. E., & Savastinuk, L. C. (2006). Library 2.0 [Electronic Version]. Library Journal. Retrieved February 4, 2007 from *http://www.libraryjournal.com/article/CA6365200.html*.

Chad, K., & Miller, P. (2005). Do Libraries Matter? The rise of Library 2.0. Retrieved February 1, 2007, from *http://www.talis.com/downloads/white_papers/DoLibraries Matter.pdf*.

Fichter, D. (2006). Library 2.0 formula. Retrieved February 12, 2007, from *http://www.flickr.com/photos/65735987@N00/114899622/*.

Ford, K. (2006). At Your Service - Basics of Routing Rules [Electronic Version]. OCLC Illiad Newsletter. Retrieved February 12, 2007 from *http://www.atlas-sys.com/products/illiad/newsletter/*.

Gilbertson, K., & Mitchell, E. (2007). Javascript code library for Illiad Web Interface. Retrieved February 4, 2007, from *http://catalog.zsr.wfu.edu/jsource.js*.

Hilyer, L. A. (2006). Introduction to Interlibrary Loan. Journal of Interlibrary Loan, *Document Delivery & Electronic Reserve, 16*(1/2).

Levine, R. (2000). The cluetrain manifesto: the end of business as usual. Cambridge, Mass.: Perseus Books.

OCLC Illiad Administrative Guide [Electronic (2006). Version]. Retrieved February 12, 2007 from *http://www.atlas-sys.com/documentation/illiad/webhelp/ILLiad_Documentation.htm*.

OCLC Illiad Document Delivery User's Guide [Electronic (2006). Version]. Retrieved February 5, 2007 from *http://www.atlas-sys.com/documentation/illiad/content/OCLCILLiadDocDelGuide.pdf*.

Yang, Z. Y. L. (2005). Providing Free Document Delivery Services to a Campus of 48,000 Library Users [Electronic Version]. Journal of Interlibrary Loan, Document Delivery & Electronic Reserve, 15 from *http://www.haworthpress.com/store/E-Text/View_EText.asp?sid=JJUGS0P5AKUW8LB38UK5MB9M9JMW4CN2&a=3&s=J474&v=15&i=4&fn=J474v15n04%5F05*.

Yu, C. (2007). Interview with Jim Toplon.

We Deliver!
Randall Express Delivery Service

Madeleine Bombeld

INTRODUCTION

Randall Library has been in the Document Delivery business since the 1998-1999 academic year. We began our service on a small scale without any promotion by copying articles from our own journal collection that had been requested by faculty. Ironically, these requests were made by faculty who failed to check holdings in the library catalog prior to submitting interlibrary loan requests. This pilot project rewarded that behavior by filling those requests from our own collection and delivering these through campus mail much more quickly than if the requests had been filled through the ILL process. Despite rewarding faculty members' propensity to overlook searching the library catalog, offering them the opportunity to ask for anything, allowing us set the acquisition method has become our gold standard. Needless to say, word of mouth communication spread quickly about this new service and requests increased significantly.

We added graduate students as eligible customers for document delivery service during the 2003-2004 academic year. Just as with the faculty pilot, we did not promote this service enhancement. The first phase of document delivery for graduate students included scanning and electronic delivery of articles from our own collection and delivery of ILL books to departmental offices. This program was successful immediately and due to numerous requests, we added delivery of our own books to the service the next semester. ILL staff and student assistants who worked with the Document Delivery service were struggling to keep up with the requests and to deliver these on a timely basis.

In the fall of 2004, Randall Library at the University North Carolina Wilmington hired an additional staff member to work twenty hours a week in Document Delivery, a part of the ILL operation. Additionally, we purchased a golf cart and our on-campus delivery service started in earnest.

The new staff member spends time filling requests in the document delivery queue of ILLiad. Specific duties including printing pull slips, locating the items in the collection, scanning for electronic delivery, check in/check out of materials through the library's ILS, packaging when necessary, and physically delivering items that circulate. Delivery methods for those items are via the use of the newly acquired golf cart or by walking to each department needing a delivery, depending on the number of items and the weather. On any given day, the work flow in the ILL/DD unit might allow a student assistant to help with document delivery duties but the majority of the work flow is accomplished by the half-time staff member.

BACK IN THE DAY

Randall Library has always prided itself on excellent customer service and the library's reputation with faculty, staff, and students is one of responsiveness and going the extra mile. The Interlibrary Loan/Document Delivery unit frequently receives praise for finding the difficult to locate item. This unit has been actively involved in seeking ways to ramp up the service and for initiating programs that allow faculty and graduate students easier access to our own collection. At the direction of the Access Services Librarian, the library's ILL/DD unit ventured into a pilot program of document delivery to faculty during the 1989-1999 academic years. At the same time plans were being developed to deliver library services to the university's first off campus facility, the Center for Marine Sciences, which was located approximately 6 miles from the main campus. First to occur was the pilot program for delivery of photocopies from library-owned journals to on and off campus faculty.

Without any publicity, ILL/DD staff started filling requests from faculty for items in the library's journal collection. Requests for copies of articles were photocopied and mailed to the campus address of the requestor. Each article delivered this way included a service slip that read "Compliments of Randall Library Express" and included ILL/DD contact information. Needless to say, this was quite an involved procedure and one that relied on student assistants spending many hours at the copy machines. Our production rates were very good, faculty reaped the rewards of this service, and they began commenting on the benefits of our efforts. Over 100 faculty members took advantage of this very successful program. The success of this pilot program and the desire to automate our processes convinced us to purchase and install Ariel® software and our first open-faced book scanner.

By 2000 the Center for Marine Sciences (CMS) faculty had a full fledged document delivery system in place just for them. Circulating material in the Randall Library collection was requested by placing a hold in our integrated library system. Circulation staff processed the hold, located the material, checked it out, and loaded it into special bins for transport to the CMS. Requests for articles from our collection were photocopied and placed in the bin as well. A call was placed to the driver of the shuttle that ran between the library and the Center for Marine Sciences informing him that there were items to be picked up at the library. The bins packed with books, articles, CDs, and videos were brightly colored and clearly marked. When materials arrived at CMS, a departmental employee emptied the bins and placed the library materials in faculty mailboxes.

The library also purchased a book drop to be placed at the CMS and developed a procedure for checking it and transferring materials to the empty delivery bins. Once these bins had library materials in them, the shuttle drivers would get a call to come inside the CMS to pick up the bins for their return trip to the campus and to deliver those back to the library. Materials were then checked in by circulation staff and returned to their collections.

Requests for copies from CMS faculty were made via a special online document delivery form that was processed by the ILL/DD staff. Initially all copies made from our collection were photocopies as the library did not yet have the hardware in place to create electronic documents. Requests for copies we did not own were routed through the ILL system. Since these two distinctly different pilots ran concurrently, both the circulation and ILL/DD staff began to build their level of confidence with the competencies required by the two programs.

MOVING TOWARD ELECTRONIC DELIVERY

During the next academic year, 2000-2001, article desktop delivery to faculty anywhere was formally instituted and actively marketed as a new program. Over 580 items were requested by faculty. Software and hardware systems were now in place that could be used to scan and deliver articles electronically and that was the next step in our plan. We were hopeful that the new technology would streamline the procedures employed during the pilot programs and result in faster turnaround time from request received to being successfully delivered. But, as most libraries have learned from their initial experiences with technology, our expectations were much higher than our actual results.

The learning curve for staff was steep initially but integrated into the workflow routine by the spring of 2001. Initial experience with the software and hardware was daunting and rather than falling behind, staff continued to photocopy some of the articles requested while struggling to become familiar with the scanning workflow. The workflow called for documents to be scanned using the Ariel® interface, converted to PDF with Adobe Acrobat® and delivered via campus e-mail. The service was named "Randall Library Express" and it quickly became a preferred and highly desired service.

Randall Library continued with this general model for the next several years but continually made changes to the service. The first change made was to review faculty ILL requests for items held by the library and to pull those and place them on the hold shelf. Once we gave up the notion that faculty were too lazy to come and find their own books, this tweak in our service became routine. Faculty were notified via telephone or email that their requested item was available for check out at the circulation desk, where they had been taken by ILL/DD staff.

Another change to our model of document delivery was instituted when faculty asked if their items could be mailed to their department. Those requests were quickly accommodated since the goal was to get the desired material into the hands of the requestor. ILLiad made this easier than ever as we could transfer requests for items we owned to the document delivery queue, specify faculty members preferred delivery method, and use campus mail service for those deliveries. ILL books for faculty were still taken to circulation for pick up and check out during this transition time but mailed to departments when requested. The signal from faculty was that most preferred items delivered to their departmental offices for easier access and we received this loudly and clearly and began the planning process that would result in the system currently in use.

Graduate students were added as eligible requestors for the article delivery service during the 2003-2004 academic year and initially, like the faculty pilot, the service was not marketed. After a successful trial, this program was formalized as well, promoted extensively and was extremely well received. Book and media delivery for graduate students was the next enhancement instituted in the fall of 2004 and it became readily apparent that our popularity was beginning to drain our available resources. There were over a thousand requests for this service during each of the years between 2002 and 2004. Not only were faculty and graduate students using the electronic delivery service but both groups were requesting that their books and media be delivered to their departmental offices as well.

As stated previously, Randall Library was engaged in full scale campus delivery of its own items as well as those obtained through ILL items by 2004. The Document Delivery statistics kept by the library were unfortunately not separated by categories of "in house item" and "ILL item" deliveries. Citing specific numbers is therefore difficult but approximately 2,400 faculty requests and 1,800 graduate students' requests were delivered between August of 2004 and February of 2007.

CONCLUSION

Starting a campus delivery service requires numerous additional resources not readily available to libraries. Randall Library was fortunate in that the university librarian was very interested in this program and worked hard to secure funding for the additional staff person and the golf cart that are integral components of our program. Additional support is provided by circulation staff members who often pull requested material from the library's collection and make them available for delivery. Having an organizational structure that places ILL/DD and circulation in the same operational unit is also helpful as it allows for cross training and better utilization of staff time.

As with any new program there are competencies to teach and new work routines to learn but starting each phase of the service as small pilot programs made it more manageable for us. Staff buy-in is a critical component for starting a new service and this staff was very supportive and helped ensure its success. The benefit for the staff with this particular program was the chance to help develop new initiatives that were popular with a key audience for the library-the faculty. Several staff members who had been in their positions for some time enjoyed the challenge of learning new skills and having a hand in redefining their duties. Staff members from ILL/DD and circulation were already accustomed to working cooperatively across boundaries in order to develop new initiatives and that made the entire process easier to implement as well.

Future plans for the Randall Express Delivery Service include expanding it to serve undergraduates. The library circulation staff is already pulling books and media requested by undergraduate and these are placed on hold and kept behind the desk for pickup. As with the other programs, we are doing this without promotion. It has already become very successful though with 196 items pulled in February and 219 in March.

Once we are able to get another half time person for ILL/DD or the equivalent in student assistant hours, the plan is to deliver library materials to all undergraduates requesting the service, perhaps even to the their residence halls and/or other local addresses. Specific delivery method is one of several issues that will need to be addressed while evaluating the students' response to this pilot. We are committed to expanding our document delivery service to include this population while also maintaining our current services in place for faculty and graduate students. Careful assessment will continue and future enhancements will be based on those results.

Delivering Library Services to Users: A Case Study of the Sooner Xpress Service at the University of Oklahoma

Molly Murphy
Shelly Franklin
Ann Raia

HISTORY OF THE SERVICE

The University of Oklahoma (OU) has offered distance learning courses for many years through its Advanced Programs (AP) department. Many of these students are overseas, serving in the military while taking classes through OU. All the students are graduate students in various degree programs. The interlibrary loan department spent several years working out the technical difficulties inherent in providing adequate library service to this diverse population. It was generally agreed that although the AP service left something to be desired, there were some advantages to the way things were done for these students. In 1995, Advanced Programs staff met with University Libraries staff to explore the possibilities of providing library services for AP students. Up to that point, distance students had to rely on the local library resources that were available to them. For the most part, few of these local options were academic or research libraries. The decision was made to expand the service to include not only AP and other distance users, but also local users. This new service was named "Sooner Xpress."

In the spring of 1998, the interlibrary loan department had an opportunity to expand its services. Because a new document delivery librarian had been hired and a new staff position had been created, it became feasible to improve the services for faculty, staff and students. Initially, if patrons ordered items owned by the library, the staff simply retrieved them. An email notice was sent, explaining what had been done and how they could pick up their items. It was very confusing for the staff and the patrons. We quickly stopped explaining the process we had gone through and, instead, simply notified the patron that the book was available. We had very few requests at first. In fact, we had so few that we didn't even bother to keep statistics.

During this time, library services continued to be provided to distance students. Some years, those requests doubled or tripled from the previous year. We continued to fax, scan, or mail articles and even began the process sending books to overseas students to their APO addresses. It was soon discovered that this was a slow process and sometimes books took four to six weeks to arrive.

Several years were spent improving services to our students overseas. Eventually, this led to an improvement in services for our students on campus and in surrounding communities. Years of figuring out technical glitches led to an overall improvement in services. In the spring of 2006, the Sooner Xpress service was further expanded. Most of the problems that had been encountered with distance students had been resolved and the next logical step was improving on and off campus delivery. What was lacking was advertisement for this service. Up to this point, patrons had to stumble upon the Sooner Xpress request form. It was "hidden" under "Access Services" and "Interlibrary Loan," which is where it was handled, although it otherwise made no sense to the average library user.

In August of 2006, a link in our library catalog was added for people to request an item they found in the OPAC entitled "Request via Sooner Xpress."

FIGURE 1.

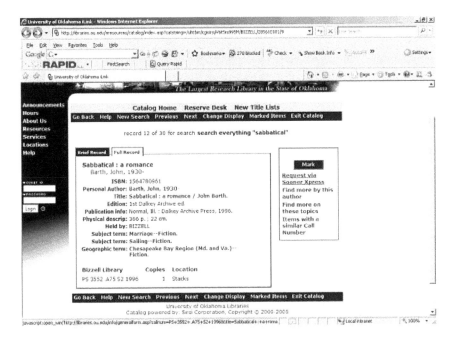

The response was a bit overwhelming at first, but once the ILL staff and students understood what the requests looked like, they became incorporated into the daily regime fairly quickly.

INCOMING REQUESTS

Requests for books and articles owned by our libraries come through the OPAC and into an Outlook Exchange account. This leads to the initial problem: since the requests remain basically e-mail requests throughout the process, they must be sorted into different folders, just as one would sort personal e-mails. The folders serve as the various status options for the requests. In addition, the ILL e-mail account receives large amounts of spam which must be deleted on a daily basis. Staff members have to be very careful not to accidentally delete emails pertaining to interlibrary loan or Sooner Xpress.

The Sooner Xpress request form presents a more serious problem. Staff members must verify the status and location of each item because the request form does not transfer that information into the e-mail. Looking up each request is time-consuming but must be done in order to verify the location (main library, branch library, annex, etc.) and status of the item (checked out to a patron or to another library, on order, in mending, etc.) None of these "extras" are captured in the request form. Requests are automatically filled in with the title, author, standard number, and call number.

Sooner Xpress service is limited to patrons who have a current affiliation with OU. They must login to the library's web site with their ID in order for the form to work. Once logged in, the patron's name, e-mail address, and phone number are automatically entered onto the form. If a patron wants to request a chapter from a book or an article from a journal, the title of the chapter or article, volume, issue, and date information has to be entered manually. Patrons have different options with regard to delivery of returnables (mail, campus mail, hold at library) and with regard to payment for non-returnables (charged to their library patron account or charged through a departmental research account). Currently, we do not charge for loans; we charge $4 for scans up to 20 pages and .15 per page after that.

VERIFICATION

Returnables

Once items have been pulled from the stacks, they are processed in a number of different ways. First, the items are divided between returnables (books) and non-returnables (copies). The returnables are further divided, depending on the patron's preference for receiving the item. The options available to the patron include "Hold at Bizzell Library," "Hold at Branch Library" (with a branch name given) or "Mail to Address Listed Above." If the patron indicated on the request form

FIGURE 2.

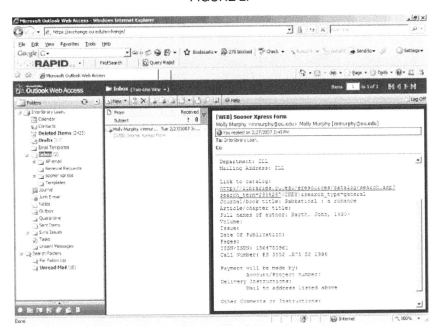

"Hold at Bizzell Library." an employee places it on hold for the patron. This automatically generates an e-mail notification stating that the item is ready to be picked up. It is then shelved on our "Holds/ILL" shelf. If the patron wants to pick up at a branch library, the item is sent to the correct branch where it is made available for pick up. If the patron selected "Mail to Address Listed Above," the item is checked out to the patron and mailed to the address provided. With all items that are sent to the patrons, a book mark that indicates it is a Sooner Xpress item is included.

When verifying the status of a request, if the status indicates that an item is not available through Sooner Xpress, it is taken care of accordingly. Items that are on loan to another library are simply ordered via ILL, because the amount of time it would take to recall the item would likely take longer than borrowing it from another library. If an item is simply checked out to another local patron, a rush recall is placed and an e-mail is sent explaining that if the patron does not hear anything within ten days, the item can then be ordered via ILL. If an item is part of a special non-circulating collection, the patron is notified by e-mail that the item will not be supplied via Sooner Xpress and that s/he must visit the collection to view it.

FIGURE 3.

Non-Returnables

For non-returnables, once the book or journal is in hand, an employee creates a record in CLIO, our ILS software. An ALA form is prepared for the request so that all Sooner Xpress requests for articles are entered into CLIO. This allows an actual request number to be associated with the Sooner Xpress form so that it can then be updated in CLIO. These requests are then scanned through Ariel and delivered to our own Ariel receive queue. They are then processed as if they were regular ILL requests. This is important for two main reasons. First, the patron will receive the article as a PDF, which will remain available to the patron for a limited time. Additionally, this allows the request to be included in the patron's ILL account. Just as a patron can monitor interlibrary loan requests; s/he will be able to see all Sooner Xpress article requests through this account as well.

UPDATING REQUESTS

There are several options for updating pending Sooner Xpress requests. Requests are initially moved from the main inbox to a subfolder called, fittingly, "Sooner Xpress." This folder contains requests that have been sent out on the daily interlibrary loan run. The requests are updated when they come back from the run. Items that are found on the shelf are placed in a "Filled Sooner Xpress" folder and the patron is notified. Items not found on the shelf are marked "NOs" and are subject to a second search. First, a second check of the catalog is conducted to verify that a branch or status was not overlooked. (In some cases, items have been found to be already charged out to the requesting patron. It seems that some patrons hope this service is instantaneous; as soon as they put in the request, it will be available to them. The reality is that several hours usually pass between the time they put in their requests and when an item becomes available.) If the item is still unable to located, it is then ordered through ILL. The patron is then notified that the item could not be found in the library and that it has been ordered through ILL instead. The "Filled Via ILL" folder is regularly converted to a spreadsheet of items that trained circulation "searchers" will look for a final time and, if not found, will be declared lost.

ADVICE

Start small if you want to test this. Begin with just staff or a limited population that you can trust to give you feedback. Always call it a "trial" so that people know they may encounter problems. Include as many tech-savvy guinea pigs as possible; they will very likely be able to show some early glitches. Consider the options available within library catalog system-the "request hold" option may be available, but not turned on.

SOLUTIONS

We are hoping to test a "request hold" option within our library catalog soon. We hope the option will include such "extras" as location and status of an item and an option to store the requests directly into a database for statistics and retrieval purposes. We are currently dragging requests in and out of email folders, which is time-consuming and prone to human error. Moreover, all of our requests are sorted by the patrons' first name, which is not an ideal way to search for anything. Another advantage to using a database for keeping track of these items is that we could tackle the searches in a more timely manner and before they might get out of hand.

CONCLUSION

Improving library services to library users is an admirable goal. It can also seem like a thankless job. However, as more patrons learn about the services and feel a need for them, the numbers will grow. (OU's requests went from a few hundred per year to close to two thousand in the first five months with the catalog link.) Obviously, as with any new service, there will be new problems and, hopefully, new solutions. The ideal would be to work out as many problems as possible and have a perfectly operating service ready to go. We found that we spent a fair amount of time explaining (and apologizing for) our service to the preliminary users. For the most part, those who use our service want us to pull the books and journals for them and allow them to pick up themselves. Most of those who prefer the "mail to address" option are truly at a distance (out of state or country) and appreciate the fact that we can offer this service. As local users become more confident of our abilities to fill requests for them, they may opt for mail delivery of their items. For now, most are content with us doing the "hard" part for them. The rest is easy.

Document Delivery to a Cast of Thousands: Free Article Delivery Service at Indiana University

Sherri Michaels

INTRODUCTION

A document delivery service has been available on the Bloomington campus of Indiana University (IU) in one form or another since 1972 when the Librarian for Economics and Political Science began providing faculty of these departments delivery of books and photocopies from the general collections. Beginning in 1982, a formalized document delivery service called Branch Delivery Service was instituted and underwent many changes until stabilizing in 1984. This service offered faculty, administrators and graduate students the ability to receive books, articles, and tables of contents. The only charge was for photocopies at ten cents per page. In 1991, more changes came due to budget restrictions and the service was limited to book delivery and tables of contents for faculty, administrators, and professional staff. Public outcry caused the full service to be re-instituted in the same year. Before being re-instituted, the service underwent a few changes, including a name change to Bloomington Delivery Service (BDS). Because the costs to the library had become prohibitive in providing the service, a fee was instituted to help subsidize some of the costs. Both books and articles were delivered through BDS. The charge for books delivered to an office via campus mail was $1. The charge for articles to be delivered in the mail or electronically was $2 for the first ten pages, and $1 for each additional increment of up to ten pages. Tables of contents were $1 each. The for-fee service was available to faculty, staff, and graduate students. In 1993, the service was expanded to allow undergraduates to place requests as well. The fee served its purpose to help offset some of the costs as well as to prevent any one person from requesting an inordinate amount of items. The number of requests dropped significantly once the fee was instituted. In December of 1990 there were 2,123 BDS requests compared to only 582 requests in December of 1991, after the fees were imposed.

The fees were not without issue however. There were problems almost from the beginning in actually collecting the fees; for example, users would sometimes supply an incorrect or invalid account number to bill. These problems were relatively minor overall. However, in 2004 the university purchased a new software system which, along with revised internal audit requirements, greatly amplified our problems in regards to charging and collecting fees from other university departments or individuals. We were able to bill individuals through the Bursar's Office, but we needed to set up accounts. Generally, we did not have the necessary personal information needed to set up accounts for individuals. Departmental billing also became an issue because an internal audit caused the university to revise its procedures concerning the charging of fees to one IU department by another. The new process required authorizations that we did not have, and we had to frequently ask for someone to authorize the bills on our behalf. The library was beginning to spend more and more time trying to collect and keep track of a small payment for a limited number of requests. By Fall of 2005, the libraries had decided that collecting the fee had become too cumbersome and that we needed to re-evaluate our options for the document delivery service. By the end of the year, the BDS service was under review once again.

A SERVICE IS RE-BORN

The libraries began the review process by taking a fresh look at all aspects of the document delivery service. First, library administration decided that document delivery was indeed a service that the library should provide. A new dean of libraries feels strongly that this service is needed to keep the library relevant to today's faculty and students. The dean feels that we cannot sit back and expect patrons to come to us; we need to be proactive in providing library materials to where users need them, when they need them. This philosophy extends to all users, so there was never a question of keeping the service available to all affiliated users including undergraduates.

Once it was decided to continue offering a document delivery service, the next issue to resolve was billing. There were no obvious forthcoming solutions to our campus billing problems. Other universities that offered fee-based services reported similar billing issues or problems collecting the fee, although perhaps not on the same scale. Since the fee had been instituted mainly as a way to prevent overuse of the system, we felt that there were other ways to achieve this outcome besides billing. Therefore, we decided to avoid the billing issue altogether and offer the service for free.

The libraries had implemented a book delivery service in 2003 called Request Delivery. Request Delivery is a service where a book from any of the eight IU campuses can be delivered to the campus library of one's choice. The requests are made through the OPAC and are part of the circulation functionality of our integrated library system. Since this book delivery option was available, it was decided to only include requests for articles in the revised document delivery service. The book delivery service provided inspiration for the name of the new service and hence, the revised article delivery service became Request Article Delivery.

Initially there were no limits such as article length or number of requests one could submit to the Request Article Delivery service. Despite the early history of the document delivery service when the department needed to curtail the number requests, we wanted to keep the policies as open as possible so as to encourage people to use the service. We have since implemented a limit of 25 requests per user per month. This was mostly in response to one user who submitted 500 requests in two days. On average, most users submit just over two requests a month, with "heavy" users averaging four. We felt that a limit of 25 would not impede anyone's research but would prevent any one person from taxing the libraries' resources. Article length has not been an issue so we have not limited that in any way. We do abide by copyright guidelines though and will not copy onerous amounts of a work. We also only deliver articles electronically. There are no other restrictions in place except that users must be a current faculty or staff member, or a student.

While we were looking at other aspects of this service, we decided to investigate ways to also streamline the workflow as much as possible. One of the reasons that the fees for the original document delivery service were initiated in the first place was because the process was a very laborious and staff-intensive one. BDS used a web form as a request mechanism, but emails and handwritten request forms were also accepted which meant that these requests needed to be manually entered into the tracking database. The BDS requests were kept in a completely separate workflow and database from the interlibrary loan (ILL) requests, even though the ILL office was handling both services. Keeping separate databases made it difficult to transfer requests to ILL when an item was not available on campus as all the information had to be re-keyed. There was a need to more seamlessly integrate the two services. The ILLiad software that the ILL office was already using had the ability to handle document delivery requests as well as ILL borrowing and lending, so it was decided to use this function of the software. Email and handwritten request forms were no longer accepted so that everything would be integrated into one system without the need to re-key any information.

As a policy, requests not filled on campus through the document delivery service due to an item missing or currently in use are transferred to the borrowing unit in ILL and sent out as an interlibrary loan request. We assume that the patron wants the item and that they do not care where the item comes from; however, it may take a little longer to receive the article through interlibrary loan than from on-campus. The ability of ILLiad to show the patron the status of their request has been helpful in keeping people informed, but a few people have complained that they did not want their request to go out on interlibrary loan if it was not available on campus because they did not want to wait. This is something that will need to be investigated in the future as to whether most want this transfer to happen or if there would be a way to automatically opt out.

In terms of people waiting for articles to be delivered, the service is billed as having a 3-5 business day turnaround. We did not want people to think of this service as a rush delivery service, nor did we want to promise anything we could not deliver. Since we were unsure of the volume of requests that we would receive, it seemed better to not promise too much. In reality, our turnaround time has averaged just over one day.

IMPLEMENTATION

Once the policies were determined and the decision made to use ILLiad as the database to track these requests, then we needed to make the necessary changes in ILLiad. The initial request screens were modified so that there were separate requests forms for materials on campus and for materials from other universities. All of the requests for articles on campus were routed to the Document Delivery "Awaiting Request Processing" queue. All of the article requests for materials from other universities were routed to the Borrowing "Awaiting Copyright Clearance" queue. Printing problems in the Document Delivery module caused us to rethink this workflow, and we changed ILLiad again so that all requests for articles were routed directly to the Borrowing module. ILL staff searches our catalog first for all articles and if it is available in print on campus, the request is moved to the Document Delivery module with the call number for the item already filled in.

ADVERTISING

Request Article Delivery went live on January 10, 2006 and was advertised beginning in the Spring of 2006. Information about the service was included in the libraries' Spring Newsletter that is sent to all faculty on the Bloomington campus. The student newspaper, The IDS, also ran a story on new library services including Request Article Delivery as well as our new self-check machine. Details of the service were advertised on the libraries' web site. Library instruction sessions included information about the service as well. The libraries have since included the Request Article Delivery service as part of its overall marketing campaign, "We Deliver," which includes advertising on buses, bookmarks, and radio ads.

RESPONSE

The response to the service has been a very positive one. Graduate students are the heaviest users of the service, followed by faculty and undergraduates. The number of requests received is much higher than when we offered the fee-based service. The Bloomington Delivery Service had received more than 3,000 requests in 2002, but by 2005 had slowed to a few hundred. The Request Article Delivery Service received more than 12,000 requests in 2006 so the service has obviously been a popular one. There was some initial concern in the first three

TABLE 1. Total Requests Received by Month

Month	Total Requests	Filled	Unfilled
January	363	290	73
February	915	786	129
March	1671	1523	148
April	1152	1100	52
May	823	778	45
June	798	772	26
July	751	729	22
August	742	732	10
September	1149	1125	24
October	1585	1541	44
November	1660	1592	68
December	631	617	14
Total	12240	11585	655

months when requests doubled or nearly doubled each month. This reflected the busiest time of the semester, though there was still relief to see that the requests evened out over the course of the year.

We averaged a 95% fill rate during 2006. Of the remaining 5%, many of them were available online. Even though we counted them unfilled for our purposes, these requests were indeed filled by sending the patron the URL for the article if there was a persistent link, or directions on how to get the article themselves in other cases. There were many more unfilled requests in the beginning months due to items being online, duplicate requests, incorrect or incomplete citation information, or even requests cancelled by the customer. These problems lessened as people became familiar with the service and the Iliad system.

COSTS TO THE LIBRARY

This service has been implemented so far with no increase in either student or staff budget. One reason is because of increased efficiencies in workflow in the ILL office. Another reason is that shortly after Request Article Delivery was implemented, we shifted some scanning responsibility to our off-site storage facility. The staff at the Auxiliary Library Facility (ALF), our off-site storage facility, now does all of the retrieving and scanning of articles for both document delivery and inter-

TABLE 2. Unfilled Reasons by Month for 2006

			Unfilled Reasons					
Month	In Use	Citation	Cancelled	Dup.	Online	Whole Item	Other	Total
Jan	1	9	5	5	44	6	3	73
Feb	3	18	13	13	67	6	2	129
Mar	0	24	20	20	88	9	1	148
Apr	4	11	8	8	22	1	0	52
May	0	12	10	10	5	6	9	45
June	1	8	11	11	3	3	0	26
July	0	14	2	3	1	2	0	22
Aug	0	2	0	3	1	3	1	10
Sep	0	3	4	5	6	6	0	24
Oct	4	6	4	6	7	17	0	44
Nov	1	8	0	5	44	6	4	68
Dec	0	3	0	3	4	4	0	14
Total	14	118	50	92	292	69	20	655
Pct	2.1%	18%	7.6%	14%	44.6%	10.5%	3.1%	100%

library loan lending for materials that are housed there, so these items never leave the building. The ALF staff scanned 2,981 articles from July (when scanning at the ALF began) through December. The ALF full-time staff has been able to absorb this extra work without an increase in budget. The libraries did however purchase a Minolta PS 7000 scanner for the ALF which cost roughly $13,000. This particular scanner was purchased because of the fragility of many of the materials housed at the ALF, as well its ability to scan oversize materials.

CONCLUSION

The libraries' decision to revise the document delivery service into a free article delivery service offered to more than 45,000 users has been a very popular one. Not only has use of the service been high, but there are frequent positive comments about this service on surveys such as LibQual and faculty surveys. There has also been strong support from Library Administration in providing this service. Efficiencies gained by moving the requests into ILLiad as well as some shifting of scanning to our off-site storage facility has helped us to offer the service without an increase in student or staff budgets. This may change as the service continues to grow, but we now have a solid foundation on which to build future enhancements.

Web Sites for Best Practices

June L. Power, Column Editor

BEST PRACTICES

Collaboration and sharing are what libraries are all about. Sharing our best practices not only helps to save us work by saving us from reinventing the wheel, but also helps to make library services better as we all strive for improvement and share ideas for doing so. Collaboration and sharing are possible through a number of different venues and tools, both online and off. It used to be that if you wanted to collaborate and share with other library professionals you joined professional associations, attended conferences and workshops, and perhaps volunteered to give a presentation–not a lot of options there, especially for access services library professionals, who often have to stay behind to man the front lines while others in the library attend the conferences and workshops.

Jump forward to librarianship in the twenty-first century, and we have email discussion lists, peer-to-peer networks, social networking software, social bookmarking, wikis, rss, online surveys, and blogs. It can be overwhelming and hard to figure out where to start or how to get involved. The websites I reviewed for this issue are all great places to get started–both in finding information and in sharing your own.

Library Success: A Best Practices Wiki

http://www.libsuccess.org

A wiki is a website that allows visitors to add, remove, and otherwise change content, typically without the need for registration, making them a truly collaborative effort and an ideal medium for exploring best practices; as it will continue to be changed and updated as new best practices are incorporated. This particular wiki invites anyone who has done something at their library that they consider a success to write about it in the wiki, or provide a link. Information in this wiki is divided into categories, with many topics pertaining to access services including management and leadership, programming, services to specific groups, and technology. The articles in each category vary some according to topic, including success stories, great ideas, blogs/websites to watch, and specific blog posts/articles to check out. For those of you that like to write, this wiki is an opportunity–it would be great to see categories created to directly reflect access services topics.

LISWiki

http://liswiki.org/wiki/

A cooperative project launched in the 2005, this site is devoted not just to best practices, but to library and information science in general– so any topic related to libraries goes, from bibliotherapy to laptop check out. A keyword search is probably your best bet, unless you know what you are looking for, as many of the articles fall into multiple categories. Many topics still need to be created or fleshed out, so additional contributors are needed. I found that many of the entries weren't really articles describing library related topics, but rather a short definition of the term needing expansions–or what's called a stub. Others, like the article on interlibrary loan, provide more information, but are dry and could have a lot more detail added. Some articles, such as the one for laptop check out, serve to aggregate links so that you can focus more on best practices and less on searching for information. "Whether you've got an old paper from library school that's just collecting dust, a brilliant newsgroup post that went unheard, or just some knowledge about libraries that's worth publishing, this is the place to do it." One nice thing about wikis is that most post the last updated date–which in my opinion every webpage should have.

Atlas Community Portal

http://www.atlas-sys.com/community/

A wonderful example of vendor/specific best practices on the web– with discussion forums, expert technical support, and software documentation blended to make this portal one stop shopping for best practices concerning the use of ILLiad interlibrary loan and document delivery software, and now Ares electronic reserves software. Guests may browse the site, or may register for membership and be able to personalize the portal to best suit their needs. The portal is logically divided into sections that make it easy to go exactly where you need for information–general information, Ares, ILLiad, Odyssey, and OCLC. The sections themselves include discussion threads for announcements, training, policies, hardware, conferences, and even fun things like recipes for those who work up an appetite while looking for information. Besides having links to the many discussion forums, the main web page also includes links to individual threads most recently updated, so if you are a frequent user of the portal you can easily see what's new.

CSDirect Innovative Interfaces Online Service Center

http://csdirect.iii.com/

Similar to the Atlas portal, CSDirect focuses specifically on Innovative Interfaces library automation system. This portal is password protected, and available only to users, but similar portals exist for other products as well. I picked this one because my library uses it and since I have password access I get to see all the good bits–like the user guides, presentations by other III users, surveys, training resources, product tutorials, and other information. Help Desk manager names, work areas, and emails are promptly placed, so that expert help can be asked for when needed. The sheer volume of information available is staggering, and can target specific needs–such as inventory control, mystery checkouts, negative fines, and more. I am especially fond of the presentations page, as it includes presentations from regional, national, and global conferences that I would otherwise never experience. I really like seeing what other institutions are doing with the software I use, so that I can make my own use of it more effective.

LISNews.org: Library and Information Science News

http://lisnews.com/

LISNews is a collaborative blog, and a source of library related current events news, and is updated frequently. Originally created in 1999, and generally supported by a handful of faithful bloggers, new authors are invited to share any news they find interesting. For those unfamiliar with blogs, this is a good way to get your feet wet without having the responsibly or maintenance worries of your own online journal. The blog defaults to a display of the current day's news, but can be navigated by date, author, or category. Categories range from the expected library topics such as circulation, bookmobiles, and online privacy to the light-hearted Friday funnies, Harry Potter Boy Wonder, and Who Dunnit? Library Thefts. A poll in the side bar allows immediate input and feedback on a library related current events question, and past polls are available for the curious.

WebJunction

http://webjunction.org/do/Home

WebJunction defines itself as "a cooperative of library staff sharing and using online resources" and the site itself blends many different online resources in providing a useful tool for library personnel. Originally started by OCLC from a Gates Foundation grant, this portal now has many partners supporting it on both the national and state levels. When you first enter the portal there are many options for finding best practices through what others are doing. Users can choose to take an online course or find training resources, connect with colleagues through discussion forums and volunteer opportunities, and collaborate through the WebJunction wiki or its niche in the blogosphere–BlogJunction. The member spotlight helps you to put a face with a name–something that is very important in an online world where networking colleagues may never meet face-to-face. The E-Learning Clearinghouse provides information on online education programs and courses for library staff and information professionals, while the E-Learning Institute aids libraries in creating, implementing, and using different forms of online learning. Live Space provides a conferencing service libraries can use as an online meeting space or classroom–great for webinars. Navigation is simple and chances for contributing content abound. A monthly newsletter keeps members updated on events and news–and if you don't find the information you want you can always ask George–WebJunction's advice columnist.

Circ and Serve–Circ. Reserves. ILL.
The view from this side of the desk.

http://circandserve.wordpress.com/

Circ and Serve is the new blogging project by Mary Carmen Chimato. Mary is the head of access and delivery services at a large university library. This blog is new, begun just this past January, so it still needs to past the test of time and blog ennui that many blogs seem to go through once started, but I wanted to include an example of a personal blog. Many library blogs exist out there, but none that specifically focuses on Access Services. With her blog, Mary hopes to share what works and what doesn't work as well as the major issues and ideas from her library so that hopefully others will benefit and share as well. Customer service, staff interactions, collaboration, and the access services triumvirate of circulation, reserves, and interlibrary loan have all made an appearance in her posts so far. While this blog is less a collaborative effort than the other websites I have discussed, visitors can comment on posts as a way to offer their input and opinions.

del.icio.us

http://del.icio.us/

Looking for a serendipitous method of finding best practices? Del.icio.us is a social bookmarking website that allows you to now only store your bookmarks and access them from anywhere with an internet connection, but also to share interesting links with other people through tagging them–a sort of linklog. By tagging your links with one-word descriptors, you can better organize and remember your links. Since you can assign multiple tags to each link, this is much more flexible than the traditional folder method used by most browsers. You can also browse other users' bookmarks in your interest areas to see what other people with similar interests are looking at and using online. The hotlist and popular tags list are quick ways to browse popular links

SurveyMonkey

http://www.surveymonkey.com/

If you are just not finding the answers you need in determining the best practices in libraries for a particular topic sometimes you need to do a little research and generate the answers yourself. SurveyMonkey provides a useful tool for easily gathering that information. This tool allows anyone to create a professional looking online survey quickly and easily, that you can then distribute the link to via email. No more poring over paper or shuffling email responses, as the results to your survey are collected in real-time and analyzed for you in graphs and charts. Your survey results can also be shared and you can download the data to Excel if you want to do more. Anyone can use the site freely–but you are limited to 10 questions and 100 responses. If you or your library get a professional subscription, a host of advanced features are possible, including being able to have more than 10 questions and 100 responses. I have found the basic subscription suits most of my needs, as generally I am looking for background information to support a project so that I can show what other institutions are doing when I look for administrative support for my ideas.

Second Life Library 2.0

http://infoisland.org/

http://secondlife.com

What's online collaboration without a little virtual reality? Exploring best practices and collaborating with colleagues doesn't always have to be accomplished through formal venues. If you haven't heard of Second Life, it is an online 3-D virtual reality community first opened to the public in 2003 and now is "inhabited" by the over 4 million alter egos created by people from all over the globe. Many librarians have joined this community and libraries have been added to the plethora of shopping malls and other buildings. Alliance Library System and OPAL are teaming up to extend the programs currently offered in Second Life, giving the substance to the virtual libraries with virtual library programs and eventually services–from storytelling to online collaboration through panel discussions . The Second Life Library 2.0 blog–now called Infoisland–helps to keep up with the latest events being sponsored by the libraries of the Second Life world. Build yourself a character called an "avatar," meet people, network, collaborate, and have virtual fun with your Second Life.

Finally, for a note of shameless and gratuitous self-promotion, check out my Access Services focused blog, The Unclassifiable Librarian, at http://www.unclassifiablelibrarian.blogspot.com/. Barring any blog ennui that finds me in the future, here you will find weekly postings on the projects I am working on, interesting things that have happened during the week, and all those little activities that unexpectedly fall in the realm of access services.

INDEX

www.ingramcontent.com/pod-product-compliance
Ingram Content Group UK Ltd.
Pitfield, Milton Keynes, MK11 3LW, UK
UKHW020346010325
455677UK00019B/323